Postmodern Gandhi and Other Essays

Postmodern Gandhi and Other Essays

Gandhi in the World and at Home

Lloyd I. Rudolph and
Susanne Hoeber Rudolph

The University of Chicago Press
Chicago and London

Lloyd I. Rudolph is professor emeritus of political science at the University of Chicago. Susanne Hoeber Rudolph is the William Benton Distinguished Service Professor Emerita at the University of Chicago. They are coauthors of several books, including, most recently, *In Pursuit of Lakshmi*, also published by the University of Chicago Press.

Portions of this book previously appeared in *The Modernity of Tradition: Political Development in India*, © 1967 by The University of Chicago.

The University of Chicago Press, Chicago 60637
The University of Chicago Press, Ltd., London
First published in 2006 by Oxford University Press, New Delhi 110 001
© 2006 by Oxford University Press and The University of Chicago
All rights reserved. Published 2006
Printed in the United States of America

15 14 13 12 11 10 09 08 07 06   1 2 3 4 5

ISBN-13: 978-0-226-73123-0 (cloth)
ISBN-13: 978-0-226-73124-7 (paper)
ISBN-10: 0-226-73123-5 (cloth)
ISBN-10: 0-226-73124-3 (paper)

Cataloging-in-Publication data have been requested from the Library of Congress.

♾ The paper used in this publication meets the minimum requirements of the American National Standard for Information Sciences—Permanence of Paper for Printed Library Materials, ANSI Z39.48-1992.

Contents

Preface

Our book is liminally positioned between a new edition of a previously published book, *Gandhi: The Traditional Roots of Charisma*, and a new work, *Postmodern Gandhi and Other Essays: Gandhi in the World and at Home*. The old book was published in 1983, the new book is to appear in early 2006. The effort that marked the passage from an old book to a new book was the creation of four new essays on Gandhi and the shedding of two of six old essays. The result is a hybrid whose strength we believe transcends the sum of its components. Before saying something in this preface about how our new essays help constitute Gandhi 'in the World' we want to remind readers of what the preface to the 1983 essays had to say about Gandhi 'at Home'.

Our interpretation of Gandhi was formed between the mid-1950s and the mid-1960s, the middle decades between decolonization and the Vietnam War and 15 years before the victory in Iran of Islamic revivalism. It was widely believed at the time that 'new nations' had to break with—even repudiate—tradition to become modern. Ancient civilizations were not so much dangerous as decadent. Scholars and statesman talked of stages of development, take-off, and the prerequisites of democracy.

Our interpretation of Gandhi expressed a countercurrent. We called the larger work in which this account of Gandhi first appeared *The Modernity of Tradition*[1] because we found that social change in India involved adaptation of its past inheritance as much as it did the destruction and displacement of that inheritance. India's indeterminant future, it seemed, was being shaped by civilizational continuities and affinities. We did not find this necessarily dangerous or undesirable, and we tried to show why.

Gandhi, who described himself in his autobiography as descended from a caste of petty merchants and was in fact the son and grandson of princely state prime ministers, became for Indians *bapu* [father] and *Mahatma* [great soul]. How was this possible? How was it done? We find the answers in the traditional roots of his charisma, the subtitle we have given to this book. Max Weber, who gave currency to the concept of charisma, found that charismatic leadership arose spontaneously and moved history in hitherto unlikely and even unanticipated directions. Charismatic leadership was a wild card that reordered the values contained in the deck of extant historical determinants. For us, Gandhi's charismatic leadership was itself in part historically determined, rooted in the aspects of tradition he interpreted for his time. Gandhi's revitalization of tradition involved breaks with its entrenched values, practices, and interests: his struggle against untouchability as a world view and social practice; his insistence on the dignity of all callings and the work they entail; and his transformation of the Indian National Congress from a body narrowly concerned with the interests of an anglicized elite to a socially concerned mass organization. In pursuing these and other transformations of Indian character, society, and politics he used traditional symbols and language to convey new meanings and to reconstitute social action.

So what does 'the traditional roots of charisma' mean? Gandhi realized in his daily life and his public actions cultural ideals that many Indians honored in their own lives but could not themselves enact. He and followers shared, for example, the traditional Hindu belief that a person's capacity for self-control enhanced his capacity to control his environment. This was the key to Gandhi's political potency. In a self-fulfilling prophecy of mutual expectations and recognitions, Gandhi and those to whom he spoke believed that the more he could realize the cultural ideal of ascetic self-control over enslaving or destructive passions, the more qualified he became as their leader.

Gandhi's 'experiments with truth', the title of his autobiography, never ceased. One result of his experiments was a self-critical, ethical, and inclusive nationalism. Gandhi frequently spoke of *swaraj* [literally *swa* 'self' and raj 'rule'], a word derived from Sanskrit and common to many Indian languages. He used its double meaning, rule thyself and national self-rule, to teach by example and precept that Indians would not be ready for or capable of national independence until they reformed themselves and their society.

Gandhi's nationalism achieved an ethical universalism that attracted—and still attracts—attention and followers outside India. It was able to do so because Gandhi placed right means [such as non-violence] above desired ends. He instructed a generation that non-violent resistance was a transforming and agentic force rather than a passive tactic of the weak. To protest injustice without hatred and violence required moral and physical courage. Gandhi showed through the practice of *satyagraha* that resolving conflicts by appealing to shared values and interests could replace enmity with community. He depicted truth as a goal rather than as an archetype or a revelation and compared it to a diamond whose many facets exposed a variety of meanings. Because Gandhi gave truth a contextual and experimental form, it could be found in all faiths and realized in the lives of all men.

Our characterization of Gandhi's view of truth as a goal rather than as an archetype or revelation in *Gandhi: The Traditional Roots of Charisma* enables us to segue to prefatory remarks about *Postmodern Gandhi*. One of the principal reasons that led us to continue our work on him in the years since 1983 when *The Traditional Roots* was published was what we regarded as his postmodern understanding of truth as experimental and situational. This is a central theme of the new edition-cum-new book, *Postmodern Gandhi and Other Essays: Gandhi in the World and at Home*.

How did Gandhi arrive at an experimental and situational view of truth? The young Gandhi we argue was influenced by what we call 'the other West'. We show how in London [1888–91] while studying to become a barrister the young Gandhi learned from the anti-modern 'other West' of John Ruskin and Leo Tolstoy, Edwin Arnold and Henry Thoreau. Starting with his 21 years [1893–1914] in South Africa[2] where he fought for minority rights and resisted the beginning of apartheid regime, extending to his 32 years [1915–47] as leader of the Indian National Congress' struggle for independence from British colonial rule, and extending beyond his death in 1948 to our own time, Gandhi's thoughts and actions have shaped the ideas and practices of the 'other west' that challenges modernity's hegemony and offers a postmodern alternative to it.

The Gandhi of the loincloth and the walking stick seems an unlikely theorist of postmodernism. We call our opening chapter 'Postmodern Gandhi' because we want to challenge a common notion of Gandhi as a traditionalist or a back number. He was neither. He challenged both the old and the new established orders—both the ritual order of upper caste Hinduism and the high modernist order of the Nehruvian Congress.

Gandhi's critique of 'modern civilization' in his 1909 book, *Hind Swaraj* was an opening salvo of the postmodern era. His autobiography, *The Story of My Experiments with Truth*,[3] and his theory and practice of non-violent collective action, *satyagraha*, articulate and exemplify his postmodern experimental and situational understanding of truth.

The four new chapters make a variety of arguments in different contexts and different levels about Gandhi's critiques of modernity and his postmodern thought and practice. We argue for example that the theory and practice of Gandhi's *ashram*s and satyagrahas showed how the elite rationality of Habermas' bourgeois 'public sphere' could be democratized; that partition might have been avoided had Gandhi's commitment to the pluralism and minority rights entailed by dominion status prevailed over the democratic majoritarianism and uniform citizenship that underlay Nehru's insistence on 'complete independence'; and that Gandhi's influence in the America has varied depending on which narrative of him was dominant: the anti-imperialist, the guru, the mahatma, or the fraud.

Gandhi was a practitioner and an activist as well as a theorist; as Marx famously put it about himself, Gandhi meant to change the world as well as interpret it, and he did. In making our case for Gandhi as a postmodern thinker and activist, we locate his version of postmodernism in the complex of meanings, many controversial, many disputed, the term postmodern has acquired. We hope to persuade readers that Gandhi's postmodernism is a postmodernism they can live with.

Kensington, California   LLOYD I. RUDOLPH
December 2005   SUSANNE HOEBER RUDOLPH

Notes

[1] The essays that constituted *Gandhi: The Traditional Roots of Charisma* originally appeared as part two of *The Modernity of Tradition: Political Development in India*.

[2] South Africa became a dominion of the British Empire in 1910, Prior to 1910, Gandhi worked as a lawyer and activist on behalf of the Indian community in Natal, a crown colony granted responsible government in 1893, and the Boer state of Transvaal. His first ashram, Phoenix Settlement, was on the outskirts of Durban, his second, Tolstoy Farm, in the countryside 21 miles from Johannesburg.

[3] Gandhi's first version of his autobiography, *The Story of My Experiments with Truth*, was as a serial publication in *Navajivan*. Asked by Swami Anand in 1925 to write his autobiography as a book, Gandhi told him that 'I have no spare time. I could only write a chapter week by week. Something has to be written for *Navajivan* every week. Why should it not be the autobiography?' The Swami agreed to the proposal, and here I am hard at work.' 'Introduction', *The Story of My Experiments with Truth*, Boston: Beacon Press, 1957, 1993, p. xxv.

Part One

1

Postmodern Gandhi[1]

Why call this essay 'Postmodern Gandhi'? One reason is to challenge a common notion of Gandhi as a traditionalist and back number. To the contrary, he challenged the established order—both the ritual order of upper caste Hinduism and the high modernism of the Nehruvian Congress[2]. A more fundamental reason is to establish Gandhi's credentials as a postmodern thinker. When, in 1909, he wrote *Hind Swaraj*, he helped to inaugurate the postmodern era by critiquing and rejecting 'modern civilization' and by articulating a civilizational alternative to it. Gandhi was a practitioner and an activist as well as a theorist; as Marx famously put it about himself, Gandhi meant to change the world as well as interpret it, and he did. Finally, in making a case for Gandhi as a postmodern thinker, I will locate his version of postmodernism in the complex of meanings that term has acquired.[3] I hope to persuade readers that Gandhi's postmodernism is a postmodernism they can live with, even live by.

The essay proceeds in five stages. It starts with 'The Meanings of Postmodernity', an exploration of historical and epistemological meanings of the term 'postmodern'. In stage two, '*Hind Swaraj*: A Text for Its Time or for Our Time?', it proceeds to examine in some detail Gandhi's critique of modern civilization and his alternatives to it. Stage three, 'Modern Civilization on Trial: Gandhi and Nehru Contest Development in an Independent India', examines the clash in October and November 1945 between Nehru's high modernist vision and Gandhi's postmodern vision of India's future. A fourth stage addresses another dimension of the clash between modernism and postmodernism in independent India by analysing 'The Fate of *Panchayati Raj*: The Eclipse and Emergence of Local Sovereignty'. 'The Prophet At Home and Abroad: Icon or Vital Signifier' returns to the question of Gandhi's standing as a 20th-century thinker and activist.

The Meanings of 'Postmodernity'

To speak of a 'postmodern Gandhi' raises the question of Gandhi's relationship to the term 'modern'. My account addresses two broad contextual meanings of modern. The first locates the modern and, by implication, the postmodern in history. In this reading, modernity has a career located in time, place and circumstance. A second way to understand modernity and postmodernity is to locate them epistemologically; what forms of knowledge and ways of knowing do they represent? In this chapter, I position Gandhi with respect to both meanings of modernity, the historical and the epistemological.

As early as 1909, in his seminal essay *Hind Swaraj*, Gandhi had identified 'modern civilization' and found it wanting. In doing so he flew in the face of prevailing world opinion. In 1909 Europe and the US were approaching the apogee of the belief in progress. Confidence in the future abounded. Accomplishments in science and technology and the capacity to use them in benign and productive ways seemed to prove that humans could master and harness nature, and direct and control social change. Before the irrationality and carnage of World War I shattered the illusion that material and social progress was inevitable and benign, progress seemed as certain as it was palpable. In formulating his inner and outer critique of 'modern civilization' in *Hind Swaraj*, Gandhi challenged this view of progress. In doing so he became an early contributor to the intellectual lineage of postmodernism.[4]

Another way Gandhi's thought foreshadowed postmodernism was its refusal to privilege modernism's commitment to the epistemology of universal truths, objective knowledge and master narratives. This 'modern' epistemological turn emerged from 17th century conceptions of natural science and foundational philosophy, the thought and practice associated with Newtonian physics, Descartean philosophy and Hobbesian liberalism.[5] Descartes abandoned scepticism's approximate and relative truths for the axiomatic certainty that, he claimed, clear and self-evident ideas provide. Seventeenth-century inventors of modernity held that laws of nature were independent of time and space, that is, were the same everywhere and always. As the Newtonian model of physics spread to other domains of knowledge, its adherents began to claim it was the only valid way of knowing. 'Science' alone can ask and answer questions. If it wasn't 'scientific' it couldn't be true.

By the 18th century, the modern view of knowing and knowledge helped to define what came to be known as the Enlightenment. Condorcet's *Historical Picture of the Progress of the Human Mind* epitomized the Enlightenment spirit.[6] He argued that scientific reasoning and scientific knowledge would increasingly displace religious thinking and spiritual knowledge. The human mind, he claimed had evolved through nine epochs. Thought and knowledge at the time of the French Revolution embodied the culminating tenth epoch. Jailed by the Revolution and about to become its victim, Condorcet's confidence in ultimate human perfection never wavered.[7]

Condorcet's Enlightenment spirit was carried forward in the 19th century by Auguste Comte. His two primitive stages of social development—theological (belief in the supernatural) and metaphysical (belief in ideas as reality)—culminated in the highest stage, positivism (phenomena explained by observation, hypothesis and experimentation), which gave science its leverage on truth. Modernity as defined by its 17th- and 18th-century lineages is epitomized by the view that scientific thinking yields objective knowledge and universal truths.

Gandhi anticipates a good deal of postmodern thinking by taking the view that, at best, humans can know partial and contingent truths. As a self-declared *karma yogi*,[8] Gandhi's epistemology was rooted in 'truth in action', a concept that locates truth in the facts and circumstance of particular situations.[9] Before launching a *satyagraha* campaign, he thoroughly familiarized himself with its particular context. In a process evocative of the discovery phase of a legal proceeding, he carefully investigated the relevant circumstances—including the attitudes and motives of the contending parties. The goal of the campaign was formulated with reference to the situation's unique problematic. In his first satyagraha in South Africa he coined the phrase, 'the minimum is the maximum'.[10] His first major campaign in India after returning from South Africa—at Champaran in Bihar—exemplifies this practice.[11] As a satyagrahi he practiced firmness in the pursuit of contextual or situational truth. And, as an adherent of the Jain doctrine of *anekanatavada*, he viewed truth as many-sided and its understanding by the human mind as 'fleeting and fragmentary'.[12]

Gandhi respected science as a form of truth and followed what he took to be scientific methods. In his autobiography, *The Story of My Experiments with Truth*, he used the word 'experiment' quite deliberately in the title of the book. In language suggestive of Karl Popper's about falsification Gandhi wrote: 'I claim nothing (more for the experiments) than does a scientist who, though he conducts his experiments with the utmost accuracy, forethought and minuteness, never claims any finality about his conclusions, but keeps an open mind regarding them.'[13]

The claim that Gandhi held a partial and contingent view of truth, a view that resembled the views of some postmodernists, has been contested by Indian scholars on Gandhi. Ajit Kumar Jha, for example, expressed a widely accepted view when he argued: 'To describe (Gandhi) as a post-modernist is a gross misunderstanding of his philosophy. One of the basic assumptions of postmodernism is the principle of ethical relativism. The Mahatma, whose entire life was dedicated to experimenting with truth, believed, in the absolute truth ....'[14]

But are these allegations valid? What does Gandhi mean when he refers to absolute truth? How does he use the term? Is it right to equate the situational truths of satyagraha or the partial and contingent truths of Gandhi's 'experiments with truth' with ethical relativism?

Gandhi's reasoning about truth starts with his commitment to the view that 'truth is God'.[15] Gandhi makes clear in a variety of ways that seeking God, like seeking absolute truth, is not the same as knowing God or knowing absolute truth. The absolute truth or God could be approached but not known by mortals. Unlike those moderns who thinks that they can know absolute truth in the form of objective truths and universal laws, Gandhi thought that making such claims was to envy God[16] and seek to be like Him. As Tom Wolfe put it in *Bonfires of the Vanities*, it is to think of oneself as a 'master of the universe'.

Gandhi compared absolute truth to a diamond which could not be seen whole but whose many facets or surfaces revealed partial truths.[17] Another way to think of Gandhi's understanding of absolute truth is to liken it to infinity in calculus, that is, as a limit that can be approached and approximated but not known or reached. The existence of infinity, like the existence of absolute truth, provides a basis for reasoning and knowledge— about mathematics and about truth. Gandhi sometimes invoked Euclid's line to illustrate the relationship between the ideal and the real. It was a line 'without breadth ... [that] no one has so far been able to draw and ... never will. All the same it is only by keeping the ideal in mind that we have made progress in geometry. What is true here is true of every ideal'.[18]

For Gandhi truth had several meanings and forms. It could be situational as in the goal of a satyagraha, contextual and contingent as in the experimental truths found in his autobiography, and absolute as in his commitment to 'Truth is God'. We have already noted that in *The Story of My Experiments with Truth* Gandhi used the word 'experiment' to invoke a version of modern science: 'I claim nothing (more for the experiments) than does a scientist who, though he conducts his experiments with the utmost accuracy, forethought and minuteness, never claims any finality about his conclusions, but keeps an open mind regarding them .... I am far from claiming any finality or infallibility about my conclusions.' He goes on to say, however, that 'I do claim that my conclusions are absolutely correct, and seem for the time being to be final. For if they were not, I should base no action on them ... for me, truth is the sovereign principle ... not only the relative truth of our conception, but the Absolute Truth ... that is God .... I worship God as truth only.' But then he says that 'I have not yet found Him ... as long as I have not realized this Absolute Truth, so long must I hold by the relative truth as I have conceived it. *That relative truth must, meanwhile, be my beacon, my shield and buckler.*'[19] This view of relative truth anticipates the postmodern turn to the contingent certainty of contextual or situational truth.

Gandhi is postmodern too in his hermeneutic. He sought meaning in context, a perspective he brought to the interpretation of practice and of texts. I show below his postmodernism in the way he interpreted vegetarianism, a core practice for someone of his religion, caste and family, and in the way he interpreted the Bhagavad Gita, a foundational text that Gandhi put at the centre of his worldview. When I say that his hermeneutic was postmodern I refer to the commitment to relative truth that we have just visited and to his avoidance of modernist hermeneutics such as the self-evidence of foundational truths or the transparency[20] of universal meta-narratives and of scientific and objective truths that claim to be independent of time, place and circumstance. Gandhi also avoided the hermeneutics of the unselfconscious universalism of revealed, sacred and immemorial truth claimed for religious texts.

Gandhi's account of his relationship to vegetarianism enacts his postmodern hermeneutic. But first, a schematic account of how he chose vegetarianism. He tells us that he started as a vegetarian by birth; it was a given of his family, caste and religion. As an adolescent he secretly rebelled against his family heritage by embracing the meat eating of what Partha Chatterjee calls 'colonial modernity', the world view and social practices of India's colonial masters, the British. It was a Faustian bargain. By eating meat he expected to become powerful like the British but in doing so he would ingest what Ashis Nandy has called the 'intimate enemy'[21] and adopt what Partha Chatterjee has called 'derivative discourse',[22] the language, concepts and world view of the colonial master. Later, in *Hind Swaraj*, he would characterize the bargain as wanting 'English rule without the Englishman. You want the tiger's nature, but not the tiger.'[23]

Determined to cross the dark waters to study in a distant and alien land, England, he overcomes his mother's objections and fears by vowing to her that he will not eat meat. Once in London, he resists intense pressure from Indian and British mentors and friends to become modern and powerful by eating meat. But keeping his vow to remain a vegetarian has the result of having to eat insipid food and suffer from chronic hunger. He breaks free from modernity's imperative to eat meat and tradition's imperative to be a vegetarianism when he finds a vegetarian restaurant and reads Henry Salt's *Plea for Vegetarianism*. Persuaded by Salt's booklet that there are good reasons to be a vegetarian, he chooses to be one. It is a choice that initiates him to the people and ideas of the 'other west' and its revolt against modernity.

Here is how Gandhi tells the story. In an act of secret adolescent rebellion, the young Mohandas violates his family's commitment to vegetarianism. He does so under the spell of his charismatic, physically powerful, meat-eating school friend, Sheikh Mehtab. Mehtab persuades him that a spirit of 'reform' is sweeping Rajkot. In the voice of colonial modernity Mehtab tells Mohandas that '... many of our teachers "[are] ... secretly taking meat and wine."' So too are 'many well-known people of Rajkot' and 'some high-school boys'.[24] 'I asked my friend the reason and he explained it thus: "We are a weak people because we do not eat meat. The English are able to rule over us, because they are meat-eaters."' Gandhi re-enforces Sheikh Mehtab's meat-eating tales of colonial modernity by quoting 'a doggerel of the Gujarati poet Narmad [which] was in vogue amongst us schoolboys, as follows: "Behold the mighty Englishman/He rules the Indian small/Because being a meat-eater/He is five cubits tall."'[25]

Gandhi then tells his readers how to interpret his secret rebellion: 'The Gandhis', he writes, 'were Vaishnavas. My parents were particularly staunch Vaishnavas. They would regularly visit the *haveli* [temple] .... Jainism was strong in Gujarat, and its influence was felt everywhere and on all occasions. The opposition to and abhorrence of meat-eating that existed in Gujarat among the Jains and Vaishnavas were to be seen nowhere else in India or outside in such strength. These were the traditions in which I was born and bred. And I was extremely devoted to my parents. I knew that the moment they came to know of my having eaten meat, they would be shocked to death .... But my mind was bent on "reform" .... I wished to be strong and daring and wanted my countrymen also to be such, so that we might defeat the English and make India free.'

A few years later a 19-year-old Mohandas who had just past his matriculation examinations was eager and determined to study in England but faced a great deal of opposition from within his family and from his caste council. Having persuaded his uncles and defied the council he needed his mother's permission to make the journey 'to cross the seas'. Fearing her son would lose his religion and abandon his way of life, she was most reluctant to give him permission to leave. She did so after he 'solemnly' took three vows '... not to touch wine, woman and meat. This done, my mother gave her permission'.[26]

Gandhi arrived in London in September, 1888. He was to study law and become a barrister. His involvement with colonial modernity started with his commitment to meat-eating and his involvement with Gujarati tradition started with the vow he took with his mother to remain a vegetarian. Gandhi spent his first month in London 'apprenticing' with English life while living with a friend of a fellow Kathiawari, Dr P. J. Mehta, to whom he had a letter of introduction and who welcomed him to London. Gandhi tells us that 'The friend continually reasoned with me to eat meat, but I always pleaded my vow and then remained silent.' The friend asked 'What is the value of a vow made before an illiterate mother, and in ignorance of the conditions here? ... But I was adamant.' The friend tries to persuade Gandhi to eat meat by reading Bentham's *Theory of Utility* to him. 'Pray excuse me, these abstruse things are beyond me. I admit it is necessary to eat meat, But I cannot break my vow .... That is how I served my apprenticeship for a month.'

Gandhi then arranges for room and board at an Anglo-Indian's house in West Kensington. His diet remains unsatisfactory: 'Everything was insipid.' And so he launches out '... in search of a vegetarian restaurant. The landlady had told me that there were such places in the city. I would trot ten or twelve miles each day, go into a cheap restaurant and eat my fill of bread, but would never be satisfied. During these wanderings, I once hit on a vegetarian restaurant in Farringdon Street. The sight of it filled me with same joy that a child feels on getting a thing after its own heart. Before I entered I noticed books for sale under a glass window near the door. I saw among them [Henry] Salt's *Plea for Vegetarianism*. This I purchased for a shilling and went straight to the dining room. This was my first hearty meal since my arrival in England. God had come to my aid.'

'I read Salt's book from cover to cover and was very much impressed by it. From the date of reading this book, I may claim to have become a vegetarian by choice .... I had all along abstained from meat in the interests of ... the vow I had taken, but I had wished at the same time that every Indian should be a meat-eater, and had looked forward to being one myself freely and openly some day, and to enlisting others in the cause. The choice was now made in favour of vegetarianism, the spread of which henceforward became my mission.'[27]

Gandhi asks us to read his rejection of meat-eating and embrace of vegetarianism not as the result of traditional obligation or self-evident modern knowledge but as a reasoned contextual choice. 'By refusing to eat the roast beef of old England', Martin Green argues, 'the vegetarians refused to join the hearty rituals of English power .... Vegetarianism', he continues, 'was then not just a diet option; it was at the center ... of an intellectual and political movement of thought and action'.[28]

Gandhi's postmodern hermeneutics can be seen too in the way he read a foundational text, the Bhagavad Gita .... Gandhi calls the introduction to his English translation of the Gita 'Anasaktiyoga' [discipline of non-attachment].'[29] Gandhi postmodern-like hermeneutic guidance about approaching the meaning of the text and authorial authority starts with his call for the Bhagavad Gita to be read as a poem [not as a sacred text or revealed or immemorial truth] whose author is a poet. 'Because a poet puts a particular truth before the world, it does not necessarily follow that he has known or worked out all its great consequences, or that having done so, he is able to express them fully. In this perhaps lies the greatness of the poem and the poet. A poet's meaning is limitless. Like man, the meaning of great writings suffers evolution. On examining the history of languages', he continues, 'we notice that the meaning of important words has changed or expanded. This is true of the Gita .... The author of the Gita, by extending the meanings of words, has taught us to imitate him.' [133]

Gandhi uses genre to guide his readers' attitudes and expectations about how to read the Gita. 'The Gita', he says, 'is not an aphoristic work; it is a great religious poem .... Nor is the Gita a collection of Do's and Don'ts. What is lawful for one may be unlawful for another. What may be permissible at one time, or in one place, may not be so at another time, and in another place .... The deeper you dive into it, the richer the meanings you get. It is meant for the people at large, there is pleasing repetition .... The seeker is at liberty to extract from this treasure any meaning he likes so as to enable him to enforce in his life the central teaching.' [134] Gandhi shapes readers' perceptions and attitudes by telling them about how he discovered the Gita. He had come to London in 1888 to study law. It was there, in London, that he first read the Gita in Sir Edwin Arnold's English translation, *The Song Celestial*, a translation that he continues to regard as outstanding. He also makes clear that he is familiar with Tilak's then famous version of the Gita: '[I] ... went reverently through the Gujarati translation of the Lokamanya's great work.' [The Lokamanya referred to here is Bal Gangadhar Tilak, 1856–1920, the 'extremist' leader who preceded Gandhi as a leader of the nationalist movement. Tilak's rival was the 'moderate' Gopal Krishna Gokhale, Gandhi's 'political *guru*'].

Gandhi then tells his readers for whom 'this rendering is designed'. First and foremost, he mentions 'this little band' of those for whom the Gita 'has become for us a spiritual reference book'. 'This rendering' is also designed 'for women, the commercial class, the so-called Shudras and the like, who have little or no literary equipment, who have neither the time nor the desire to read the Gita in the original, and yet who stand in need of its support'. Gandhi here is defying Hindu orthodoxy which confines reading and hearing of the sacred texts to the 'twice born' [males spiritually reborn at the *uppanaya* or donning of the sacred thread ceremony at puberty] uppers castes, particularly Brahmins. 'Women, Shudras [lower castes] and the like' [a euphemism for 'untouchable' castes?] are not to hear much less read sacred texts.

Gandhi turns next to the relationship of his interpretation to the many who have gone before. He 'does not mean any disrespect to the other renderings' of the Gita but he goes on to distinguish his version by saying that, unlike other translators/interpreters of the Gita, he has tried to enforce the meaning of the Gita in his own life. He is, he says, a practitioner who has tried to enforce 'the meaning in my own conduct for an unbroken period of forty years'.

Having positioned himself with respect to the text and his intended audience he turns to the text's message. He starts by taking advantage of the poetic license his postmodern trope of the Gita as poem subject to changing interpretations and meaning allows. He makes clear that the momentous battle on the field of Kurukshetra between the related Pandava and Kaurava clans which Arjuna, with Krishna's transcendent vision and voice at his side, witnesses and participates in is 'not a historical work'. The Gita, he says should be read as metaphor and not as history, figuratively, not literally.

'Even in 1888–89 .... I felt it was not a historical work, but that under the guise of physical warfare, [the *Gita*] described the duel that perpetually went on in the hearts of mankind and that the physical warfare was brought in merely to make the description of the internal duel more alluring.' [127] Gandhi makes his point about metaphor more decisive by arguing that 'In the characteristics of the perfected man of the Gita, I do not see any to correspond to physical warfare.' [127–8]

Gandhi postmodern hermeneutic can also be seen in the way he addresses the question of the literalness and/or historicity of the perfection of Krishna. 'Krishna of the Gita', he says, is perfection and right knowledge personified; but the picture is imaginary. 'That does not mean', he is quick to add, 'that Krishna, the adored of his people, never lived. But the perfection is imagined. The idea of a perfect incarnation is an aftergrowth.' [128]

His postmodernity is again evident in the way he discusses the idea of incarnation in Hindusim in order to show that the point of Gita is not to show Krishna as perfection incarnate but rather to show that 'self-realization is the subject of the Gita.' At the same time Gandhi argues the Gita's author 'surely did not write it to establish' the doctrine of self-realization. 'The object of the Gita', Gandhi continues, 'appears to me to be that of showing the most excellent way to attain self-realization .... *That matchless remedy is renunciation of fruits of action*'. [italics in the text] [129]

Gandhi then addresses the seeming contradiction between the necessity of action and every action being tainted. The 'taint of sin', he says, is inherent in all action. How can one avoid the taint of sin that action entails and at the same time meet the requirement to act? 'The Gita', he says, 'has answered the question in decisive language; "By desireless action ..."' [129]

If Gandhi tells us to read the Gita as saying that its object is to show the way to self-realization, what ways does he have in mind and which one is the best means to approach self-realization? Right knowledge is essential. So too is devotion which must not only accompany knowledge but also 'given the first place'. [129] But Gandhi asks us to read the Gita as saying that while knowledge and devotion are essential for self-realization, they are not sufficient. Gandhi asks us to read the Gita as saying that 'No one has attained his goal without action ... all activity, whether mental or physical, is to be included in the term action. Then how is one to be free from the bondage of action, even though he may be acting? The manner in which the Gita has solved the problem is to my knowledge unique. The Gita says: "Do your allotted work but renounce its fruit—be detached and work— have no desire for reward and work …. He who gives up action falls. He who gives up only the reward rises."' [131]

In the context of acting without desiring the fruits of action, Gandhi critiques and rejects a core characteristic of modernity, instrumental rationality, the kind rationality found in reason of state and the calculations of micro-economics. 'He who broods over results', he says, 'is like a man given to objects of senses; he is ever distracted, he says goodbye to all scruples, everything is right in his estimation and he therefore resorts'. As John Maynard Keynes also put it, 'to means fair and foul to attain his ends'.[30] 'when there is no desire for fruit', he says, 'there is no temptation for untruth of *himsa*. Take any instance of untruth or violence, and it will be found that at its back was the desire to attain the cherished end.' [132]

Having located Gandhi within postmodern epistemological space, I turn to locating him within postmodern historical space. Gandhi's 1909 critique and rejection of 'modern civilization' in *Hind Swaraj* anticipates recent scholarly arguments for the historicity of modernity. Stephen Toulmin makes a strong case for its historicity in *Cosmopolis; The Hidden Agenda of Modernity*. He finds modernity's origins in Descartean modern philosophy, Newtonian modern science and Hobbesian modern state theory. For Toulmin the modern era like the classical, medieval or renaissance eras has a discernible historical career, a beginning in the mid-17th century, an apogee before World War I, and a sputtering close somewhere between the end of World War II and the close of the Cold War. Gandhi's challenge to modern civilization in the context of the British empire should be counted as part of the beginning of the end of the modern era.

John McGowan's *Postmodernism and Its Critics* also helps us to recognize the resemblance between Gandhi's historical critique of modernity and the postmodern turn. McGowan asks 'what the word (postmodernism) could possibly mean'. It is used, he answers, 'to designate a specific form of cultural critique …', a critique that 'is resolutely anti-foundationalist—eschewing all appeals to ontological or epistemological or ethical absolutes—while proclaiming itself resolutely radical in its commitment to the transformation of the existing Western social order.'[31] Gandhi too rejected modernity's claims about absolutes and was 'resolutely radical' in his commitment to transform the existing social order. Satyagrahis know 'truth in action', not absolute truth, and are committed to radical social change.

By 1992 Vaclav Havel, an architect and hero of the non-violent revolution in Eastern Europe, could pronounce an epitaph for modern civilization. In 'The End of the Modern Era',[32] Havel interpreted the 'end of Communism' as signalling the passing of 'a major era in human history'. Like Toulmin's interpretive narrative of modernity's 300-year career, Havel spoke of the close of 'the modern age as a whole'. That age, he said, 'has been dominated by the culminating belief ... that the world—and Being as such—is a wholly knowable system governed by a finite number of universal laws that man can grasp and rationally direct for his own benefit.' This confidence 'gave rise to the belief that man ... was capable of objectively describing, explaining and controlling everything that exists, and of possessing the one and only truth about the world.'

A postmodern Havel in 1992, spoke as a prescient postmodern Gandhi had 67 years earlier in *Experiments* of the value of situational truths. Such truths Havel said enabled humans to recognize 'an elementary sense of justice', gave them 'the ability to see things as others do' and 'a sense of transcendental responsibility ...', and made them recognize politics as 'morality in practice'.[33]

Unlike his turn-of-the-century contemporaries in India, Gandhi did not succumb to the allure of colonial modernity. Nor did he, like most of his contemporaries in Europe and the US succumb to the allure of modern civilization's claim of progress or to its siren call of high modernism, that scientific knowledge and Enlightenment rationalism translated into practice by technocrats, engineers, and managers made it possible for man to conquer and command nature, perfect society, and replace poverty with abundance. Nor did he share his contemporary, Max Weber's, tragic view of modernity as an iron cage. Rationalization in the form of instrumental or means-ends rationality, Weber argued, promoted not only objectifying efficiency but also disenchantment—leaving no place in life for religion and myth. Gandhi rejected not only modernity's triumphal progressivism but also its erasure of religion and myth.

Hind Swaraj: A Text for its Time or for Our Time?

How do these readings of modernity's career relate to Gandhi's 1909 critique in *Hind Swaraj* of modern civilization? It is a critique that has gained new currency as doubts about the viability and moral standing of modern civilization[34] have grown. Doubts arose soon after the publication of *Hind*

Swaraj as a result of the seemingly meaningless and senseless carnage, cost and destruction of World War I. Two generations later in the 1960s, the cultural hegemony of modernist discourse began to unravel.

In the 1960s, postmodern thinkers began to ask whether modernity should continue to be accepted as *the* master narrative for our era. The counter-cultural challenges of the 1960s undermined modernity's credibility and moral standing: Rachel Carson's *Silent Spring* [1962] about the dangers of pesticides in the food chain became the seminal work of the environmental movement. Betty Frieden's *Feminine Mystique* sparked the feminist movement. When the students at Berkeley revolted in 1963 they took as their motto the warning on IBM punch cards, 'do not bend, staple or mutilate'. Perhaps the most decisive turning away from modernity to postmodernity came in 1968, the *annus mirabilis,* when students in Paris, Seoul, across the US, and around the world revolted against the modern state's violence and oppression, not least in Vietnam.

Post 1968, as the 'counter-cultural' challenge to modernity entered mainstream discourses at home and globally,[35] Gandhi's 1909 challenge and alternative to modern civilization began to resonate with wider circles of thought and opinion. In 1909 *raj* censors declared Gandhi's challenge and alternative to modern civilization in *Hind Swaraj* politically subversive but they didn't even notice its cultural subversions.[36]

The British Empire was at its apogee before World War I during Gandhi's formative years (1888–1914) as a law student in London and a barrister activist in South Africa. Its unrivalled industrial, commercial, military and cultural power was taken to epitomize modern progress.[37] As *Hind Swaraj* was being written, the Empire was regarded by its votaries and emulators as the world's greatest power, the guarantor as well as the beneficiary of a global *pax Britannica.* Its triumphal voice and symbols were used by its agents at 'home' in England and in the far-flung reaches of a global empire to legitimize, even naturalize, its rule.[38] The agents and votaries of the British empire shared an 'illusion of permanence',[39] an illusion built on confusing power with civilization and culture with biology. The empire's products and services, fleets and armies, ideas, and practices circled the world. In an era that believed in and pursued progress, the Empire's splendour and seeming invincibility exemplified the modern civilization that Gandhi was to characterize, critique, and reject.

When Gandhi wrote *Hind Swaraj* on board the *Kildonan Castle* on his way back to South Africa from London,[40] he not only advanced a critique of modern civilization, he also offered an alternative moral understanding of civilization. Gandhi wrote, in Ashis Nandy's phrase, 'from outside the Imperium', outside, that is, the then-dominant world view of modern civilization. According to Nandy, Gandhi had freed himself from the 'intimate enemy', the alien but domesticated mentality that colonial modernity had implanted in the consciousness of educated Indians.[41]

Gandhi's critique of modern civilization in 1909, when progress was thought of as both desirable and inevitable, seemed to some hopelessly utopian, to others wrong-headed, deluded, and dangerous. His political guru, the liberal Gopal Krishna Gokhale, visiting him in South Africa in 1912, told him he would soon regret having written it, and Nehru, who paid it little attention, thought it perverse. In India it was only in the 1980s, when Nehru's modernist vision and economic legacies began to lose their lustre, that *Hind Swaraj* took on a new life as text for our time.

In 1888, as a 19-year-old from Porbandar, a backwater on the Kathiawar peninsula jutting into the Arabian sea, Gandhi had crossed the 'dark waters' to spend three years as a law student in London. By 1909 he had spent 15 years in South Africa as a successful barrister and a uniquely inventive civil society opponent of an apartheid regime in the making.[42] Still, it wasn't until April 1919, after soldiers of the Indian Army under the command of General Dwyer killed 400 peaceful protestors gathered in Amritsar's Jallianwala Bagh [garden], that Gandhi says he abandoned his belief in the justice of British law and gave up describing himself as a loyal citizen of the Empire.

Was *Hind Swaraj* intended as a nationalist tract for its time, a text designed to address the exigencies of nationalist politics at that moment? Or is it a text meaningful over time, indeed for our time, because it addresses the dark side of modern civilization in ways that have proved relevant a century later? Dietmar Rothermund, a leading historian of India and a Gandhi scholar, reads it as a 'time-bound', 'strategic' document whose interpretation should be confined to the political circumstances under which it was written.[43] Gandhi wrote in response to two constituencies, Rothermund argues, the violent revolutionaries[44] with whom he was in contact during his four-month stay in London, and his friend from student days in London, Dr Pranjivan Mehta, whom he makes his interlocutor and foil in *Hind Swaraj*'s dialogue.

Rothermund makes a 'modern' argument about how to read *Hind Swaraj*: Use archival research to ascertain the 'objective truth' about it. He tells us to treat *Hind Swaraj* as a 'strategic document', a 'nationalist tract' of and for its time. Doing so would not do justice to Gandhi's intentions which are made clear in the 1909 foreword to the Gujarati version of *Hind Swaraj* and in the 1910 preface to the English translation, *Indian Home Rule*. Nor would it do justice to the text's context, meaning, and consequences.

The 1909 foreword and 1910 preface make clear that Gandhi saw himself as part of a larger movement of European thought. In its time and subsequently, that movement has proved to have a global reach. To reduce *Hind Swaraj* to an Indian nationalist tract impoverishes and distorts it. Gandhi learned from and identified with Europeans who doubted, dissented, and resisted empire and modernity. It was they who motivated and helped him to formulate his critique of modern civilization and to articulate his alternative to it.[45]

Gandhi thought of the European dissenters as the 'other' West. It was a West that shaped his civilizational hybridity and countercultural mentality. It was a West to which, in time, he made major contributions. The 'other' West was defined in part by the 14 authors and 20 books Gandhi listed in an appendix to *Hind Swaraj*. It was also defined by public figures of the late 1880s who shaped the climate of opinion he encountered on his arrival in London in 1888—William Morris, George Bernard Shaw, Annie Besant, the labour leader John Burns, the Marxist Maurice Hyndman as well as appendix authors Edward Carpenter and Henry Salt.[46] The authors and public figures imagined another way to live and marched to a different drummer. Gandhi's co-conspirators said no to modernity's siren call of progressivism and maximalism and to empire's awesome violence and splendour.

In the preface and in the foreword of *Hind Swaraj*, Gandhi tells us what he learned from and shared with the other West: 'Whilst the views expressed in *Hind Swaraj* are held by me, I have but endeavoured humbly to follow Tolstoy, Ruskin, Thoreau, Emerson and other writers besides the masters of Indian philosophy. Tolstoy has been one of my teachers for a number of years. Those who want to see a corroboration of the views submitted in the following chapters, will find it in the works of the above-named masters. For ready reference some of the books are mentioned in the Appendices.'[47] And in the foreword he tells us, 'These views are mine, and yet not mine. They are mine because I hope to act according to them. They are also part of my being. But yet, they are not mine, because I lay no claim to originality. They have been formed after reading several books. That which I dimly felt received support from these books.'

Gandhi goes on to make clear that he is aware of the existence and importance of a constituency in India free of the 'intimate enemy' created by colonial modernity and of an 'other west' opposed to the hegemony of modern civilization: 'The views I venture to place before the reader are, needless to say, held by many Indians not touched by what is known as civilization, but I ask the reader to believe me when I tell him that they are also held by *thousands of Europeans*' (emphasis mine).[48]

Clearly, Gandhi believes that what he has to say about modern civilization in *Hind Swaraj* is explicitly or tacitly shared by 'many Indians' and 'thousands of Europeans'. Gandhi did not stereotype or essentialize the West of Western civilization or equate it with modern civilization. He knew that the colonialism and imperialism of Britain, Tsarist Russia, and other European powers and the modern civilization they perpetuated and imposed did not eliminate the possibility of a Ruskin or a Tolstoy speaking from within the West for an 'other' West. For Gandhi in 1909, the countercultural dissent and resistance to the hegemony of modern civilization were already global phenomena.

The twenty books Gandhi recommends for further reading in the appendix of *Hind Swaraj*, cannot, as Dieter Rothermund would have it, be characterized as time-bound by the early 20th-century concerns of Indian nationalism. Four were by Tolstoy (including *The Kingdom of God is Within You*), two by Thoreau (including *Civil Disobedience*), and one each by Ruskin (*Unto This Last*), Plato (*Defence and Death of Socrates*), Giuseppe Mazzini (*Duties of Man*), R.C. Dutt (*Economic History of India*), Henry Maine (*Village Communities*), and Edward Carpenter (*Civilization: Its Cause and Cure*). No doubt Gandhi had written a tract for his times but it is equally clear that he meant to link *Hind Swaraj* to enduring questions, in Tolstoy's phrase, about how we should live. The circumstances surrounding the writing of *Hind Swaraj* suggest that Gandhi meant to create a text that spoke not only to his time but also over time to a world in the thrall of modern civilization.

Gandhi wrote the initial Gujarati version of *Hind Swaraj* and translated Tolstoy's 'Letter to a Hindoo' into Gujarati while travelling on board *The Kildonan Castle*. He tells us that the writing of *Hind Swaraj* was profoundly influenced by Tolstoy's letter. Nominally, the letter was addressed to Taraknath Das,[49] a participant in the violent movement against the partition of Bengal in 1905. In 1909 Das was a political exile living in Vancouver, Canada. His journal, *Free Hindustan*, advocated revolutionary violence.

The addressee suggests the contemporary relevance of the letter but its philosophic and moral content makes clear that it was addressed to Gandhi. Tolstoy's recognition a year later of Gandhi as his spiritual heir substantiates this view. Gandhi wrote *Hind Swaraj* on shipboard after three intense and challenging months in London at the centre of the British Empire. In the Preface, Gandhi tells us that, as he wrote aboard ship during his return journey to South Africa, he 'could not restrain' himself. Eighty years later, in a biography of his grandfather, Rajmohan Gandhi speculates that 'the way the text flowed onto the ship's notepaper and the confidence it exudes suggest that *Hind Swaraj* was felt by Gandhi to be something in the nature of a discovery' about the relationship of violence and non-violence to civilization.[50] Gandhi's Preface to his translation of Tolstoy's 'Letter to a Hindoo' supports this view: the letter's central principle of non-violence, Gandhi says, was exactly his own. For both Gandhi and Tolstoy, non-violence is fundamental to their view of courage and civilization, not a convenient tactic or a weapon of the weak.

What is the nature of this bond between Gandhi and Tolstoy and how was it established? In the opening decade of the 20th century, Tolstoy was the pre-eminent figure of the 'other west,' those who said no to modern progress and violent empire. Max Weber, a leading voice in the discourse about modernity, recognized Tolstoy's challenge to the modern world view in one of his most evocative and provocative essays. 'Science as a Vocation'. It was delivered as a lecture at Munich University in 1918 at the close of World War I and not long before Weber's death.

The war had shattered modernist illusions about progress, mastery, and perfection. Weber first credits Nietzsche's 'devastating criticism of those "last men" who invented happiness' with 'dispelling the illusions' that art, religion or nature can show the way to happiness. 'Who believes in this?' he asks. Can science as a vocation provide an answer? 'Tolstoy', Weber writes, 'has given the simplest answer, with the words; Science is meaningless because it gives no answer to our question, the only question important to us: "What shall we do, and how shall we live?"' Weber is quoting here directly from Tolstoy's 'A Confession'. Weber goes on to argue that science can clarify choices but cannot specify which is the right choice. Near the end of his life Weber was deeply divided between an inevitabilist view of modernity and a tragic view of its consequences. When he imagined a non-modernist alternative it was Tolstoy's way of framing ethics.[51]

Gandhi first wrote to Tolstoy in 1908[52] on the occasion of his 80th birthday. On 1 October 1909, before he sailed for South Africa from London, Gandhi wrote again asking whether he could publish Tolstoy's 'Letter to a Hindoo', which the Rangoon-based Dr Pranjivan Mehta, the previously mentioned friend from Gandhi's student days in London [1888–91] had recently brought to his attention.[53] When Tolstoy agreed, Gandhi had 20,000 copies printed, and published Gujarati and English versions in *Indian Opinion*.[54]

Tolstoy, via his 'A Letter to a Hindoo' told Gandhi that Indians must resist England non-violently; to resist violently would be to yield to the conquerors' world view. Mankind must try to move to a new level of consciousness. The law of love must replace the law of violence. Is it not clear, Tolstoy asked in words that would reappear in *Hind Swaraj*, that '... it is not the English who have enslaved the Indians, but the Indians who have enslaved themselves'.

On 11 November 1909, Gandhi, still in London, had sent Tolstoy 'a copy of a book written by a friend (Joseph Doke) ... in connection with my life, in so far it has a bearing on the struggle with which I am so connected .... As I am very anxious to engage your active interest and sympathy I thought that it would not be considered by you out of the way for me to send you this book'.[55] Tolstoy responded to Doke's biography of Gandhi on 7 September 1910. It was probably Tolstoy's last letter (he died in November). 'Your work in the Transvaal', Tolstoy told Gandhi, 'Which seems to be far away from the center of our world, is yet the most fundamental and the most important to us, supplying the most weighty practical proof in which the world can now share and with which we must participate, not only the Christians but all the peoples of the world.'

These events bonded Tolstoy and Gandhi. Before he died on 20 November Tolstoy had recognized Gandhi as his 'spiritual heir'. Gandhi in turn had launched his first satyagraha from a newly established ashram he called Tolstoy Farm, pledging, 'so far as possible, and so far as we understood it, to follow ... (Tolstoy's) teaching'.

Hind Swaraj can be read at many levels and in several ways. In so far as it links Tolstoy to Gandhi and both to an effort that continues to this day to replace violence with non-violence as the basis for civilization it seems limiting to view *Hind Swaraj* solely as a time-bound or nationalist tract. Hind Swaraj goes well beyond timely political artifice. By embracing and synthesizing the 'other west' *Hind Swaraj* lays out the fundamentals of Gandhi's 'other project', a project beyond Indian nationalism and independence, transforming and transcending 'modern civilization'. *Hind Swaraj's* postmodernism can be found in its ability to reject and go beyond modernity.

Modern Civilization on Trial: Gandhi and Nehru Contest Development

Jawaharlal Nehru, like America's New Deal President Franklin Delano Roosevelt, thought that one should 'make no little plans'; little plans 'have no magic to stir men's blood'.[56] Nehru like Roosevelt, preferred big plans and big dams. He admired the US multipurpose TVA (Tennessee Valley Authority) and tried to replicate it in the Bhakra-Nangal complex and the Damodar Valley Authority.[57] Nehru expected big dams to become the temples of modern India. In this section I explore Gandhi's postmodernism by revisiting his October–November 1945 clash with Nehru over the meaning and practice of 'development'.

Big dams, pre-eminent symbols of high modernist development thinking, are under fire these days—in India, at the Sardar Sarovar on the Narmada[58], at Tehri on the Bhagirathi, and in the world beyond India at the Three Gorges on the Yangtze in China.[59]

Opposition to big dams symbolizes a crisis in the kind of modern development thinking that captured the imagination of Nehru's generation. After World War II and decolonization, Nehru-like development thinking was conceptualized by social scientists as modernization. In 1951 Talcott Parsons and Edward Shils theorized modernization in six pattern variables.[60] In one version or another, the variables dominated social science thinking about development until the 1980s when postmodern critiques began to challenge their hegemony. Beginning in the 1980s and with increasing force in the 1990s, development and its hand-maiden, the developmental state, have become associated with environmental destructiveness, social disorganization, and human oppression.[61] The World Bank has tried to salvage modern development by continuously modifying economic, cost-benefit paradigms, and criteria to include equitable distribution of benefits, basic human needs, sustainability, environmental friendliness, protection of human rights, and benefiting the poorest.[62]

The agent of development, the modern nation state, has come under a cloud too. For Nehru and his inter-war years generation the modern state was enlightened, benign, and effective; a suitable instrument for economic and social transformation. Today, as money, commodities, services, ideas, images, persons, disease, drugs, and terrorism circle the globe with accelerating speed and deeper penetration, the modern state is increasingly seen as obsolescent, less and less able to cope. With decreasing effectiveness, its exclusivist claims to sovereignty and the use of force have lost credibility and legitimacy.[63] At the other extreme is the unbounded sovereignty of the Bush administration's unilateralism. Decreased state effectiveness and legitimacy, and the modern state's apparent inability to reduce, much less eliminate, poverty, the most widely agreed-upon development objective,[64] has cast doubt on the developmental state, an idea and practice that Nehru whole-heartedly embraced and that Gandhi for the most part rejected.

The Gandhi–Nehru debate over development and the modern state began in 1928. Nehru had recently returned from a tour of Western Europe and the Soviet Union. The trip left a deep impression on him, reviving and sharpening his high modernist proclivities. The debate resumed briefly in 1940 and culminated on the eve of Independence in October and November 1945 when the two men clashed over their respective visions of an independent India.

Fifty-five years later, from the perspective of the end of the 20th century, we can see more clearly than most of their contemporaries how and why these nationalist comrades in arms differed. When they first met in December 1916 in Lucknow at the annual meeting of the Indian National Congress, Gandhi was 47, Nehru 27. Gandhi had recently returned to India after 21 years in South Africa, a colony on the periphery of the British empire. His reputation as a satyagrahi on behalf of Indians' civil rights and against racism preceded him. Nehru had returned to India in 1912 after seven years in the homeland of empire, England. He had been a public school boy at Harrow, then done science tripos at Cambridge and studied law at the Inner Temple, an education common to the empire's governing class.[65] From 1920, when Nehru began playing an important role in Indian politics, Gandhi was his mentor. It was through Nehru that Gandhi 'captured the imagination of the younger people ....'[66] By 1926 when Nehru left for an extended tour of Europe, it was clear that Gandhi had chosen him as his political heir.

Why did Gandhi choose Nehru 'despite the latter's known basic differences with him'?[67] In retrospect, it seems clear that their world views were poles apart: Gandhi championed the village, civil society, craft production, and simple living, Nehru the city, the modern state, industrial production, and material well-being.

The apogee of their positive relationship appears to have been in 1929[68] when Gandhi signalled that Nehru was to be his successor by proposing him for the presidency of the Congress. Gandhi famously said at that time, 'the nation is safe in his hands'.[69] Nehru took office and presided over the 'historic' Lahore Congress in December. But he soon reports himself as 'bored' with Gandhi's rather uneventful 'constructive program' and not pleased with Gandhi's reference to 'an idyllic Ram Raj'. In the mid-1930s, Nehru recorded in his diary, 'I am getting more and more certain that there can be no cooperation between Bapu and me. We had better go our own different ways.' And Gandhi wrote to his English friend, admirer and collaborator, Agatha Harrison, that 'Jawaharlal's way is not mine. I do not accept his methods'. But in 1942, when Gandhi launched the Quit India movement, the kind of political action Nehru liked, Gandhi could tell the Wardha session of the AICC that 'when I am gone he (Nehru) will speak my language'.

In an exchange of letters and one meeting in October and November 1945 Gandhi tried to determine if Nehru would in fact speak his language when he was gone. The exchanges focused on what kind future each man envisioned for independent India. Put another way, they exchanged views on what kind of development would be best for an independent India.

Despite the profound differences in October and November 1945 over development that we are about to examine, in June 1946 Gandhi persuaded Vallabhbhai Patel, who held a 6 to 1 lead over Nehru in Provincial Congress Committee nominations, to withdraw from the crucial Congress presidential contest. As a result of Patel's withdrawal, Nehru was unanimously elected Congress president, an event that paved the way for Nehru to head a transitional interim government. After Independence in 1947, the leadership of the party and government that Gandhi had arranged for Nehru meant more than Patel's superior hold over the Congress Parliamentary Party. As a result, Nehru became independent India's first Prime Minister.

Nehru quickly rejected Gandhi's call, in his 'Last Will and Testament', to convert the Indian National Congress from a political party seeking power in the new state into a *Lok Sevak Sangh*, a People's Service Association. In the Constituent Assembly, Nehru avoided addressing Gandhi's request to provide for a 'predominately non-violent state' and saw to it that 'village swaraj' was watered down to non-justiciable panchayati raj clauses in the Constitution's Directive Principles of State Policy.

In 1957, nine years after Gandhi's death, Nehru made an aspect of his differences with Gandhi public when he told a Commonwealth Parliamentary Conference that his government was not, 'pacifist or Gandhian in international or national affairs'. Two years earlier, in a private conversation that Lester Pearson, then Foreign Minister and later Prime Minister of Canada, reports in his memoirs, Nehru described Gandhi as 'an awful old hypocrite'.[70]

Even though Gandhi was acutely aware of these and other differences with Nehru, until his death on 30 January 1948 he supported Nehru over Vallabhbhai Patel for leadership of the Congress party and the government of independent India. Both men regretted their differences and tried to overcome them. Until the end Gandhi persisted in asking Nehru to reconsider his commitments to 'modern civilization'.

Gandhi's assassination put an end to their personal dialogue but not to the discourse it represented. When Gandhi died, two of his letters to Nehru about India's future remained unanswered. Nehru believed that state-directed and-controlled industrialization would solve India's poverty problem and make it a power in the world. State patronage of science, higher education, and research would promote and establish what Nehru sometimes referred to as a 'scientific temper', a modern secular culture that would do for India what the renaissance did for Europe.

The differences between Gandhi and Nehru came to the surface in October and November 1945 when Gandhi asked Nehru to discuss his goals for an independent India.[71] The story, based on extant correspondence, reveals Nehru's incomprehension of and indifference to *Hind Swaraj*, the primary text for understanding Gandhi's critique of modern civilization and the kind of development and state it entailed. Gandhi started with the village and the villager, with local autonomy and employment, with work in small-scale industries, crafts and agriculture. Nehru started with the city and urban life, with centralized state planning, and with production and work in large-scale, impersonal industry and offices.

Gandhi wrote to Nehru that the essence of what he said in *Hind Swaraj* 'is that the things required for human life must be individually controlled by every person ....' 'You will not understand me' he continued, 'if you think that I am talking about the villages of today'. 'My villages ... exist in my imagination.' As if to warn Nehru against privileging or naturalizing his vision of a modern industrial India, he continued with the remark that 'After all, every person lives in the world of his own imagination.'

'The villager in this imagined village', Gandhi continued, 'will not be apathetic .... He will not lead his life like an animal in a squalid dark room. Men and women will live freely and be prepared to face the whole world .... No one will live indolently or luxuriously'. The village of his imagination would be self-reliant, not self-sufficient. 'I can think of many things which will have to be produced on a large scale. Maybe there will be railways, so also post and telegraph. What it will have and what it will not, I do not know, nor do I care. If I can maintain its essence, the rest will mean free facility to come and settle.' Gandhi's imagined village was to be voluntary, another of his experiments with truth. He ended his letter to Nehru by suggesting that they find time to sort out the issues between them.

Nehru agreed that they should meet, adding, 'I don't know when to fit this in. I shall try'. Promising to reply at greater length, he sent off a short answer on 9 October.

'Briefly put, my view is that the question before us is not one of truth versus untruth or non-violence versus violence .... I do not understand why a village should necessarily embody truth and non-violence. A village, normally speaking, is backward intellectually and culturally and no progress can be made from a backward environment. Narrow-minded people (Nehru's conception of Gandhi's imagined villagers?) are much more likely to be untruthful and violent.'

After arguing that 'we must find out specifically how to attain (a sufficiency of food, clothing, housing, sanitation, etc.) speedily', Nehru continued: 'It is many years since I read *Hind Swaraj* .... But even when I read it 20 years ago it seemed to me completely unreal .... It is 38 years since *Hind Swaraj* was written. The world has completely changed since then ... consideration of these questions must keep present facts, forces and the human material we have today in view, otherwise it will be divorced from reality.'

Nehru then reminded Gandhi that '... the Congress has never considered that picture (portrayed in *Hind Swaraj*) much less adopted it. You yourself have never asked to adopt it except for minor aspects'. He then questioned whether it was desirable for 'Congress to consider these fundamental questions .... I should imagine', Nehru continued, 'That a body like the Congress should not lose itself in arguments over such matters which can probably produce great confusion in people's minds resulting in an inability to act in the present.'

On 12 November 1945, Nehru found the time to discuss what development should mean and be in independent India. The only account we have of this conversation is the memo Gandhi sent to Nehru summarizing what he took to be the gist of their discussion. 'I have realized', Gandhi wrote, 'after our talks of yesterday that there is no great difference between us with regard to our modes of thinking and understanding things', He then recorded what he understood to be their areas of agreement.

1. In your view the real question is how to enhance the intellectual, economic, political and moral power of every human being. In mine too.

2. And every person therein have a similar right and opportunity to rise higher.

3. The condition of the country and the city should accordingly be similar in respect to food and water, habitation, clothing and recreation ....

4. ... To ensure that one person does not ride another, the basic unit must be an imaginary village or group that can remain self-sufficient[72] and within the group there needs to be mutual dependence. This way of thinking provides a picture of the relationship among human beings inhabiting the entire world.

Nehru did not respond but his silence speaks for itself; we can infer that he did not accept Gandhi's summary and wanted to exit silently. Gandhi, for his part, didn't press for more meetings nor did he, as Nehru seemed to be daring him to do, attempt to have their differences over the nature of development in free, post-colonial India considered by a meeting of the Congress Working Committee. Perhaps he thought that this was not a time to weaken Nehru's leadership (we known that six months later, on 6 June 1946, he backed Nehru against Patel for Congress president) and that he should wait for a more favourable moment. With the rush of events surrounding Independence, the violence of Partition, and Gandhi's assassination, that moment never came.

Gandhi died in 1948, Nehru in 1964, but the debate about development and modernization continues. At the official level Morarji Desai's Janata government (1977–9) and V.P. Singh's Janata Dal government

(1989–91) gave more credence and weight to Gandhian ideas about development than did Indira Gandhi's (1966–77; 1980–4) and Rajiv Gandhi's (1984–9) Congress governments. Nehruvian discourse and practice about development remained the official creed of the Congress until June 1991, when the advent of economic liberalization changed both discourse and prctice.[73] In the 1970s and with increasing force in the 1980s and 1990s, Gandhi's postmodern version of development became more relevant and salient.[74] His imagined village gained in plausibility and viability even as Nehru's imagined urban, industrial society became increasingly unworkable, unliveable, and unsustainable.[75]

Gandhi's postmodern emphasis on human capital, decentralized production, and 'appropriate technology', challenged modernity's emphasis on physical capital and its efficiency when deployed in Fordist mass production assembly lines.[76] Gandhi's view of machines gained ground too. He welcomed machines when they served rather than enslaved workers. Gandhi's praise for the Singer sewing machine as liberating and productivity-enhancing suggests that he would have welcomed the computer and the information technology revolution. That revolution has made it possible to work at home in the kind of amenity-rich 'villages' that Gandhi imagined.

Economic liberalization in 1991 changed the terms of debate by privileging the market over the centralized planning of the Nehruvian state.[77] The magic of Nehru's imagined India already had begun to fade in the 1970s and faltered in the 1980s as what Nehru called 'the temples of modern India',[78] the big dams and state enterprises, attracted fewer devotees and more employees. Private investment, both domestic and foreign, and market relations began to displace state investment and bureaucratic authority as the driving forces of development. Gandhi's call for the Congress to transform itself from a political party into *Lok Sevak Sangh* [a peoples' service organization] up to a point had happened as NGOs displaced government agencies or helped them with development. From a *Hind Swaraj* perspective, substituting the high modernism of market capitalism for the high modernism of state industrialism may intensify rather than reduce development's destructive and oppressive consequences. The NGO and IT revolutions show some promise of moving beyond the high modernism of the Nehru era to something like the postmodernism of Gandhi's 'imagined village' but not enough to remove the need for *Hind Swaraj's* radical critique of modern civilization. As we leave the 20th and enter the 21st century *Hind Swaraj* remains a text for our time.

The Fate of Panchayati Raj: What Happened to Sovereignty from Below?

The Gandhi–Nehru correspondence of October and November 1945 revealed not only their differences over the meaning of development but also their differences over what kind of state an independent India should have. As we have seen Gandhi argued for 'village *swaraj*'; Nehru, particularly after the Viceroy, Lord Louis Mountbatten, declared for Partition on 3 June 1947, argued for a centralized modern state.

Gandhi was a minimalist about the state; the less the better. In *Hind Swaraj* he had argued that states that govern least, govern best. Gandhi's constitutional ideas were radically decentralist; if there had to be a state (and he accepted that there had to be one) then let it start from the bottom with self-reliant, self-governing village communities.[79]

Nehru's ideas are more familiar. He wanted a modern state. That meant something like the centralized colonial state of the British raj in India but modified after independence by parliamentary democracy, what is often referred to as the Westminster model. For Nehru the Westminster model meant parliamentary sovereignty and party government, that is, electoral mandates that gave disciplined parties a license to rule for five years.[80]

On 21 November 1945, at a time when he chose not to reply to Gandhi's effort to find common ground for India's future, Nehru made his views about a future Indian state quite clear to Sir Benegal Rau, the distinguished civil servant and judge who played a major role in shaping the Indian Constitution.[81] Nehru told Rau that he anticipated 'an expansion of governmental activities .... I should like the new constitution to lay the greatest emphasis on State activities such as planning, industrial development ... nationalization of key industries, etc. ...'[82]

Before 3 June 1947, when the new Viceroy, Lord Louis Mountbatten, announced that the British government would recognize two independent states on the subcontinent, India and Pakistan, Nehru's hopes and plans for an expanded, activist, centralized state had been checked by efforts to institutionalize the sovereignty-sharing arrangements that Mohammed Ali Jinnah and the Muslim League believed would assure Muslims a seat at the table. The only hope of maintaining a common state for Hindus and Muslims lay in projecting a Union government with minimal powers and autonomous provinces with ample powers. The effort failed. In this context Nehru welcomed partition; it meant an activist, centralized state was once again possible.

The Constituent Assembly minus the Muslim League was dominated by the Indian National Congress and Nehru was master of the Congress. He was now free to construct the kind of state he had projected for Rau in November 1945; it was not the kind of state that would have figured in Gandhi's dreams.

Gandhi wanted a decentralized bottom-up state built on a foundation of 'village *swaraj*'. Nehru, along with key 'strong state' allies in the Constituent Assembly such as Vallabhbhai Patel, the 'iron Sardar', and B.R. Ambedkar, India's first Law Minister, Dalit leader and 'father' of the Indian Constitution, wanted a centralized top-down state capable of planned development. Patel, no socialist, wanted centralized powers for the sake of reason of state. Nehru was an urban as well as an industrial person. He would have agreed with Karl Marx about 'the idiocy of rural life'. And Nehru shared Ambedkar's view that village India is 'a sink of localism, a den of ignorance, narrow-mindedness, and communalism'.[83] This troika led the way in blocking and marginalizing efforts by Gandhians in the Constituent Assembly to add in the form of *panchayati raj* institutions, a third autonomous tier in India's 1950 Constitution.[84]

Marginalizing local government is an old story for modern states. Today it is being countered by a postmodern concern for community and local knowledge and empowerment. Although there were important counter-currents (for example, Malcolm Darling's efforts in the Punjab),[85] the British Raj too marginalized rural local government. Its collectors and magistrates were more than willing to be 'kings of the district'.[86] Silencing and patronizing the countryside reflects the modern state's pursuit of centralized power and rationalized administration at the expense of efforts by ordinary citizens to govern themselves locally.

The story of the fate of panchayati raj in the Constituent Assembly and since shows how local knowledge and local power were kept in the wings for almost 50 years.[87] The Gandhians in the Constituent Assembly had to settle for Article 40 of the non-justiciable Directive Principles of State Policy, a constitutional feature that expresses aspirations rather than mandates action. It called upon the Indian state to 'organize village panchayats and endow them with such powers and authority as may be necessary to enable them to function as unit of self-government'.[88] After Independence, bureaucratic establishments supported by powerful and entrenched state-level politicians succeeded, until the passage in 1992 of the Constitution (73rd Amendment) Act, in frustrating attempts to implement

Article 40's objective of establishing an autonomous, constitutionally validated and protected 'third tier' of government.[89]

Panchayati raj, like Gandhi's conception of development in *Hind Swaraj*, made a comeback in the 1990s. Indian intellectuals and activists increasingly recognize that Gandhi anticipated the 'crisis of the nation state'.[90] India in the 1990s began to dismantle its tutelary Nehruvian central planning state. After economic liberalization was launched in 1991, the Indian state began to retreat from the commanding heights of the economy. Moving in the direction of a regulatory state that makes and enforces economic and political rules of the game in a transparent and accountable manner,[91] many Indian politicians and intellectuals welcomed the economic rebirth of the federal system[92] and of local government.

The protracted post-Independence efforts to give substance to Article 40 were renewed in 1992 when the provisions of the 73rd Amendment Act began to be implemented. Part IX, 'The Panchayats', consisting of Articles 243–243 'O', was inserted into the Constitution. These articles provide inter alia for independent state-level elections and finance commissions for panchayats and for one-third reservation of panchayat seats for women. The total number of village panchayats is projected as 225,000. With 10 members each, the number of persons participating at the primary level would be 2.25 million. Total blocks, the next level, comes to 5000 with 25 members each for a total participation at the second tier of 125,000. The 465 30-member, district-level local governments will engage 13,950 persons. With one-third of the seats reserved for women, the total number of women representatives will come to 795,000.[93]

Madhya Pradesh was the first state to conduct panchayat elections under the provisions of Part IX of the Constitution. Some were hopeful that Madhya Pradesh would lead the way to the realization of the 45-year-long effort to implement Gandhian-style local government in India. But early successes bred resistance. By 1994 ministers were reported as 'not happy about relinquishing powers' and bureaucrats as showing 'lack of interest'. Thwarting efforts to establish local government goes back to Munro's and Elphinstone's initiatives in Madras and Bombay under the East India Company and is as recent as resistance to the Balwantry Mehta-inspired reforms of the late 1960s and early 1970s.[94] Ministers and MLAs in Madhya Pradesh resisted plans to turn over control and resources of 25 of the state governments' 49 departments to elected village, block, and district bodies.[95] Madhya Pradesh's then Chief Minister, Digvijay Singh, had persisted in the years after 1993 in efforts to make panchayati raj institutions work, particularly as a means to make primary and school education effective. He used panchyati raj institutions to release primary and school education from the clutches of state-level bureaucracies and bureaucrats, and put them in the hands of local governments.

Gandhi's alternatives to Nehruvian high stateness,[96] self-help and self-rule, truth in action in civil society, and sharing sovereignty in imagined villages,[97] were overshadowed for forty years by Nehru's vision of a modern developmental state. Nehru foresaw a state that was benign, disinterested and enlightened, a state whose moral purposes were to bring 'modern civilization' to India, to make it a respected world power and, by occupying the economy's 'commanding heights', not only to 'eradicate' poverty but also to enhance national power. His vision has been tarnished and eroded by purposes and practices of a different kind. The Soviet Union's high state exemplar which had influenced Nehru's aspirations for Indian economic institutions failed in 1989–91. The instrumentalities of high stateness in India, the dams, the public sector industries, the elaborate network of state controls, and the politics of centralization, were gradually discredited. The dams silted, the PSUs lost money, the permit/licence raj choked the economy, and political centralization stifled the states of the federal system and blocked the realization of panchyati raj.

Gandhi's imagined village, his commitment to appropriate technology and non-violent means, his postmodern vision of swaraj as self-help, self-rule and social capital, may not be a permanent solution for the multiple crises of the modern state. As the world seems to have learned from the achievements and failures evident in the career of the modern nation-state, today's cure often becomes tomorrow's disease; depending on context and the problem at hand, centralization or decentralization can be appropriate responses. But these days and for some time the Gandhi-like postmodern slogan of thinking globally and acting locally seems suited to the needs and temper of the 21st century.

The Prophet at Home and Abroad: Icon or Living Signifier?

It is sometimes said that Gandhi is a prophet honoured more abroad than at home. In the early decades that followed Independence, when hopes for a brighter future were dogged by the trauma of Partition, Gandhi was not widely understood or appreciated. The Nehruvians constructed Gandhi as, at best, a past number and, at worst, a crank who engaged in costly simple living, useful for a time but a traditionalist who nurtured an archaic belief in the potentialities of village India in an industrializing age.

Much of his reception in the first three decades of Independence was formalistic, iconographic, and hagiographic. Statues of Gandhi can be found throughout India, in big city squares and at small town crossroads. Gandhi's walking staff can be heard tapping through the pages of the ubiquitous *Chitra Kathas*, comic books that tell the stories of India's great men and women. Gandhi is featured too in primary school readers. His face stares at us from 10- and 100-rupee notes and from three-rupee stamps. Was Gandhi's fate in independent India to be an icon, in sight but out of mind, a dead monument rather than a living memory?

Gandhi's image and reputation in India began to recuperate in the 1980s when a postmodern Gandhi began to take shape. Books by Ashis Nandy and other scholars contributed to the turn-around.[98] The critical and box office success of Richard Attenborough's 1983 film, *Gandhi*, with Ben Kingsley playing Gandhi, fed back to India and helped to change perceptions and consciousness.[99] A newly-remembered Gandhi began to inspire and legitimize a burgeoning civil society of social and political movements and not-for-profit, non-governmental and voluntary organizations. They supported a variety of goals and causes, including non-violent activism on behalf of the environment, the poor, marginalized minorities, civil and human rights, peace, opposition to nuclear weapons, limiting growth, and panchayati raj.[100]

Several of India's most influential intellectuals—Rajni Kothari, Ramashray Roy, perhaps Partha Chatterjee and, in the diaspora, Bhikhu Parekh, joined Nandy in reading a postmodern Gandhi into the record of India's nationalist movement and postcolonial consciousness. He was shown as crafting an authentic Indian voice by disentangling his ideas and vocabulary from those of the raj's colonial modernity and by reforming and revitalizing tradition. Nandy said that Gandhi spoke from 'outside the imperium' and had freed himself from an 'intimate enemy'; Chatterjee that more than any others of his time and since, Gandhi's discourse came closest to being non-'derivative'.[101] He was acknowledged as a key author of India's civil society and many of its associated movements. The secular-rationalist left, disposed to be suspicious of Gandhi's spiritual aspect, softened its critique. The Hindu right, disposed to suspect his religious inclusivism, began to stress his commitment to Hinduism. Indeed, as Gandhi the icon and monument faded from view and a revitalized Gandhi emerged to occupy considerable political space, he became an increasingly contested multivalent signifier. Ashis Nandy's four Gandhis were no longer enough to accommodate his multiplying meanings.

Gandhi's ideas and persona has been put to many uses at home as well as abroad. Abroad, by 1934, Gandhi had become sufficiently well known for Cole Porter to sing, 'You're the top!/You're Mahatma Gandhi/You'r the top/You're Napolean brandy.' A generation later Albert Einstein wrote that 'I believe that Gandhi's views were the most enlightened of all the political men of our time.' And a decade after Einstein the Gandhi image had moved from high to popular culture; Bob Dylan could sing [in the first of five verses about Gandhi] that 'There was a man named Mahatma Gandhi/He would not bow down, he would not fight/He knew the deal was down and dirty/And nothing wrong could make it right away/But he knew his duty and the price he had to pay/Just another holy man who tried to be a friend/ My God, they killed him.'

At home in India, by 1995, the then Uttar Pradesh Dalit Chief Minister, Mayawati, thought there was political mileage to be gained form Gandhibashing.[102] She replaced his statues with those of notable Dalits and Dalit defenders. An important faction within the BJP hijacked Gandhi to legitimize its *swadeshi* (economic nationalist) political economy policy advocacy. India's influential neo-realist nuclear 'hawk', K. Subrahmanyam, in an article on 'Nuclear Imperialism; A Gandhian Response to NPT and CTBT', used Gandhi to oppose India's participation in the Comprehensive Test Ban Treaty (CTBT). Ramachandra Guha replied in 'Gandhi and the Bomb', and Subrahmanyam riposted with 'Gandhian Strategy'.[103]

Gandhi's recuperation in India had been helped by his growing significance abroad. Not least among those he influenced was Martin Luther King.[104] King adopted Gandhi's methods of non-violent civil disobedience in his leadership of the civil rights movement in the United States. The Montgomery, Alabama, Bus Boycott that launched the civil rights movement in the United States began on 1 December 1955 when Rosa Parks refused to yield her seat on a crowded bus to a white man. Her refusal defied the city segregation ordinance. Her act of civil disobedience had a Gandhian inspiration; six months earlier she had attended a workshop in Monteagle, Tennessee where she had learned about Gandhi and was trained in Gandhian techniques.[105]

Four days later, on 5 December, the young untested King gave 'the most decisive speech of my life, a speech that helped to launch the Montgomery Bus Boycott'.[106] As leader of the Southern Christian Leadership Conference, King made Gandhi a household name in the US by embracing his ideas and methods. In his by now well-known passage about his commitment to Gandhi, he said: 'Gandhi was probably the first person in history to lift the love ethic of Jesus above mere interaction between individuals to a powerful and effective social force on a large scale .... The whole concept of "Satyagraha" was profoundly significant to me.'[107]

In the 1980s Gandhi began to influence European public life. He was acknowledged by non-violent revolutionaries in Eastern Europe—Lech Walesa in Poland and Vaclav Havel in Czechoslovakia.[108] In the 1990s the Dalai Lama began to invoke Gandhi in his non-violent effort to gain autonomy for Tibet. In the 1990s Nelson Mandela was in position publicly to acknowledge that 'the Gandhian influence dominated freedom struggles on the African continent right up to the 1960s'.[109] At the close of the 20th century, *Time* chose Gandhi along with Albert Einstein and Franklin Roosevelt as the three most influential persons of the century.

Gandhi's postmodernism has become increasingly visible and relevant on the Indian and world stage. He has become a pre-eminent voice for civil society and against the modern state. After the state directed carnage of World War I, Gandhi's advocacy and practice of non-violence attracted world wide attention and support[110] and after the Cold War his ideas about civil society as an arena for self-help and social change gained prominence. In the 20th century the modern nation-state reached an apogee and then began to lose its ascendancy. Fading, failing, and failed states became more common.[111] Gandhi's presence grows and his voice amplifies as civil society, often for the better, sometimes for the worse, comes to occupy space in an increasingly active and expanding public sphere.[112] NGOs, voluntary organizations, and social movements count Gandhi as a progenitor whose ideas and methods provide inspiration, legitimacy, and guidance. NGOs provide alternatives to or supplement state programmes and give voice to and empower victims of modernization and development.[113]

Gandhi was pre-eminently a person of civil society. Two of his most important creations, satyagraha, non-violent but militant pursuit of truth in action, and *sarvodaya*, service on behalf of others or for the common good,[114] occurred within the mental and physical space of civil society. He was a tireless theorist and practitioner of self-help. The less individuals and local communities relied on state authority and support the better. Civil society would be recognized as the site, the arena, the space, for addressing not only injustice, inequality, hatred and violence but also development.[115] It is a site distinct from the state and the family where resistance, empowerment and self-help can happen, where persons can take responsibility for themselves and others.

In *Hind Swaraj*, Gandhi used the concept of swaraj or 'self-rule' in a variety of postmodern ways. One way was as a critique of modern formal organizations such as corporate and state bureaucracies, entities that Max Weber said reduced humans to cogs in the bureaucratic machinery. Gandhi was anti-'Fordist' well before the academy invented its negative analysis of mass production and mass consumption.[116] As he put it, he was for production by the masses and against mass production, that is, production on assembly lines.[117] Gandhi saw early on that assembly line production made workers slaves rather than masters of the machine and that the endless multiplication of wants made consumers slaves rather than masters of their desires.

Gandhi's inventions for action in civil society, satyagraha and sarvodaya, often identified the state as the problem, not the solution. In 2005, almost 15 years from the collapse of the Soviet Union's centrally planned economy and state owned economy, we should not imagine that Gandhi would have embraced the globalized market economy as an alternative to state planning and ownership. Well before Karl Polanyi made the case in *The Great Transformation*, Gandhi viewed the market economy's commodification of man and nature as alienating and exploitative.[118]

Gandhi's alternatives to the state and the market were swaraj, individual and group self-rule, and stewardship—not ownership—of property and of nature. Swaraj was a means or process that could, at one level, generate trust and social capital and, at another, lead to 'national independence'. We find versions of swaraj practiced these days by NGOs to constrain and orient states and markets not only 'inside', within states, but also 'outside', among states, in the burgeoning transnational civil society of issue and epistemic communities.[119]

As technology continues to improve efficiency and increase growth, as productivity continues to increase, societies move toward an automated future with fewer jobs and more consumption and pollution. Increased production is premised on increased consumption; there is a negative synergy between them. The more consumption of natural resources and global warming, the more limits on growth become imperative.[120]

Gandhi took from the Bhagavad Gita that mastering desire was essential for swaraj. Translated into the world of man and nature, that meant simple living, serving others, and stewardship. Less was more. Small-scale industry and craft production based on appropriate technology, the kind of production that E.F. Schumacher described in *Small is Beautiful* and that Alvin Toffler, in *The Third Wave*, called 'Gandhi with Satellites'. Gandhi asked for machines that empowered rather than enslaved, and that created rather than eliminated work.

He was a minimalist, not a maximalist, about happiness; limitless desire was enslaving, not liberating. He was a minimalist about nature too; in contemporary language, endless growth puts the biosphere at risk of what contemporary scholars call counter-finality,[121] an uncertain but possible point of no return. Man was part of nature, its steward, not its master.[122]

Gandhi also anticipated postmodern discourses on war and violence, for example, that violence was not only wrong and degrading but also self-perpetuating, self-destructive, and cowardly;[123] on gender, for example, that maleness and femaleness were qualities, not biological essentialisms, that men should be more like women rather than the reverse and that in principle androgyny was the superior form of gender orientation;[124] on the professions, for example, that their goals were easily displaced and corrupted; on lawyers, for example, that they too often fomented conflict for profit;[125] on doctors, for example, that they too readily objectified and dehumanized patients, treating them as objects rather than as persons, and concentrated on curing diseases rather than preventing them by promoting health and practising preventive medicine; on food, for example, that what and how much one ate had a powerful effect on health and well-being; on difference, for example, that inclusivity, shifting the boundaries of identity and truth outward, what Gandhi called brotherhood and Vaclav Havel spoke of as seeing things as others do, was a strategy that fostered non-violence, cooperation, and 'velvet revolution', and that exclusivity, shifting the boundaries of identity and truth inward, was a strategy that fostered violence, civil war and ethnic cleansing; on cooperation, social capital and love, for example, that their supply is neither fixed nor limited and that they are likely to increase with use.[126] Most important, his way of talking and doing, his rhetoric and action, sought to rescue truth from the monopoly claims of science by restoring the autonomy and validity of transcendent, imaginative and subjective truth. His postmodern voice and pursuit of truth in action sought to chart a course away from a failing modernity.

Notes

[1] The earliest version of this essay was delivered as a talk at the Rajendra Prasad Academy in New Delhi on 22 January 1996. I spoke there on the invitation of the academy's director, Bimla Prasad. His books on Gandhi or his circle include *Gandhi, Nehru and J.P.; Studies in Leadership*, Delhi: Chanakya, 1985, 2000 and (ed.) *Jayaprakash Narayan; Selected Works*, New Delhi: Manohar, 2000. Prasad was a close associate of the Gandhian activist, Jayaprakash Narayan.

Many of the ideas for this essay began and matured in connection with a course on 'Gandhi' that I taught at the University of Chicago from 1989 to 2002. Each class was a new adventure in ideas that added to the challenge of understanding and interpreting Gandhi at home and in the world. Because the undergraduate and graduate students in each class were self-selected and highly motivated, their contributions were unusually important to an evolving contextual view of Gandhi. I mention only two from this galaxy, Daniel Klingensmith and Shankar Ramaswami.

[2] The reference to 'high modernism' is meant to invoke the meaning James Scott gives to the term in his book, *Seeing Like a State: How Certain Schemes to improve the Human Condition Have Failed*, New Haven: Yale University Press, 1998. His introduction and chapter on Chandigarh locate Jawaharlal Nehru in the high modernist camp—among those rationalists whose schemes to improve the human condition have failed.

[3] There has been a cascade of outstanding reconsiderations of Gandhi in recent years including work by several scholars who have begun to consider Gandhi as a theorist if not a postmodern theorist. They include Ronald J. Terchek, *Gandhi: Struggling for Autonomy*, Lanham, MD: Rowman & Littlefield, 1998; David Hardiman, *Gandhi in his time and ours*, Delhi: Permanent Black, 2003; Claude Markovits, *The Un-Gandhian Gandhi: The Life and Afterlife of the Mahatma*, Delhi: Permanent Black, 2003; Bart Gruzalski, *On Gandhi*, Belmont, CA: Wadsworth/ Thomas Learning, 2001; Anthony Parel (ed.) *Gandhi, Freedom, and Self-Rule*, Lanham, MD: Lexington Books, 2000, including essays by Parel, Antony Copley, Ronald J. Terchek, Dennis Dalton, Judith M. Brown, Fred Dallmayr, Sudarshan Kapur, and Stephen Hay; Bhikhu Parekh, *Gandhi's Political Philosophy; a Critical Examination*, Notre Dame, Indiana: Notre Dame University Press, 1989 and *Gandhi*, Oxford: Oxford University Press, 1997; and; Vinit Haksar, *Rights, Communities and Disobedience; Liberalism and Gandhi*, New Delhi: Oxford University Press, 2001. Fred Dallmayr has pioneered the field of comparative political theory, a context in which Gandhi becomes a major figure because he transcends the East/West divide. For more on comparative political theory, see Fred Dallmayr, *Beyond Orientalism: Essays on Cross-cultural Encounter*, Lanham, MD: Rowman and Littlefield, 1996.

[4] Gandhi, of course, was not alone in his early critique of modernity and articulation of a postmodernist alternative. As several of Martin Green's books make clear, he was deeply influenced by Leo Tolstoy and, more generally, a child of *fin de siecle* new age thinking, what I call in what follows, 'the other West'. See Martin Green, *The Origins of Nonviolence: Tolstoy and Gandhi in their Historical Settings*, University Park and London: The Pennsylvania State University Press, 1886; Martin Green, *Mountain of Truth; The Counterculture Begins, Ascona, 1900-1920*, Hanover: University Press of New England, 1986; Martin Green, *Gandhi; Voice of a New Age of Revolution*, New York: Continuum, 1993.

Gandhi learned from Tolstoy's critique and repudiation of modern civilization but was an unintended beneficiary of Nietzsche's. Gandhi, as well shall see in some detail, learned from his times even as he added value and broke new ground.

[5] For the modern epistemological turn see Stephen Toulmin's *Cosmopolis: The Hidden Agenda of Modernity*, New York: Free Press, 1990. For an in-depth discussion of Newtonian physics, see Stephen E. Toulmin and June Goodfield, *The Architecture of Matter*, Chicago: Chicago University Press, Phoenix Edition, 1982. For more on Newton's location in the history of ideas see James Gleick, *Isaac Newton*, New York: Pantheon Books, 2003. Gleick locates Newton by saying, 'He was the chief architect of the modern world .... He made knowledge a thing of substance: quantitative and exact', p. 3.

Descartes' *Discourse on Method* was first published in 1637 in a Paris dominated by sceptical philosophy. See Richard Henry Popkin, *The History of Skepticism from Erasmus to Descartes*, New York: Humanities Press, 1964, for a discussion of Descartes' relationship to and ultimate break with scepticism. The theme of Richard Watson's recent biography, *Cogito, Ergo Sum: The Life of Rene Descartes*, Boston, MA: David R. Godine, 2002, is Descartes' 'quest for certain knowledge .... The objective is in, the subjective is out. Descartes triumphed precisely because his method of treating all natural objects—even human bodies—as machines works. He promised that with his method we could become masters and possessors of nature. And he delivered the goods', p. 3.

[6] See Carl Becker's, *The Heavenly City of The Eighteenth Century Philosophers*, New Haven: Yale University Press, 1932.

[7] See Keith M. Baker, *Condorcet; From Natural Philosophy to Social Mathematics*, Chicago: University of Chicago Press, 1975, and Marie Jean Antoine Nicholas Caritat, Marquis de Condorcet, *Sketch for A Historical Picture of the Progress of the Human Mind*, 1795.

[8] Gandhi describes himself as a Karma yogi in 'Anasaktiyoga; The Message of the Gita', his introduction to Mahadev Desai (ed.), *The Gospel of Selfless Action or the Gita According to Gandhi*, Ahmedabad: Navajivan Publishing House, 1929, pp. 125–34. In his introduction to the Gita, Gandhi reviews the claims of the various paths to truth, *moksha*, knowledge, devotion/faith, ritual and action, and concludes that the greatest of these is action.

His Gita presents the war/battle between the Pandavas and the Kauravas as a metaphor for moral struggle in the mind, heart, and soul, i.e. as an exemplar of truth in action.

⁹ See Margaret Chatterjee, *Gandhi's Religious Thought.* South Bend, IN: University of Notre Dame Press, 1983.

¹⁰ M.K. Gandhi, *Satyagraha in South Africa*, Ahmedabad: Navajivan Publishing House, 1971.

¹¹ See M.K. Gandhi, *The Story of My Experiments With Truth*, Boston: Beacon Press, 1957, Part V, Chapters XII–XIX for Gandhi's version of the Champaran story.

¹² See Anthony Parel (ed.), *Gandhi. Hind Swaraj and Other Writings*, Cambridge, UK: Cambridge University Press, 1997, p. xlvii.

¹³ M.K. Gandhi, *Experiments*, p. xiii. Karl Popper was probably the most influential propagator of the doctrine that falsification, being subject to disproof, was a fundamental aspect of science. *The Open Society and its Enemies*, Princeton, NJ: Princeton University Press, 1971.

¹⁴ *The Times of India*, 29 January 1996.

¹⁵ Gandhi attributed his shift from 'God is Truth' to 'Truth is God' in part to his effort to count truth-seeking atheists such as Charles Bradlaugh, whom Gandhi admired and respected, as God-seekers. 'Not even atheists have demurred to the necessity and power of truth ...,' Gandhi wrote. 'I recall the name of Charles Bradlaugh ... I would never regard him as an atheist, I would regard him as a God-fearing man ....'

Gandhi reconstructs a conversation with Charles Bradlaugh, the determined preacher of atheist doctrine, in the Hyde Park of Gandhi's student days: 'His face would redden if I would say, "Mr Bradlaugh, you are a Truth-fearing man and therefore a God-fearing man." I would automatically disarm his criticism by saying Truth is God ....' Anand T. Hingorani (ed.), *Gandhi for 21st Century; 1, God is Truth* by M.K. Gandhi, Mumbai: Bharatiya Vidya Bhavan, 1998, p. 30. See also R.K. Prabhu (ed.), *Truth is God*, Ahmedabad: Navajivan Publishing House, 1956, p. 165.

¹⁶ I take the idea—and the term—'the envy of God' from Haskell Levy's Ph.D. dissertation, 'The Envy of God; on the theology of modern social thought', Department of Political Science, University of Chicago, 1988.

¹⁷ See Stephen Hay, 'Jaina Goals and Disciplines in Gandhi's Pursuit of Swaraj', in Peter Robb and David Taylor (eds), *Rule, Protest, Identity, Aspects of Modern South Asia*, London: Curzon Press/Humanities Press, 1978, pp. 120–31, for Gandhi's relationship to Jain concepts and practices.

The film *Rashomon* is one of the more persuasive performance representations of truth as affected by subjectivity in the form of psychological, physical and moral 'location'.

[18] The quotation is from 'The Sarvodaya State', first published in *Harijan*, 9 January 1940, and republished in M.K. Gandhi, compiled by R.K. Prabhu, *India of My Dreams*, Ahmedabad: Navajivan Publishing House, 1947, p. 80.

[19] M.K. Gandhi, *Experiments*, Introduction, pp. xxvii–xxviii. See also David Edmonds and John Eidinow, *Wittgenstein's Poker: The Story of a Ten-Minute Argument Between Two Great Philosophers*, New York: Ecco/HarperCollins, 2001, where falsification and falsifiability are discussed throughout in the context of Popper's critique of positivism.

[20] I find Deirdre N. McCloskey's characterization of transparency felicitous: 'The theory of reading adopted officially by economists and other scientists is that scientific texts are transparent, a matter of "mere communication", "just style", simply "writing up" the "theoretical results" and "empirical findings". Communication is seen as the transmission of unaltered little messages through intermental pipes, in the manner of the hydraulic tube at the drive in bank, or a sewer. The pipes occasionally get clogged up. That's a "communication problem". Then a Roto-Rooter of "let's be clear" reams out the pipes and lets the flow surge through.' *If You're So Smart: The Narrative of Economic Expertise*, Chicago: University of Chicago Press, 1992, pp. 36–7.

[21] See Ashis Nandy, *The Intimate Enemy, Loss and Recovery of Self under Colonialism*, New Delhi: Oxford University Press, 1983.

[22] See Partha Chatterjee, *Nationalist Thought and the Colonial World; A Derivative Discourse*, Minneapolis, MN: University of Minnesota Press, 1993.

[23] M.K. Gandhi, *Hind Swaraj and Other Writings*, Anthony J. Parel (ed.), Cambridge: Cambridge University Press, 1997, p. 28.

[24] Mohandas K. Gandhi, *The Story of My Experiments with Truth*, Boston: Beacon Press, 1957, 1993, pp. 19–20.

[25] Gandhi, *My Experiments*, pp. 20–1.

[26] Gandhi, *My Experiments*, p. 39.

Gandhi's postmodern hermeneutics can also be seen in his 'observations about the interpretation of vows or pledges .... Interpretation of pledges has been a fruitful source of strife all the world over .... Selfishness turns them a blind eye, and by use of the ambiguous middle they deceive themselves and seek to deceive the world and God. One golden rule is to accept the interpretation honestly put on the pledge by the party administering it .... My mother's interpretation of meat was, according to the golden rule, the true one for me, and not the one my wider experience or my pride of better knowledge might have taught me.' pp. 57–8.

[27] Quotes from Part I, Chapter XIV. The Choice, Gandhi, *My Experiments*, pp. 46–8.

[28] Martin Green, *Gandhi: Voice of a New Age Revolution*, New York: Continuum, 1993, pp. 94–5.

[29] Mohandas K. Gandhi, 'Anasaktiyoga; The Message of the Gita', in Mahadev Desai, editor and co-translator, *The Gospel or Selfless Action or The Gita According to Gandhi*, Ahmedabad: Navajivan Publishing House, 1946.

[30] 'For at least another hundred years', Keynes said, 'we must pretend to ourselves and to every one that fair is foul and foul is fair; for foul is useful and fair is not. Avarice and usury and precaution must be our gods for a little longer still.' http://www.Brainyquote.com/quotes/j/johnmaynar152o46.html.

[31] John McGowan, *Postmodernism and its Critics*, Ithaca, NY: Cornell University Press, 1991, p. ix.

[32] *The New York Times*, 1 March 1992. An address by Vaclav Havel, then President of Czechoslovakia, to the World Economic Forum in Davos, Switzerland, 4 February 1992.

[33] The last phrase about politics being 'morality in practice' is from Vaclav Havel's 1995 Harvard commencement address, 'Civilization's Thin Veneer', *Harvard Magazine*, July–August 1995.

[34] In 1997, Cambridge University Press launched its 'Cambridge Texts in Modern Politics'. Gandhi's *Hind Swaraj*, edited and introduced by Anthony Parel, was chosen to inaugurate the series. The series is designed to provide 'editions in English ... of texts which have been important in the politics of Latin America, Africa and Asia in the later nineteenth century and twentieth century, and which will continue in importance into the twenty-first'.

Other recent interpretations of *Hind Swaraj* can be found in Chapter 5 of Rajmohan Gandhi's *The Good Boatman; A Portrait of Gandhi*, New Delhi: Viking Penguin India, 1995; Nageshwar Prasad (ed.), *Hind Swaraj; A Fresh Look*, New Delhi: Gandhi Peace Foundation, 1985; Makarand Paranjape, *Decolonization and Development; Hind Swaraj Revisioned*, New Delhi: Sage Publications, 1983; and David Hardiman, Chapter 4, 'An Alternative Modernity', in his *Gandhi*.

[35] For the 1960s as an age of dissent see Theodore Roszak, *The Making of a Counter Culture; Reflections on Technocratic Society and its Youthful Opposition*, Garden City, NY: Doubleday, 1969; and Roszak (ed.), *The Dissenting Academy*, New York: Vintage, 1968.

It wasn't until a decade or so after 1968 that postmodernism surfaced in academic teaching and scholarship. See, for example, McGowan, *Postmodernism and Its Critics*, for an early account of postmodernism as an academic subject.

For Gandhi as 'voice of new age revolution' see Martin Green's *Gandhi* which makes this phrase its subtitle.

[36] The Government of India banned the book in 1910. Parel, *Gandhi; Hind Swaraj*, p. lviii.

[37] For accounts of the British Empire at its apogee see James Morris, *Pax Britannica; the Climax of an Empire*, London: Oxford University, 1968; Francis Hutchins, *The Illusion of Permanence; British Imperialism in India*, Princeton, NJ:

Princeton University Press, 1967; and Martin Green, *The Origins of Nonviolence; Tolstoy and Gandhi in their Historical Settings*, University Park and London: The Pennsylvania University Press, 1986.

[38] For how British Empire 'triumphalism' was articulated and shaped attitudes towards self and other, see Martin Green's *The Origins of Nonviolence*.

[39] The title of Hutchins' book, in which he examines the mentality of the agents of the British Empire in India.

The fading and failure of that illusion in the years just before and during World War II is portrayed in Paul Scott's four-volume work *The Jewel in the Crown* republished as *The Raj Quartet*, 4 volumes, Chicago, IL: University of Chicago Press, 1998, and in a 14 hour PBS television series.

[40] Gandhi tells us his version of writing *Hind Swaraj* in *Satyagraha in South Africa*, Ahmedabad: Navajivan Publishing House, 1928, 1950, 1961, 1971; and in his *Experiments with Truth*.

Gandhi had been in London as part of a delegation whose objective was to negotiate better conditions for 'Indian' communities in Natal and Transvaal, political entities that in 1910 became provinces in a self-governing dominion of South Africa.

For an insightful and detailed account of the circumstances that influenced the writing of *Hind Swaraj* see Parel's introduction to his *Gandhi: Hind Swaraj*, Martin Green's *Gandhi*, Chapter V, 'Johannesburg and Satyagraha: 1902–1914', and James D. Hunt, *Gandhi in London*, Revised Edition, New Delhi: Promilla & Co., 1993, Chapter Four, '1909, The Unwilling Petitioner', and Chapter Five, 'The Renunciation of London'.

Gandhi's 1909 visit to London took place at an historical moment when violent methods were attracting the younger generation in India, particularly in Bengal and London. Gandhi was keenly aware of violence's appeal and wrote *Hind Swaraj* in part to counter its appeal and to provide an alternative to it. A leading figure who was at the centre of a Maharashtrian group committed to violent methods was Pandit Shyamji Krishnavarma. He was sufficiently well established to fund scholarships for Indian students. Vinayak Rao 'Veer' Savarkar, Gandhi's nemesis, inventor of 'Hindutva', and like Krishnavarma, linked to Tilak, was a leading advocate and practitioner of violence. Savarkar had arrived in London in July 1906. Gandhi visited Krishnavarma at India House where he met and spoke with Savarkar. For a detailed account see Green, *Gandhi*, 'From Durban to London,' and 'London 1906', pp. 162–7.

[41] Ashis Nandy, 'From Outside the Imperium; Gandhi's Cultural Critique of the West', in *Traditions, Tyranny and Utopias; Essays in Political Awareness*, Delhi: Oxford University Press, 1987, pp. 127–62. In 1967, Susanne Hoeber Rudolph and I had made a similar argument in Part II of *The Modernity of Tradition* on Gandhi in the section entitled 'Gandhi and the New Courage'. That section appears below as Chapter 6.

[42] Joseph J. Doke, *M.K. Gandhi; an Indian Patriot in South Africa*, London: London Indian Chronicle, 1909; M.K. Gandhi, *Satyagraha in South Africa*, Chapter xx; Deepak R. Tamasker, 'The New Radicals: Indian African Political Unity in Mid-Twentieth Century South Africa,' B.A. paper, The College, University of Chicago, 1999; Robert A. Huttenback, *Gandhi in South Africa*; *British Imperialism and the Indian Question, 1860–1914*, Ithaca and London: Cornell University Press, 1971; Maureen Swan, *Gandhi: The South African Experience*, Johannesburg: Ravan Press, 1985.

[43] Commentary at Conference on Contemporary Meanings of Gandhi, Rajendra Prasad Academy, New Delhi, 22 January 1996. These remarks reflect Rothermund's positioning of *Hind Swaraj* in his shorter English and longer German biographies, *Mahatma Gandhi: An Essay in Political Biography*, New Delhi: Manohar, 1991, and *Mahatma Gandhi: Der Revolutionaer der Gewaltlosigkeit* (Mahatma Gandhi; The Revolutionary of Non-Violence), Munich: Piper, 1989.

Although Rothermund sometimes recognizes Gandhi's civilizational critique and writes sympathetically about it, his dominant interpretive frame for *Hind Swaraj* is Gandhi's political tactics and strategy. For example, he tells us that '*Hind Swaraj* was relevant only for India and contained no position with respect to the problems of Indians in South Africa. Gandhi purposely avoided this theme and even pointed out that he would have preferred not to publish *Hind Swaraj* because it might burden his battle in South Africa .... However he felt himself obliged to make clear his position on the spectrum of Indian politics.' *Der Revolutionaer der Gewaltlosigkeit*, p. 70. Translation by Susanne Hoeber Rudolph.

[44] V.D. Savarkar came to London as a young activist in 1906 and was arrested and sent to the Andamans for revolutionary activity, He was believed to be the person who incited Madan Lal Dhingra to assassinate William Curzon-Wyllie, ADC to the Secretary of State for India. Pandit Shyamji Krishnavarma was a linguist, lawyer, and full-time worker in London for Indian nationalist causes. He organized the Indian expatriates in London for violent revolution. Green, *Gandhi*, Chapter 5. Johannesburg and Satyagraha, pp. 145–210 and Parel, *Gandhi; Hind Swaraj*, pp. xxvi–xxvii.

[45] See Green, *Mountain of Truth*, and Parel, Editor's Introduction to *Hind Swaraj*, pp. xiii–lxii.

[46] Green, *Gandhi*, p. 91.

[47] 'Appendices' start on page 120 of Parel's edition of *Hind Swaraj* with 20 entries under I. Some Authorities. I have added the first names in *italics* of the authors listed.

'The following books are recommended for perusal to follow up the study of the foregoing:

The Kingdom of God Is Within You—Tolstoy, *Leo*

What is Art?—Tolstoy, *Leo*

The Slavery of Our Times—Tolstoy, *Leo*
How Shall We Escape?—Tolstoy, *Leo*
The White Slaves of England—Sherard, *Robert H.*
Civilization; Its Cause and Cure—Carpenter, *Edward*
The Fallacy of Speed—Taylor, *Thomas F.*
A New Crusade—Blount, *Godfrey*
On the Duty of Civil Disobedience—Thoreau, *Henry David*
Life Without Principle—Thoreau, *Henry David*
Unto This Last—Ruskin, *John*
Duties of Man—Mazzini, *Giuseppe*
Defence and Death of Socrates—From Plato
Paradoxes of Civilization—Max Nordau
Poverty and Un-British Rule in India—Naoroji, *Dadabhai*
Economic History of India—Dutt, *R. C.*
Village Communities—Maine, *Henry Sumner*

In *Gandhi* and in *Mountain of Truth*, Green pioneered the study of the 'other West' that, from his student days in London, helped to shape Gandhi's outlook and to which Gandhi subsequently contributed.

[48] Parel, *Hind Swaraj*, pp. 6 and 10–11.

[49] A 25-year-old in 1909, Das had fled to Canada from the US where, with others, he tried to rouse American public opinion against British rule in India. 'At the instigation of the British government' he had been imprisoned by the US government 'for advocating the overthrow of the Raj in India by violent means'. Backed by Irish-Americans and the organized labour movement and with the help of the American Civil Liberties Union, he was freed. After World War I, when American opinion began to support Gandhi, Das returned to the US, earned a Ph.D. at Georgetown University in 1924, married a wealthy American, Mary Keatings Morse, became a Gandhi spokesperson to the US public, and, in 1930, established the Taraknath Das Foundation to help Indian students study in US and Germany. He died in the US in 1958. S.P.K. Gupta, *Apostle John and Gandhi; The Mission of John Haynes Holmes for Mahatma Gandhi in the United States of America*, Ahmedabad: Navajivan Publishing House, 1988, pp. 250–1.

[50] Rajmohan Gandhi, *The Good Boatman*, pp. 153–4. Rather than being 'dashed off', as Dietmar Rothermund suggests (*Mahatma Gandhi*, p. 23), *Hind Swaraj* seems to be the creative culmination of an intense, personally challenging four-month stay in England.

[51] For Weber's 'Science as a Vocation' see Max Weber, *From Max Weber; Essays in Sociology*, edited and translated by H.H. Gerth and C. Wright Mills, p. 143. For

Tolstoy's 'A Confession ...' see Leo Tolstoy, *A Confession and Other Religious Writing*, translated by Jane Kentish, London: Penguin, 1987.

I owe thanks and credit to Deborah Wheeler's 'The Tolstoy-Weber Dialogue— a Quest for Meaning', Qualifying Paper, Political Theory, Department of Political Science, University of Chicago, 2/6/1990, p. 24ff, for alerting me to the Weber–Tolstoy connection.

Paul Honingsheim tells in his memoir of 'Max Weber in Heidelberg' that Weber anticipated 'Science as a Vocation' in a 'little known' article, 'Zwei Moralen' (Two Ethics), where he argued that Tolstoy 'had attempted to realize his ideal (of pacifism and living according to The Sermon on the Mount) only in the last period of his life when he actually left his estate and his family and lived as a wandering beggar. Only the man who lives as Tolstoy did in his last weeks can invoke the Sermon on the Mount and proclaim the merits of pacifism and disarmament.' Honingsheim 'interrupts' his account of Weber's voice to say that '... this was written during the war and is to be explained by the situation at that time. On the other hand, I must emphasize that *before the war* (emphasis added) Weber told me that some day he would have to take a stand on Tolstoy.' Paul Honingsheim, *The Unknown Max Weber*, New Brunswick, NJ: Transaction Publishers, 2000, Edited and with introduction by Alan Sica, p. 207.

52 The Gandhi–Tolstoy correspondence is conveniently brought together in *Mahatma Gandhi and Leo Tolstoy Letters*, edited with Introduction and Notes by B. Srinivasan Murthy, Foreword by Virginia Hartt Rinder, Long Beach, CA: Long Beach Publications, 1987. Most quotations from the letters are taken from this publication.

53 A typescript of Tolstoy's 1908 letter was circulating in Indian revolutionary circles in Paris in 1909. Dr Pranjivan Mehta sent a copy to Gandhi in London from Paris and later joined him in London. Parel, *Hind Swaraj*, p. xxix.

54 According to Parel, the English and Gujarati versions of Tolstoy's *Letter to a Hindoo* appeared in December 1909 and January 1910. Unknown to Gandhi, Taraknath Das published the letter at about the same time in the Boston monthly *The Twentieth Century* together with 'a searing refutation of Tolstoy's thesis'. V. Chattopadhyaya wrote his own refutation of Tolstoy in *Bande Mataram*, which was serialized in April 1910 in the *South African Chronicle*, a Durban weekly run by 'Gandhi's Indian rivals in Natal.' Parel, *Hind Swaraj*, p. xxix.

55 The first version of Joseph Doke's biography of Gandhi was published in the *London Indian Chronicle* in 1909. Presumably, this is the edition Gandhi sent to Tolstoy in 1909. The first Indian edition appeared in 1919. The 1909 version carried an introduction by Lord Ampthill supporting Gandhi's efforts during his 1909 London visit to have Indians recognized as citizens of the empire and to secure their rights as citizens in the then self-governing Transvaal.

Joseph Doke, Minister of the Johannesburg Baptist Church, supported Gandhi's non-violent movement against the Transvaal government. In 1908 when '... Gandhi was the victim of a murderous assault by a fellow-Indian .... (Doke and his wife) nursed him back to health in their own home.' See the most recent edition, *M.K. Gandhi, An Indian Patriot in South Africa*, New Delhi: Government of India, Publication Division, Ministry of Information and Broadcasting, 1967. See also James D. Hunt's chapter on 'Gandhi and the Johannesburg Clergy' where he discusses the Gandhi–Doke relationship, pp. 98–123.

[56] The aphorism, which has been attributed to the city planner Daniel Burnham, was said to be one of Franklin Roosevelt's favourites. 'The quotation', a Bartlett footnote says, 'is now doubted'. See Henry M. Saylor, 'Make No Little Plans: Daniel Burnham Thought It but Did He Say it?', *Journal of the American Institute of Architects*, 27 (1957), 3. See *Bartlett's Familiar Quotations*, Sixteenth Edition, Justin Kaplan, General Editor, Boston: Little Brown and Company, 1992, p. 555.

[57] See Daniel Klingensmith's 1998 Ph.D. dissertation in the Department of History, University of Chicago, '"One Valley and a Thousand:" Remaking America, India and the World in the Image of the Tennessee Valley Authority, 1945–1970' (Oxford University Press, forthcoming), for how Nehru, and those of his generation who thought as he did, understood development. Klingensmith argues that what was established through the US–India exchange was '... a set of common metaphors, tropes, symbols and terms, a "poetics" of development. But there is no need,' he continues, 'to assume that ... those ... who invoked the developmental model meant the same thing by it. TVA was ultimately not so much a blueprint as a signifier ... open to a variety of usages and ... meanings, in discourses about the state, civil society, the economy and the environment.' Dissertation Abstract, pp. 2–3.

[58] See K.K. Oza, 'Saga of Failed Dams', *Mainstream*, 8 July 1995, pp. 11–16 for an overview. Amita Baviskar's *In the Belly of the River; Tribal Conflicts over Development in the Narmada Valley*, Delhi: Oxford University Press, 1995, gives an account of the lives of Bhilala adivasis in the Narmada Valley who are fighting displacement by the Sardar Sarovar dam.

For a defence of big dams see Bharat Singh, Water Resources Development Training Centre, University of Roorkee, UP, 'Sardar Sarovar Project—more beneficial than baneful', the *Hindu*, 12 December 1996. Singh argues that the project 'is one of the most thoroughly investigated and meticulously planned projects in this country. It is unfortunate that it is being opposed in India and abroad. The controversy over technical matters such as dam stability, water availability, water logging and siltation rate has no real validity as these aspects fall within the experts' domain .... No development since civilization began has taken place without changing environmental and social conditions. The only criterion is whether the gains are commensurate with the costs. The Sardar Sarovar Project is particularly advantageous in this respect .... For every tribal displaced seven tribals in the command area will benefit'.

The contest over the Sardar Sarovar dam on the Narmada river in Gujarat is reviewed critically, including an account of the World Bank's withdrawal from the project on 30 March 1993, by a leading opponent, Arundhati Roy, in *The Greater Common Good*, Mumbai: India Book Distributors, 1999.

For a recent account of the national controversy over dams on the Narmada river see Robert Jensen, 'The Narmada Gave Us Life; They Have Turned Her Against Us'. *Counterpunch*, 21 September 2004.

[59] If completed, the $24 billion Three Gorges Dam on the Yangtze will be the largest hydroelectric dam in the world. It would span nearly a mile across and tower 575 feet above the world's third longest river. Its reservoir would stretch over 350 miles upstream and force the displacement of close to 1.9 million people. Construction began in 1994 and is scheduled for completion by 2009.

The project is currently facing massive corruption problems, spiralling costs, technological problems, and resettlement difficulties. One million people have been displaced by the dam as of early 2005; many are living under poor conditions with no recourse to address outstanding problems with compensation or resettlement.

[60] The six pattern variables were presented in Talcott Parsons and Edward Shils, *Towards a General Theory of Action*, Cambridge, MA: Harvard University Press, 1951. The pattern variables were expressed as affective versus affect-neutral relationships; particularistic versus universalistic norms; collective versus self-orientation in identity and action; ascription versus achievement in determining status; functional diffuseness versus functional specificity in role determination.

The notions that there are comprehensive and definitive pattern variables that explain human action, a 'general theory of action' and a knowable and perfectible 'social system' (Parsons' first big book was called 'The Social System') continue Condorcet's Enlightenment spirit, a spirit that runs through Marx, Comte, Durkheim and Parsons.

[61] See Meredith Woo Cumings (ed.), *The Developmental State*, Ithaca: Cornell University Press, 1999. For a critique of American scholarship about the Nehruvian developmental state, see Paul R. Brass, 'How American Political Scientists Experienced India's Developmental State', in Lloyd I. Rudolph and J.K. Jacobsen, (eds), *Experiencing the State*, New Delhi: Oxford University Press, 2006.

[62] For a recent evaluation of World Bank doctrine and performance over time, see John Lewis, Devesh Kapur, and Richard Webb, *The World Bank; Its First Half Century*, Washington, D.C.: The Brookings Institution, 1997.

[63] Istvan Hont's essay, 'The Permanent Crisis of a Divided Mankind: "Contemporary Crisis of the Nation State" in Historical Perspective', in John Dunn (ed.), *Contemporary Crisis of the Nation State?*, Oxford, UK and Cambridge, MA: Blackwell, 1995. 'There are two obvious dangers threatening "nation-states": either they cannot preserve their territorial integrity, or they cannot provide the people within their territory with adequate welfare and comfort.'

Hont's theory of two dangers does not, in my view, adequately confront and theorize the 'inside' and 'outside' crises raised by the monopoly sovereignty claims of modern states. For the argument that the modern state has become obsolescent but not obsolete, see R.B.J. Walker, *Inside/Outside: International Relations As Political Theory*, Cambridge, UK: Cambridge University Press, 1993.

For the hollowness of modern state sovereignty claims, see Stephen Krasner, *Sovereignty; Organized Hypocrisy*, Princeton: Princeton University Press, 1999.

[64] In 'The Beautiful Expanding Future of Poverty; Popular Economics as a Psychological Defense', *International Studies Review*, vol. 4, no. 2 [Summer 2002] Ashis Nandy distinguishes between poverty and destitution. Before development undertook to eradicate poverty, large sections of the population were poor but not destitute. The commons, the community, and their kin and neighbours kept most above a subsistence line. Karl Polanyi in *The Great Transformation*, makes a similar argument. Nandy distinguishes pre-modern poverty from modern destitution in another way. In pre-modern societies, the poor and the rich lived differently; their lifestyles were distinguishable. In modern societies the destitute and the affluent share lifestyles but not income, pp. 107–21.

[65] See Rupert Wilkinson, *Gentlemanly Power*, New York: Oxford University Press, 1964, for the tight relationship between education and power before World War I when the Empire seemed to be at its apogee.

[66] Madhu Limaye, *Mahatma Gandhi and Jawaharlal Nehru; A Historic Partnership 1916–1948*, Delhi: B.R. Publishing Corporation, 1989, 4 volumes; vol. I, 1916–31, p. 80.

[67] Limaye, *Mahatma Gandhi*, I, p. vii. These are the words of Madhu Limaye, whose four-volume work is devoted to trying to answer this question.

In his preface, Limaye says, 'The freedom movement drew into its fold the finest elements from the various Provinces of India. Gandhi's magic touch made them into heroes. I often asked myself as to why did Gandhi pick up from among half a dozen eminent leaders—Rajaji, Vallabhbhai, Rajendra Prasad, Abul Kalam Azad, Jawalarlal Nehru and Subhas Chandra Bose—Jawaharlal Nehru as his heir despite the latter's known basic differences with him? This question troubled me because it was difficult for me to conceive Jawaharlal rising to pre-eminence either without Gandhi's decisive intervention in India's politics or Gandhi's deliberately and persistently promoting his succession. This question has interested me and mystified me, in turns, these last fifty years.'

[68] For why Gandhi and Nehru only appear to be close in 1929 see Chapter 2 'The Road Not Taken'. In 1927 Gandhi blocked a Motilal Nehru effort to make his son, Jawaharlal, Congress president. Gandhi and Nehru fought over whether Congress' goal should be dominion status or complete independence. Gandhi told Nehru to unfurl his own flag, that is, leave the Congress on the issue and to set up his own organization. Nehru declined to leave and asked for forgiveness. In the

process it became clear to Gandhi that Nehru spoke for a younger generation that had to be accommodated if Congress was to remain united and strong. At the December 1929 Lahore annual meeting Congress resolved that unless Britain granted dominion status, Gandhi's position, within one year Congress would adopt immediate independence, Nehru's position, as its goal. Dominion status was not granted and in 1930 Congress abandoned dominion status for complete independence.

[69] Tendulkar, *Mahatma*, New Delhi: Government of India, 1962, vol. II, p. 490.

[70] S.C. Gangal says in 'Gandhi and Nehru: A Love-Hate Relationship', the *Hindu*, 28 November 1995, that 'none of Nehru's successors nor any of the Nehru family members or aides has contradicted Pearson's published record'. Gangal concludes his account with the observation that 'within less than a decade of Gandhi's passing away Nehru was totally alienated from Gandhi—not only politically and ideologically ... but personally and emotionally'.

[71] Gandhi's attempt in 1945 to engage Nehru about their respective visions of post-Independence India first came to my attention when I read Nehru's *A Bunch of Old Letters*, London: Asia Publishing House, 1960, which reproduces their exchange of letters in October and November, 1945. The late Raj Krishna's article, 'The Nehru-Gandhi Polarity and Economic Policy' in B.R. Nanda et al. (eds), *Gandhi and Nehru*, Delhi: Oxford University Press, 1979, was also particularly helpful. An early account of the October/November 1945 exchange of letters can be found in Bimla Prasad's *Gandhi, Nehru & JP*, Delhi: Chanakya Publications, 1985, pp. 274–8. I would not agree with his statement that 'the correspondence only shows difference in emphasis but agreement on fundamentals.' Also helpful for constructing the relationship is B.R. Nanda's chapter on 'Man versus Machine' in his *Gandhi and His Critics*, New Delhi: Oxford University Press, 1985. Martin Green's accounts in *Gandhi* particularly pp. 196–8, of Gandhi–Nehru relations are telling.

In writing about the Gandhi–Nehru debate in 1945 about development I have also drawn on Sudhir Chandra's '"The Language of Modern Ideas"; Reflections on an Ethnological Parable', Thesis Eleven (an MIT Press Journal), Number 39, 1994, pp. 39–51. Parel's edition of *Hind Swaraj*, pp. 149–56, provides the complete texts.

[72] Gandhi here refers to village communities as 'self-sufficient', a usage frequently followed by Gandhi commentators and interpreters. I have remarked in the body of the text above that Gandhi viewed village communities as self-reliant, not self-sufficient. As quoted above, he wrote to Nehru, 'I can think of many things which will have to be produced on a large scale. Maybe there will be railways, so also post and telegraph'. I take these remarks as supporting self-reliance over self-sufficiency. They also suggest that Gandhi accepted some of the technologies and economies of scale of his time and that he anticipated similar conditions and their consequences in the future.

[73] Faced with the threat of national bankruptcy in the form of a balance of payments crisis, a newly elected Narasimha Rao Congress government with

Manmohan Singh as Finance Minister responded by 'liberalizing' the economy internally by abandoning *inter alia* the 'permit-licence raj', and externally by abandoning economic nationalism and autarchy, lowering tariffs and moving toward participation in world markets and the global economy.

[74] See Sumit Roy, 'Development, Environment and Poverty; Some Issues for Discussion', *Economic and Political Weekly*, 27 January 1996, pp. 29–41. Roy addresses environmental concerns that have modified 'traditional' development goals and led to the concept of 'sustainable development'. He also takes account of 'a shift in emphasis from state to market forces in shaping development policies'.

Roy's analysis encompasses the 1972 UN Conference on Human Environment held in Stockholm where Prime Minister Indira Gandhi played a prominent role in ushering in the environment on the international agenda.

[75] By 2005, the time of this writing, China and India were contributing to the limits of growth crisis by gobbling up ever larger amounts and proportions of world commodities and to the global warming crisis by burning ever larger amounts and proportions of fossil fuels.

[76] The move from work, production, and markets based on the mass production and mass consumption of what David Harvey calls Fordism to what he calls 'flexible accumulation' can be found in Chapters 8 and 9 of his *The Condition of Postmodernity*, Cambridge, MA: Blackwell, 1990, pp. 125–72. Harvey derives his ideas about Fordism from Charles Sabel's *Work and Politics: the Division of Labour in Industry*, Cambridge: Cambridge University Press, 1982.

[77] In June 1991 when the Narasimha Rao Congress government took office the country was on the verge of bankruptcy. An IMF bailout was accompanied by Manmohan Singh's 'reform' measures that signalled an end to Nehruvian-style state-led development. The implosion of the Soviet imperial state, the bankruptcy of communist ideology and, perhaps most important, the discrediting of centrally planned economies in the Soviet Union and Eastern Europe set the stage for India's turn to liberalization.

[78] See Baren Ray's 'The burden of population', the *Hindu*, 1 June 1995, where he argues that the swaraj path established by millions of Gandhian activists was abandoned for a Nehruvian pursuit of 'science and technology (that) led to a concentration and over-centralization of all the entrepreneurial effort—of all the eggs being put in the same basket—namely in what Jawaharlal Nehru called the temples of modern India'.

[79] Village adults would directly elect panchayats, local councils. Higher-level bodies at the *taluka* and district levels would be composed of *sarpanches* (representatives) elected from the level below and exercise advisory powers. Members from district and municipal levels would make up provincial- (now state)-level panchayats which would elect presidents of provincial governments. They in turn would form an All-India Panchayat whose internally-elected president would serve

as head of state and of government. Like the clause in the US Constitution that makes it incumbent on the US President 'to faithfully execute the laws', the president of the All-India Panchayat would act primarily as an implementing agent. This sketch is from Shriman Narayan Agarwal's *Gandhian Constitution for a Free India*, Allahabad: Kitabistan, 1946, as glossed by Granville Austin, *The Indian Constitution*, New York: Oxford University Press, 1966, p. 30. Gandhi said that he had not checked every word in Agarwal's book but hadn't found anything jarring in what he had read. Even so he had asked Agarwal to make some alterations. It seems Gandhi approved of the book's general approach.

[80] See B.N. Rau, *India's Constitution in the Making*, edited by B. Shiva Rao, Mumbai: Orient Longman, 1960.

[81] Rau was under instructions from the then Viceroy, Lord Wavell, to sound out Nehru about his expectations concerning the Constitution to be framed by the Constituent Assembly that would convene on 6 December 1945.

[82] *India's Constitution in the Making*, quotation form B. Shiva Rao's Foreword, pp. xxxiii and xxxiv.

[83] I am not so much disputing this view as implicitly calling attention to Gandhi's 'imagined village', the kind of village his constructive programme and social reforms were meant to realize. Nehru's imagined state had not yet revealed its pathological face, that is, as self-serving, corrupt, inefficient, rent-seeking, predatory, and violent, so Nehru had the advantage in 1945–50 in the contest between him and Gandhi over visions of the future.

Ambedkar's image of village India does capture part of the truth even today. Investigations conducted in the early 1990s of the role of lower castes and classes in local structures suggest that 'traditional oligarchies' were—and are—more powerful at local than at district or provincial/state levels. Thus James Manor's 1994 finding that Scheduled Castes participate least in the most local levels of *panchayati raj* but gain voice and influence at the district and particularly at the state levels, where local oligarchies count less. Richard Crook and James Manor, 'Enhancing Participation and Institutional Performance: Democratic Decentralization in South Asia and West Africa', Report to ESCO, the Overseas Development Administration (Great Britain), 1994, Chapter II, Karnataka.

[84] For a detailed, carefully researched account of the story see Austin, *Indian Constitution*, Chapter 2, 'Which Road to Social Revolution', pp. 26–49.

[85] For an insightful account of Darling see Clive Dewey, *Anglo-Indian Attitudes: the mind of the Indian Civil Service*, London: Rio Grande/Hameldon Press, 1993.

[86] For the mentality and perspective of Raj administrators see Philip Mason (pseudonym Woodruff), *The Men Who Ruled India*, London: Cape, 1963, 2 vols, vol. 2, *The Guardians*.

[87] See James Scott's *Seeing Like a State; How Certain Schemes to Improve the Human Condition Have Failed*, New Haven: Yale University Press, 1998, where he

discusses the importance of local knowledge, how it is scorned by objective truth modernism, and examines, in a chapter on Chandigarh, the ideas and practices of Nehru's 'high modernism'.

[88] For a recent historical and analytical account of panchayati raj that views its future as promising, see George Mathew, *Panchayati Raj: From Legislation to Movement*, New Delhi: Concept Publishing Co., 1994.

A short version of the tangled story of Gandhian-inspired efforts to make panchayati raj the third tier of India's federal system is given in Robert L. Hardgrave, Jr and Stanley A. Kockanek, *India; Government & Politics in a Developing Nation*, Fifth Edition, Fort Worth: Harcourt Brace Jovanovich College Publishers, 1993, 'Village Government: Panchayati Raj', pp. 112–15.

Their story ends with Rajiv Gandhi's abortive effort in 1989 on the eve of the ninth parliamentary election to appropriate his opponent's issue by making the 64th Amendment Bill a key feature of his campaign. Nominally yet another effort to reinvigorate moribund panchayati raj institutions, it 'would have created a nationwide program of centralization' by controlling local government funds from Delhi thereby bypassing the state governments, many of which were in opposition hands. The move would have converted panchayati raj into a tool of centralization[.] pp. 268–9.

[89] For an overview of efforts to establish panchayati raj institutions in several states, see Mathew, *Panchayati Raj*. The story of aborted efforts to establish panchayati raj as an independent and parallel structure of the Indian state is told in a Rajasthan context by James Warner Bjorkman and the late Het Ram Chaturvedi in 'Panchayati Raj in Rajasthan: The Penalties of Success', in Karine Schomer, Joan L. Erdman, Deryck O. Loderick, and Lloyd I. Rudolph, *The Idea of Rajasthan; Explorations in Regional Identity*, vol. II, *Institutions*, New Delhi: Manohar and Columbia, MO., South Asia Publications, 1994, pp. 132–58. Bjorkman and Chaturvedi speak of 'the thwarted revolution' and a '"failure" of success', referring to the backlash on the part of ministers and MLAs to loss of power, resources, and patronage to local communities and their governments.

[90] Since the end of the Cold War and the national security state, many academic and policy intellectuals have written about the modern nation-state being in deep trouble. Noted Cambridge political theorist John Dunn entitles his edited book *Contemporary Crisis of the Nation State?* Mathew Horman and Andrew Marshall entitle their 1995 book *After the Nation-State*, and Ash Narain Roy asks in the *Hindustan Times* of 3 March 1996 'Is the nation-state doomed?' In the second half of the 1990s, with the rise of amorphous processes collectively known as 'globalization', the modern nation-state has found itself even more embattled. For one of many globalization processes and its relation to the sovereignty claims of the modern state, see Susanne Hoeber Rudolph and James Piscatori (eds), *Transnational Religion and Fading States*, Boulder, CO: Westview Press, 1997.

[91] See Lloyd I. Rudolph and Susanne Hoeber Rudolph, 'Redoing the Constitutional Design; From an Interventionist to a Regulatory State', in Atul Kohli

(ed.), *The Success of India's Democracy*, Cambridge, UK: Cambridge University Press, 2001.

[92] For the economic rebirth of the federal system, see Lloyd I. Rudolph and Susanne Hoeber Rudolph, 'The Iconization of Chandrababu; Sharing Sovereignty in India's Federal Market Economy', *Economic and Political Weekly*, XXXVI, 5–11 May, pp. 1541–52.

[93] See the *Pioneer*, 7 March 1996, 'Change in women's lives; a social transformation is taking place due to the reservation for women in rural bodies', which gives these estimated numbers at the various levels of panchayati raj.

[94] For an analysis of the causes of the defeat of the Balwant Rai Mehta reforms see James Warner Bjorkman and Het Ram Chaturvedi, 'Panchyati Raj in Rajasthan: The Penalties of Success', in Lloyd I. Rudolph et al. (eds), *The Idea of Rajastan: Explorations in Regional Identity, Volume II. Institutions*, New Delhi: Manohar/American Institute of Indian Studies, 1994, 2001, pp. 117–58.

[95] V. Venkatesan, 'Great expectations; Panchayati raj in Madhya Pradesh', *Frontline*, 19 July 1994, pp. 30–2.

As George Mathew remarked in *Panchayati Raj*: '... had it not been for the fact that the state legislatures were created along with the Parliament our respected MPs would not have allowed even the state legislatures to come up, once they had tasted power in the initial years.'

[96] For the concepts of high and low stateness and their application to Third World countries as well as Europe and the US, see J. Peter Nettl, 'The State As Conceptual Variable', *World Politics*, XX, July 1969, pp. 559–79.

[97] Gandhi's postmodern imagined village as a critique or an alternative to modernity's pathologies and failures is evident in Ashis Nandy's follow-up to the 22 January 1996 seminar at the Rajendra Prasad Institute where Susanne Rudolph and I contrasted Gandhi's and Nehru's visions of what 'the village' is and might be. In 'The Village; Its Decline in the Imagination' (*Times of India*, 18 March 1996) Nandy lamented that the village as created by Gandhi, Satyajit Ray, R.K. Narayan, and M.N. Srinivas was collapsing. 'As a collectivity we are in the process of losing that imagination' and in doing so impoverishing the Indian civilization.

[98] For a broad review of Gandhi's influence and standing in 1969, the hundredth anniversary of his birth, see Pran Chopra, *The Sage in Revolt: A Remembrance,* New Delhi: Popular Prakashan for the Gandhi Peace Foundation, 1972. Chopra's book may have been a turning point in that he spoke *inter alia* of what Gandhi had to contribute to India's present and future.

No doubt the publication of two of Ashis Nandy's early books, *At the Edge of Psychology; Essays in Politics and Culture*, Delhi: Oxford University Press, 1980, and *The Intimate Enemy: Loss and Recovery of Self Under Colonialism*, Delhi: Oxford University Press, 1983, gave a kick start to the Gandhi turnaround in India. So did the revival of interest in *Hind Swaraj* by less well known authors such as Makarand

Paranjpe, *Decolonization and Development; Hind Swaraj Revisioned*, 1983, Nageshwar Prasad (ed.), *Hind Swaraj: A Fresh Look*, 1985; and, most importantly, the study that recognized Gandhi's *Hind Swaraj* as a classic in political thought, Anthony Parel's *Gandhi. Hind Swaraj and Other Writings*, 1997.

The Nehruvian perspective was strongly entrenched in official Indian circles. When I gave the required lecture on Gandhi at the Lal Bahadur Shastri National Academy of Administration at Mussoorie in 1962, I anticipated the message of this book by interpreting him as a 'post-industrial critic'. The probationers listened in disbelief. These about-to-be Indian Administrative Service [IAS] officers, successors to the ICS, the raj's 'steel frame', were steeped in the Nehruvian world view. I was given a very hard time in the question period that followed. Only two of the one hundred or so probationers spoke to be afterward about their admiration for Gandhi.

[99] For the politics of the reception of Attenborough's *Gandhi* see Lloyd I. Rudolph, 'The *Gandhi* Controversy in America', in Robert M. Crunden (ed.), *Traffic in Ideas Between India and America*, Delhi: Chanakya, 1985.

[100] By 1989 the sixteen essays in John H. Hicks and Lamount C. Hempel (eds), *Gandhi's Significance for Today; The Elusive Legacy*, New York: St Martin's Press, 1989, captured something of the Gandhi revival in India. So too did Mark Juergensmeyer, *Fighting With Gandhi*, San Francisco and New York: Harper and Row, 1984; and B.R. Nanda, *Gandhi and His Critics*, Delhi: Oxford University Press, 1985.

[101] 'Chatterjee was asked by Nermeen Shaikh about his book, *Nationalist Thought and the Colonial World*. You suggest, Shaikh says, "that nationalist thought operates 'within a framework of knowledge whose representational structure corresponds to the very structure of power it seeks to repudiate.' In other words nationalism may succeed in liberating the nation from colonialism but not from the knowledge system of the post-Enlightenment West, which may continue to dominate maybe even more powerfully. Could you elaborate this argument?'

Chatterjee's reply with respect to Gandhi was: '... the whole Gandhian way of thinking was clearly very interesting. My answer .... Yes, this was clearly *an attempt to think of the state and forms of rule in very different terms.* But it was effectively a failure. Having raised the question and *having produced completely new conditions* through which people could be mobilized for the anti-colonial movement, the Gandhian intervention in effect completely failed to reach the sorts of objectives that it had placed before the nation ... because of the way in which it tried to deal with the fundamental problem of violence in society .... The original and distinctive contribution of Gandhian politics was to evolve *amazingly effective techniques of non-violent resistance* by an unarmed people against the institutions of state violence. But it never managed to propose a theory .... By which a state could legitimately employ violence against wrongdoers.' (My emphasis.) "Towards a Postcolonial Modernity: AsiaSource Interview with Partha Chatterjee." http://www.asiasource.org/news/special_reports/chatterjee_print.html.

I have underlined phrases that suggest how Gandhi devised means to resist and colonial rule and gain independence. Chatterjee, it seems, is among those who, as Gandhi said in *Hind Swaraj*, 'want the tiger's nature, but not the tiger ...', that is the violence of British rule without the British. Parel (ed.), *Hind Swaraj*, p. 28.

More broadly, it seems that Chatterjee's modernism leads him to accept the violence of the modern state. Gandhi rejected the centrality of violence to the modern state but accepted the need for armed forces to defend the country and the necessity of *artha* [which entails a functioning state] to the creation and existence of the good society. For Gandhi the *karma yogi* virtuous conduct included engaging in public life. He agreed, he said, with Thoreau, 'that government is best which governs the least'. *Collected Works*, v. 62, p. 92. He insisted at the second Round Table Conference that 'a nation that has no control over her own defense forces, and over her external policy is hardly a responsible nation. Defense, its army, is to a nation the very essence of its existence ....' *Collected Works*, v. 48, p. 304.

[102] One of the strategies Mayawati pursued as UP chief minister during her six-month term in 1995 was to promote the Dalit cause through symbolic politics. For example, she had statues of Dalit heroes erected at the center of Lucknow, the state capital. Foremost among them was a statue of E.V. Ramaswami Naicker, leader in Madras, now Tamil Nadu, in the 1920s and 1930s of the lower-caste anti-Brahmin movement that became, in the 1950s, the regional nationalist DMK (Dravida Munnetra Kazhagam) party. She also saw to the tearing down of Gandhi statues throughout the state. Gandhi was a target *inter alia* because, while not a Brahmin, pictured as the principal oppressor of Dalits he was, as a *baniya* (*vaishya* or merchant caste), among the 'twice born' (spiritually reborn via the uppanaya ceremony at which a sacred thread is donned) upper castes. The attack on Gandhi along with the broader attack on Brahmins and upper castes more generally led the then upper caste-dominated BJP (Bharatiya Janata Party) to withdraw its support to Mayawati's BSP (Bahujan Samaj Party) led government.

[103] *Times of India*, 24 January, 30 January, 1 February 1996.

[104] For a more elaborate account of the Gandhi–King relationship, see Chapter 3. "Gandhi in the Mind of America" in this volume.

[105] See Clare and Harris Wofford, *India Afire*, New York: J. Day and Co., 1951. Wofford gives an account of how his friend, the Gandhian Socialist, Ram Manohar Lohia, had visited the US and, *inter alia*, helped to set up a Gandhian-oriented training institution for civil rights workers at the Highlander Folk School in Monteagle, Tennessee Harris Wofford, *Of Kennedys and Kings; Making Sense of the Sixties*, Pittsburgh: University of Pittsburgh Press, 1980, pp. 112 and 190.

Rosa Parks worked as a tailor assistant in Montgomery Fair, a local department store. She had joined the NAACP in 1943, worked with the NAACP state president, Edgar Daniel Nixon, and was elected secretary of the Montgomery chapter. It had been looking for a test case to challenge the legality of segregated bus seating and to gain public support by launching protests against it. See http://www.africanaonline.com/rosa_parks.htm.

[106] Martin Luther King, *Stride Toward Freedom: The Montgomery Story*, New York: Harper, 1958, p. 45.

[107] King, *Stride Towards Freedom*, pp. 78–9.

[108] For some measure of Gandhi's influence on resistance in Eastern Europe, see Rainer Hilderbrandt with collaboration from Hans-Jurgen Dyck, *From Gandhi to Walesa; Nonviolent Struggle for Human Rights; A Documentation with 181 Photos*, Berlin, Publishing House at Checkpoint Charlie, 1987.

See also several of Vaclav Havel's essays in *Living in Truth*, London: Faber and Faber, 1986; and E. Kriseova, *Vaclav Havel. The Authorized Biography*, New York: St Martin's Press, 1993.

[109] For the Dalai Lama see T. Gyatso, *Freedom in Exile; The Autobiography of the Dalai Lama*, New York: HarperCollins, 1990.

Mandela wrote in 1999, 'I followed the Gandhian (non-violent) strategy for as long as I could ... (the ANC) chose sabotage because it did not involve loss of life, and it offered the best hope for future race relations'.

Both ANC Nobel Prize for Peace recipients Albert Luthili and Desmond Tutu were followers of Gandhi. See *Time*, 31 December 1999.

[110] Chapter 3 of this volume, 'Gandhi in the Mind of America', details his reception in the US after World War I. Claude Markovits does something similar for Gandhi's reception in Europe. The vehicle was Nobel Prize winner Romain Rolland's 1923 biography of Gandhi. It was translated from the French into several European languages, including German, and English and sold well. 'Romain Rolland's prestige was then at its peak: his critical attitude towards the great butchery of 1914–18 had elevated him to the status of keeper of the conscience of the world, in the manner of Tolstoy prior to the Great War .... The combination of deep empathy and literary skill explains why the text had such an impact and helped make Gandhi a well-known figure beyond India and the English speaking countries .... Rolland's most important contribution to the birth of the Gandhian legend was the link he established between the European intelligentsia's pteoccupation with peace and Gandhi's teaching ....' Claude Markovits, *The Un-Gandhian Gandhi: The Life and Afterlife of the Mahatma*, Delhi: Permanent Black, 2003, pp. 17–19.

[111] For more on fading states see Susanne Hoeber Rudolph, 'Introduction: Religion, States, and Transnational Civil Society', in Susanne Hoeber Rudolph and James Piscatori (eds), *Trnasnational Religion & Fading States*, pp. 1–24.

[112] For a recent systematic analysis of the civil society concept in the context of political theory, see Neera Chandhoke, *State and Civil Society; Explorations in Political Theory*, New Delhi: Sage Publications, 1995, where *inter alia* she considers civil society's conceptual history, the constitution of the civil sphere, and civil society as an arena for contestation.

[113] For an effort a decade ago to enumerate the often Gandhi-inspired or legitimized burgeoning world of NGOs in South Asia, see Todd Nachowitz (ed.), *An Alternative Directory of Nongovernmental Organizations In South Asia*, revised edition, Syracuse, N.Y., Maxwell School of Citizenship and Public Affairs, Syracuse University, 1990. Approximately 1000 NGOs are listed in this booklet under headings such as alternative travel and tourism; animal rights; anti-nuclear alternatives; appropriate technology; Bhopal; children and youth; consumer rights; occupational safety; cottage industries; education; environmental; food and hunger; forestry; health; human services; human rights; media; organic farming; peace and disarmament; people's empowerment; refugees; research and documentation; rural development; tribals; urban development; women.

Since 1990 the number of NGOs has increased exponentially and their range geometrically. The Union and state governments have come increasingly to rely on NGOs to implement as well as to inaugurate programmes. This has meant that large sums are available, a condition that has led to corruption as spurious or non-performing organizations have multiplied. Support from outside India has come under increasing attack. Voluntary service has given way to salaried professionalism. Such development have cast a cloud over the NGO world but not succeeded in dimming its lustre.

For defence of the forests in the Garhwal region of Uttar Pradesh, particularly the paradigmatic Chipko movement and its progeny in Garhwal, see Antje Linkenback, 'Ecological Movements and the Critique of Development: Agents and Interpreters,' *Thesis Eleven* (an MIT Press journal), No. 39, 1994, pp. 63–85. Medha Patkar and Arundhati Roy's efforts on behalf of the displaced peasants of the Narmada dam basin continues the Gandhian resistance tradition

[114] For a comprehensive account of Gandhi's views on and programmes for self-help constructive work at the village level, see M.K. Gandhi, *India of My Dreams*, Ahmedabad: Navajivan Publishing House, 1947, particularly chapters 15–20.

In the 1990s, as self-help in the form of NGOs and voluntary associations became more active and influential, a backlash against their influence as 'parallel governments', conduits for foreign influence and channels for fraudulent and corrupt use of government funds began to develop. Such abuses were the exception rather than the rule, clearly a failure of success. Nevertheless the abuses began to give NGOs a bad name, opening the way for a discourse about the contestation over Gandhian versions of civil society as swaraj and self-help.

For an example of this kind of contestation, see 'CBI probe into fund bungling by 61 NGOs', the *Pioneer*, 5 March 1996. A critical but supportive editorial on the standing and contribution of NGOs appeared on the same day, 'Towards accountable NGOs', the *Pioneer*, 5 March 1996.

[115] Sunderlal Bahuguna, founder of the Chipko movement and a senior voice from India's civil society, spoke about people's movements aimed against 'the

aggression of development projects born of centralised planning'. Such projects, Bahuguna wrote, benefit the affluent while robbing the common people of their water resources, forests and land—the basis of their survival'.

Today marginalized hill people, tribals and fishermen have united for action in people's movements (e.g. the Narmada Bachao Andolan; Fishermen's Movement; Save Chilka Movement; Himalaya Bachao Andolan; Azad Bachao Andolan). They declare that 'the gifts of nature cannot be treated as saleable commodities. All living beings (not only humans) have the first right over these resources'. 'This is', Bahaguna argues, 'a challenge to the existing concept of development, which regards nature as a commodity and society as only of human beings'. Sunderlal Bahuguna, 'India corrupted', the *Indian Express*, 11 April 1996.

[116] For an early influential statement about the break from mass to craft-like production for niche rather than mass markets see Michael Piore and Charles Sabel, *The Second Industrial Divide: Possibilities for Prosperity*, New York: Basic Books, 1984. For the advantages and problematics of post-fordist production and marketing, see Gary Herrigel, *Industrial Constructions: The Sources of German Industrial Power*, Cambridge, UK: Cambridge University Press, 1996 and Harvey, *The Condition of Postmodernity*.

[117] Gandhi in *Hind Swaraj* and Chaplin in *Modern Times*, had much earlier critiqued mass production. Thinking they had something in common, they met in 1931 in London when Gandhi was attending the Second Round Table Conference. The meeting was not a success—perhaps because Gandhi's asceticism and seriousness didn't mesh with Chaplin's cynicism and mockery.

[118] This is a central argument of Karl Polanyi's *The Great Transformation*.

[119] For transnational issue communities, see Stephen Toulmin, 'The Role of Transnational NGOs in Global Affairs', draft paper for a conference on 'The UN and Japan in an Age of Globalization', and Stephen Toulmin, 'The Twilight of Sovereignty: Subject/Citizen/Cosmopolitan', *Graven Images; A Journal of Culture, Law, and the Sacred*, vol. 1, 1994. For the concept and practice of epistemic communities, see Peter Haas, 'Introduction: Epistemic Communities and International Policy Coordination', in a special issue of *International Organization*, 46, 1, Winter 1992.

[120] For a recent update on Dennis L. Meadows' seminal 1972 work, *The Limits of Growth*, and the associated Club of Rome studies see Keith Suter's 2005 article, 'Fair Warning? The Club of Rome Revisited', http://www.abc.net.au/science/slab/rome/default.htm.

[121] See Ronald Herring, 'Interests in Nature; Common Property, Common Dilemmas and the State', Working Paper Series No. 7, October 1991, Harvard Center for Population and Development Studies for the discourse on the risks of counter-finality, an uncertain but possible point of no return for the biosphere.

For a recent review of the literature related to the prospect of counter-finality in relation to the willingness and capacity of modern states to share sovereignty in ways appropriate to dealing with local, regional, and global threats to environmental viability, see Andrew Hurrell, 'A Crisis of Ecological Viability? Global Environment Change and the Nation State', in John Dunn (ed.), *Contemporary Crisis of the Nation State*, pp. 146–65.

[122] See Richard Watson, *Cogito, Ergo Sum: The Life of Rene Descartes*, where he tells us that 'with his [Descartes] method we could become masters and possessors of nature. And he delivered the goods', p. 3.

[123] See for interpretation and commentary, Richard B. Gregg, *The Power of Non-Violence*, Philadelphia, Lippincott Company, 1935 and Thomas Merton, (ed.), *Gandhi on Non-Violence*, New York: New Directions, 1965.

[124] For more on our views of Gandhi on gender, see Chapter 6. Gandhi and the New Courage. For a careful analysis and interpretation of Gandhi's views on gender see Ashis Nandy, 'The Psychology of Colonialism: Sex, Age and Ideology in British India', in *The Intimate Enemy*.

[125] Gandhi's critique of the professions, particularly his critique of the legal profession, seems to have anticipated Robert Merton's theory of the displacement of goals 'whereby "an instrumental value becomes a terminal value".' Gandhi argued that instead of resolving conflicts lawyers too often generated them. See Robert Merton, 'Bureaucratic Strucure and Personality', in *Social Theory and Social Sturcture*, New York: The Free Press, 1968, p. 253.

[126] I have chosen to cast Gandhi's ideas on cooperation, social capital, and love in economic terms to take advantage of Albert Hirschman's parallel thoughts about them in his remarkable essays, 'Against Parsimony: Three Ways of Complicating Some Categories of Economic Discourse,' one of which is '"Love": Neither Scarce Resource Nor Augmentable Skill', in *Rival Views of Market Society and Other Recent Essays*, Cambridge, MA: Harvard University Press, 1992, pp. 153–7.

Something similar could be said, and Hobbes did so, about violence and hatred; that they are neither limited nor scarce and that the more they are used the more the more they grow. The difference is that their negative synergy leads to chaos and annihilation. As Gandhi put it, 'an eye for an eye and the whole world will be blind'.

2

The Road Not Taken
The Modernist Roots of Partition

Two roads diverged in a yellow wood,
And sorry I could not travel both
And be one traveler, long I stood
To where it bent in the undergrowth

...

I shall be telling this with a sigh
Somewhere ages and ages hence;
Two roads diverged in a wood, and I—
I took the one less traveled by,
And that has made all the difference.

The Road Not Taken by Robert Frost

The road not taken was dominion status, a form of polity in which an independent and sovereign India would remain part of the Empire/Commonwealth.[1] India would have joined Australia, Canada, New Zealand and South Africa in the British Commonwealth of Nations. It was a path Gandhi favoured for postmodernist reasons, some of which I explored in Chapter I, 'Postmodern Gandhi',[2] and others of which will become apparent as this chapter progresses.

In December, 1929, at the Lahore annual session of the Indian National Congress, the dominion status that Gandhi advocated was replaced by *purna swaraj* or complete independence. Complete independence was strongly advocated by Jawaharlal Nehru. He presented the resolution, made the arguments and mobilized the support for it. With Gandhi's approval the annual session had chosen Jawaharlal Nehru as its president for the coming year. Subsequently Gandhi was to choose Jawaharlal as his political heir and successor.

The success of the 'complete independence' resolution and Nehru's selection as president signalled the coming of age of a younger generation in the Congress. Sometimes referred to as 'Young Turks', sometimes as 'extremists',[3] it included, in addition to Nehru, Subhas Chandra Bose from Bengal, and Srinivasa Iyengar from Madras. At this juncture of Congress' career its younger generation was dissatisfied with Gandhi's leadership.

Some of the reasons for the younger generation's dissatisfaction with Gandhi are reflected in Jawaharlal Nehru's story. In 1927 and 1928, he had travelled abroad, first to Brussels where he had been a delegate to the International Congress Against Colonial Oppression and Imperialism, then to the Soviet Union where he had been impressed by what had been accomplished in the ten years since the Bolshevik revolution. Many Nehru scholars[4] date the change in Nehru's world view from being a 'Gandhian' to being an anti-imperialist and a socialist from this trip. The trip seems to have re-kindled his admiration for the 'rationality' of science that his Cambridge *tripos* had instilled and launched what proved to be a growing commitment to the efficacy of industrial technology and the developmental state.

For high modernist reasons to be explored below, Nehru and his younger generation colleagues carried a resolution over Gandhi's objections making purna swaraj, 'complete independence', the Congress's political objective. India was to break its ties with the Empire/Commonwealth. Those ties had helped Gandhi during his 21 years in South Africa in his efforts to secure and protect the rights of the Indian minority there and, for better and for worse, gave the British governments in London and in New Delhi a voice in managing the modalities of the transition to independence. Through an exercise in counter-factual history I shall argue that the change of Congress' political goal from dominion status to complete independence made the partition of India into two successor nations, India and Pakistan, more likely. Two roads diverged in 1929. Dominion status was the 'road not taken' and not taking it 'has made all the difference'.[5]

The partition of India into two successor states, India and Pakistan, imposed a high cost on both parties. Much has been said, represented and written about the trauma of partition itself, not least the lives lost and ruined,[6] and I will not say more about the memory and consequences of partition here. As of this writing, 58 years have gone by since partition on

15 August 1947. India and Pakistan have fought four wars, if we count the Kargil war in April–June 1999. In May–June 1998 they both became overt nuclear powers. Since Partition they have found it impossible to trust each other enough to cooperate for their mutual advantage. Was it necessary? Was it inevitable?

Partition, Modernity's Child

In the previous chapter I advanced a variety of arguments in support of the view that Gandhi was a species of postmodern, indeed that he was among the earliest to advance a critique of 'modern civilization' and an alternative to it. In this chapter I take up an important strand of his postmodernism, how the struggles over nationalist goals reveal another face of Gandhi's postmodernism. Modernists like Jawaharlal Nehru embraced the scale, uniformity and centralization of high stateness.[7] Postmodernist like Gandhi rejected all three, preferring the small, the plural and the local.[8] Advocates of high stateness such as Nehru embraced a strong unitary state, uniform citizenship, and majoritarian democracy. Gandhi, an advocate of low stateness and civil society, embraced a federalized and localized state, minority rights and representation and shared sovereignty. Nehru the high modernist was state-centric in his thought and actions; Gandhi the postmodernist was civil society-centric in his thought and actions.

Partition: Unimaginable or Imaginable?

In 1929, when the Congress abandoned the goal of dominion status and adopted the goal of 'complete independence', partition wasn't imaginable. What happened on the midnight of 14 August 1947 was, Mushirul Hasan tells us, 'unthinkable a decade before that date'.[9]

India's British rulers and their rivals for sovereignty on the Indian subcontinent, preeminently the Indian National Congress and Muslim voices, particularly that of the Muslim League led by Mohammed Ali Jinnah, were committed to achieving some form of 'transfer of power' to an Indian entity. Various procedures and entities were imagined, Annie Besant's World War I era 'home rule', the goal of Montagu-Chelmsford post World War I reform, 'responsible government', or, a decade later, the [Motilal] Nehru Report's objective, 'dominion status'.

True, a year after Nehru carried his 'complete independence' resolution at Lahore, a small cloud appeared on the horizon. In 1930 the Cambridge-educated philosopher, lawyer, poet and politician, Mohammed Iqbal, proposed the creation in northwestern India of a self-governing state within the British-Indian empire. Iqbal launched his proposal at Allahabad as president of the All-India Muslim League. It was an idea on offer that, at the time, attracted little attention and had few takers; the annual meeting, like others before and after, couldn't muster the required quorum of 75.[10]

The outbreak of World War II in September 1939 radically changed political equations on the Indian subcontinent. After Britain declared war on 3 September 1939, Lord Linlithgow, the Viceroy, committed India's men and resources to the war effort without consulting the Indian National Congress or gaining its support. Congress withdrew its cooperation and the Congress governments which had been in charge of eight of eleven provincial governments since the party's success in the 1937 provincial elections, resigned. By 1942, after the failure of the Cripps Mission in March, and the Congress' Quit India movement in August,[11] all Congress leaders were in jail. Britain needed political support to manage the country and its war effort, and it needed Muslim recruits for the Indian Army. Mohammed Ali Jinnah and the Muslim League, seeing an opportunity to strengthen the League politically and its bargaining position with the raj, offered political cooperation.

Encouraged by the results of cooperation with the raj, Jinnah resurrected Iqbal's idea at the 1940 session of the Muslim League in Lahore. Moving what in retrospect has been called the Pakistan resolution, he advanced the idea of an autonomous 'Muslim homeland' in India.[12]

Until the outbreak of World War II in September 1939 the Muslim League had been a letter-head organization. Nevertheless, the British Raj found it useful because it afforded it a way of showing concern for the country's largest minority—what the Raj liked to speak of as its Muslim subjects. Jinnah, who aspired to be the 'sole spokesman' for India's Muslims, proved useful in that role to several Viceroys. But the League had few members and little electoral support. In the 1937 elections for provincial legislatures, it attracted only 5 per cent of the vote in the separate constituencies reserved for Muslims.[13] Most Muslim voters were located in the great Muslim majority provinces, Punjab and Bengal, whose regional parties and leaders rejected and resisted Jinnah's efforts to forge a national Muslim constituency.[14] The Muslim League's elite, composed mainly of large UP landlords, was 'fragmented, battered and bruised by frequent splits caused by feuds'.[15] Returning from England in 1934 after a five-year hiatus, Jinnah continued to be perceived as 'liberal, eclectic and secular to the core'; committed to India's unity, he was thought of by the Viceroy, Lord Linlithgow, as 'more Congress than the Congress'.[16]

So what happened? How could so cataclysmic an event as partition occur when it couldn't be imagined as little as a decade earlier? How did the 'ambassador of Hindu–Muslim unity', the liberal constitutionalist and Indian nationalist, Mohammed Ali Jinnah, become, in Lord Wavell, the Viceroy's phrase, a 'Frankenstein monster',[17] ready in this telling to destroy the world that created him? Many able scholars have laboured long and hard to penetrate the Jinnah enigma[18] and to provide plausible narratives for why and how partition happened.[19] I do not propose to rehearse the narratives or to evaluate the answers here because it is not my purpose to examine Jinnah's post-war role or partition's endgame. Instead, I want to use the pre-endgame story to engage in a version of counter-factual history. The counter-factual story shows, I argue, that the victory in 1929 of Nehru's high modernist goal of complete independence over Gandhi's postmodernist goal of dominion status made partition more likely. Telling the story of partition in this way makes it possible to locate this cataclysmic event in the context of a theme of this book, the clash between modernity and postmodernity.

Nehru, Gandhi, and Sovereignty: Should Jinnah be Given a Seat at the Table?

The first public clash between Gandhi and his political heir-to-be, Jawaharlal Nehru, occurred in December 1927 at the Congress's annual session in Madras. The issue that divided them was whether the Indian National Congress should keep dominion status as its political goal or abandon it and adopt a new goal, 'complete independence'. Gandhi was for dominion status, Nehru for complete independence. The struggle went on for two years. It was resolved in 1929 at the annual session in Lahore with Nehru's installation as president of the Indian National Congress and the Congress' adoption of complete independence as the national movement's political objective.

While both goals involved sovereign autonomy, they brought with them different expectations and commitments. Dominion status carried with it allegiance to the Crown, participation in imperial institutions and engaging with British politics and public opinion. Dominion status meant that there would be negotiations about the conditions in India under which the transfer of power would occur. For example, the British were likely to insist on provisions for minority rights and representation. Complete independence, on the other hand, carried overtones of anti-imperialism, unitary nationalism and majoritarian democracy. It implied a political rupture that would destroy symbolic and ceremonial ties and leave the shape of the successor state in nationalist hands. By abandoning the path of dominion status for complete independence, the Congress signalled that it was more concerned with majority rule and uniform citizenship than with minority rights and representation. Complete independence also meant and that the successor state was unlikely to share sovereignty with the minority community.

Gandhi and Nehru brought different historical understandings to the concept of dominion status. Gandhi spent the first 21 years of his political life in South Africa as a member of an Indian minority fighting for rights in the face of an incipient *apartheid* regime. The British Crown and imperial citizenship figured as a potential source of rights and redress against oppression. Gandhi made two trips to London from South Africa seeking legal help. He raised and led a medical corps to aid the English in the Zulu and Boer Wars and recruited for the British Army in World War I. A generation younger than Gandhi, Nehru, as we have seen, viewed imperialism and capitalism as evil forces in world politics. He liked English ways and had English friends but politically the British empire was the enemy.

The issue of dominion status became urgent in 1927. The time was fast approaching for the decennial review of constitutional change mandated by the Montagu-Chelmsford reforms of 1919. Stanley Baldwin's Conservative government anticipated that the Labour Party would soon be able to form a government and that a Labour government would produce a Commission whose members would be sympathetic to Indian self-rule. The Baldwin government acted early and preemptively in 1927 by appointing a seven member statutory commission that excluded Indians but included a majority of Tory imperialist opposed to Indian self-rule.[20]

In December 1927 Congress resolved on a total boycott of the Commission. So too did the Muslim League and the Swarajists. Gandhi, Jinnah, Sapru, indeed all prominent political leaders, agreed that the Commission was an abomination and an insult. As Ian Wells put it, 'The Simon Commission reminded the nationalist movement of its common foe and many Indian politicians, including Jinnah, who had moved away from the Congress returned to its fold .... Jinnah', Wells continues, 'was at the centre of the protest and promoted a united front for the boycott of the commission'.[21] Jinnah like Gandhi, Motilal Nehru and Sapru were agreed that the time had come for Britain to grant India dominion status. In the event, the Commission's report of May 1930 confirmed the worst fears of nationalist Indians by rejecting all ideas of transfer of power and made no mention of Dominion Status.

Anticipating this result, both the Viceroy, Lord Irwin, and nationalist leaders of various tendencies worked to repair the damage the Simon Commission was expected to cause. On 31 October 1929 the Viceroy announced that a Round Table Conference would be held in London on Indian constitutional reform and held out the prospect of the conference advancing the cause of Dominion Status for India.[22] Indian nationalists for their part launched the All-Parties Conferences that eventuated in a Congress' version of constitutional reform, the 1928 Nehru Report. One of its principal recommendation was Dominion Status for India. This was the context for Jawaharlal Nehru's successful effort at Congress' annual meeting in Madras in December 1929 to repudiate Dominion Status as Congress' political objective and to replace it with purna swaraj or complete independence.

Gandhi declared 'Hindu–Muslim unity' to be highest priority in 1927; remaining committed to dominion status would help to foster and maintain that unity but would not insure it. Gandhi worked on other measures to promote Hindu–Muslim unity. One was to work tirelessly on behalf of Dr A.M. Ansari, a distinguished and much respected Muslim elder statesman, to bring about his election as Congress president at the Madras annual meeting. Even though electing a prominent Muslim president of the Congress was not a way of sharing sovereignty or guaranteeing the community a seat at the table, Ansari's election would, it was hoped, serve to reassure the Muslim community. And, in an echo of the 1916 Lucknow Pact, Gandhi did expect Ansari to contribute to a pact among the communities, something along the lines that Jinnah came close to realizing in early 1927 via his 'Delhi Proposals'.[23]

Gandhi's plan was cross-cut by a request from Motilal Nehru, a Gandhi confidant and Congress stalwart, to have his son, Jawaharlal, elected Congress president. Gandhi told Motilal that it was premature for this to happen. At this conjuncture, Gandhi was convinced that Hindu–Muslim unity took precedence over another pressing concern, generational change in Congress' leadership. Ansari was elected.[24] Jawaharlal was accommodated by being moved from being one of several INC general secretaries to being *the* 'working secretary', a more elevated post.

Jawaharlal had other priorities. He had returned from an extended European tour toward the end of December 1927, just in time for the Congress annual session in Madras. Seemingly his consciousness had been transformed by his experience as a delegate to the International Congress Against Colonial Oppression and Imperialism in Brussels and by travel with his father, Motilal, in a Soviet Union only a decade away from its Bolshevik revolution. With his new consciousness of imperialism and revolutionary change, Nehru now found Gandhi's 1920's concentration on constructive work in India's villages and on spinning *khadi* on a *charkha* tame and humdrum. Six years had passed since the momentous Gandhi-led non-cooperation campaign for self-rule. Nehru and others thought it was about to succeed when Gandhi, fearing the escalation of violence after Chauri Chaura, called it off.

As Madhu Limaye put it, 'the Jawaharlal who returned to India at the end of 1927 was a changed person. He had drunk deep at the fountain of Marxism, and was full of anti-imperialism, complete independence and socialism'.[25] Class politics, not communal harmony, was uppermost in his mind.

Against Gandhi's advice to stay with the moderate course in INC-Raj relations, Nehru took the lead at the 1927 annual session in pressing for and passing radical resolutions. One resolution replaced dominion status with complete independence as the Congress's objective, another attacked imperial wars.

Gandhi reacted sharply to Nehru's attack on his carefully crafted strategy. In a letter dated 4 January 1928,[26] he told Nehru:

'You are going too fast. You should have taken time to think and become acclimatized. Most of the resolutions you framed and got carried could have been delayed for one year.[27] Your plunging into the "republican army" [by replacing dominion status, which called for allegiance to the British Crown, with "complete independence" which didn't] was a hasty step.'[28]

Then came a less than veiled attack on Nehru's new-found revolutionary fervour:

'But I do not mind these acts of yours [the badly-timed, ill-judged resolutions] so much as I mind your encouraging mischief-makers and hooligans. I do not know whether you still believe in unadulterated non-violence. But even if you have altered your views, you could not think that unlicensed and unbridled violence is going to deliver the country. If careful observation of the country in the light of your European experiences convinces you of the error of the current ways and means, by all means enforce your views, but do please form a disciplined party ....[29] Until that day, it is your duty as working secretary of the Indian National Congress to devote your whole energy to the central resolution, i.e., Unity ...'

An angry Nehru replied on 11 January 1928:

'It amazes me to find you [... who are always so careful with your words and language] using language which appears to me wholly unjustified ... you have ... specially selected some resolutions for ... criticism and condemnation ....

You have referred to discipline .... May I remind you that you are member of the Working committee and it is an extraordinary thing for a member on the morrow of the Congress to criticize ... its principal resolutions.'

Nehru then cut to the substance:

'You have described the Independence Resolution as "hastily conceived and thoughtlessly passed". [Given the attention that Nehru and others over the last five years and at the annual session have given to the subject] ... no stretch of language can justify the use of the words "hastily conceived" [or] ... "thoughtlessly passed".

... a demand for independence and all that implies has come to mean a very great deal for me and I attach more importance to it than to almost anything else .... I doubt if anyone outside a small circle understands your position ....

The liberals [for example, Sir Tej Bahadur Sapru, and Motilal Nehru] and the Muslims [such as, Jinnah] may have their doubts about independence,' Nehru admitted, 'and say they prefer dominion status' but 'whether they like it or not, it passes my comprehension how a national organization can have as its ideal and goal dominion status. *The very idea suffocates and strangles me*'[emphasis supplied].

Nehru then turned to the more general questions of Gandhi's ideas and leadership, questions which bear more directly on the modernity–postmodernity divide.

'You know how intensely I have admired you and believed in you as a leader .... I have done so in spite of the fact that I hardly agreed with anything that some of your pervious publications—*India Home Rule [Hind Swaraj]*, etc.—contained. I felt and feel that you were and are infinitely greater than your little books.

[S]ince you have come out of prison [February 1924] something seems to have gone wrong .... You ... repeatedly changed your attitude ... most of us were left in utter bewilderment .... I have asked you many times what you expected to do in the future and your answers have been far from satisfying ... you ... said that ... you expected the khadi movement to spread rapidly [but] ... the miracle has not happened ....

I am beginning to think, if we are to wait for freedom till khadi becomes universal in India we shall have to wait till the Greek Kalends[30] ... our khadi work is almost wholly divorced from politics ....[31]

What then can be done? You say nothing ... you only criticize and no helpful lead comes from you ....'

Nehru then turns directly to world view.

'Reading many of your articles in *Young India*—your autobiography, etc.— I have often felt how very different my ideals were from yours .... You misjudge greatly, I think, the civilization of the West and attach too great importance to its many failings .... I neither think that the so-called *Ramaraj*[32] was very good in the past, nor do I want it back. I think that western or rather industrial civilization is bound to conquer India .... Everybody knows these defects [of industrialism] and the utopias and social theories are meant to remove them.'[33]

Nehru then juxtaposed his modern understanding of the cause and cure for India's poverty to Gandhi's post-industrial view.

'You have advocated ... claims of ... the poor in India .... I doubt very much if the fundamental causes of poverty are touched by [your remedy of village employment and constructive work].[34] ... You do not say a word against the semi-feudal zamindari [landlord] system ... or against the capitalist exploitation of both the workers and the consumers.'

Let us pause to underline some of the positions Nehru takes in his 11 January 1928 letter. Industrial or modern civilization is bound to conquer India; its defects will be removed by western [read Fabian and/or Marxian] 'utopias and social theories'; charkha spinning and the making and wearing of khadi deadens rather then awakens the spirit and practice of *swaraj*; feudalism and capitalism must be attacked and removed if India is to overcome its poverty; and Gandhi is 'infinitely greater than [his] ... little books ...' [for example, *Hind Swaraj*] whose reading makes Nehru realize 'how very different my ideals ... [are] from yours ....'

It wasn't always this way. In the early and mid-1920s, before his European trip, Nehru spoke as if he held Gandhian views. He condemned violence and affirmed the efficacy of nonviolence. 'The choice for us', he said in 1923, 'is between Lenin and Mussolini on the one side and Gandhi on the other'. Free India should not become a 'cheap replica' of Western countries. Bringing the message of khadi to the people was a way of avoiding such a result.[35]

On 17 January 1928, Gandhi responded to Nehru's denial of his Gandhian self. He tells Nehru that he must have been 'heroically suppressing' his true self all these years. He is 'free' to 'revolt against me'. The articles[36] criticizing Nehru and the work of the Madras annual session 'were a misfire all around'. 'I had no notion of the terrible extent of [our] differences.' 'While you were in that state [of self-suppression], you overlooked the very things which appear to you now as my serious blemishes.' Similar criticisms on previous occasions weren't noticed because, while 'you [were] under stupefaction, these things did not jar you as they do now'.

Gandhi was clear about what was to be done.

'... if [as you say] I am wrong I am evidently doing irreparable harm to the country ... it is your duty to rise in revolt against me ....'

Then follows what seems to me a remarkable statement from Gandhi, a person known for trying to bridge differences by finding or making common ground:

'The differences between you and me appear to me to be so vast and radical that there seems no meeting ground between us. I can't conceal from you my grief that I should lose a comrade so valiant, so faithful, so able and so honest as you have always been .... But this dissolution of comradeship—if dissolution must come—in no way affects our personal intimacy.'

Gandhi then turned to how to begin their separation and rivalry.

'I suggest a dignified way to unfurl your banner. Write to me a letter for publication showing your differences. I will print it in *Young India* and write a brief reply .... If you do not want to take the trouble of writing another letter, I am prepared to publish the letter [of 11 January 1928] that is before me .... I consider that letter a frank and honest document.'[37]

Nehru was 'shocked and pained' by Gandhi's 17 January 1928 letter.[38] But he quickly decided not to accept Gandhi's invitation to go into opposition, a positioning that would have meant challenging his mentor and patron. Instead, Nehru backed down. His 11 January letter was impulsive and ill-considered. Gandhi was not to publish it. He pledged not to intentionally or directly criticize Gandhi's views or positions.

'No one has moved me and inspired me more than you .... There can be no question of our personal relations suffering. But even in the wider sphere am I not your child in politics, though perhaps a truant and errant child?'

What lay behind this remarkable exchange between Gandhi and Nehru? I want to interpret its meaning not only as a prelude to their differences in October/November 1945 over *Hind Swaraj* and an imagined future for an independent India discussed in Chapter 1, but also as a way to understand how the resolution of their differences over dominion status and complete independence led to the partition of India.

The Negotiating Positions: Dominion Status versus Complete Independence

At the overt level the January 1928 conflict between Gandhi and Nehru was an argument about the Congress' grand strategy. Should the country's goal be dominion status or complete independence? Answers were being prepared for the Simon Commission, appointed to look into constitutional advance, which was about to arrive in India on 22 February1928.[39] Its composition—as we have seen its seven members included no Indian and it was dominated by conservative Tories—was an insult to Indian nationalists and particularly infuriated the younger generation of which Nehru was a leader.

Gandhi wanted the Congress to have a version of dominion status on offer. It would, unlike Nehru's 'complete independence' demand, help to reassure the minorities, particularly the Muslims, that self-government would include minority rights and representation as well as majority rule. And it would help to assure the great Muslim majority provinces, Punjab and Bengal, and the princely states, both important parts of the independence equation, that the new state would find a way to provide for their autonomy in the shared sovereignty of a federal system.

Another reason for Gandhi preferring dominion status over complete independence was his awareness that the Indian negotiating position should be within striking distance of British parliamentary and public opinion. Like it or not, the British Parliament would have to legislate on the subjects of Indian constitutional reform and self-government.[40]

Such a negotiating position, proposing advances that had some chance of being accepted by Parliament, had in fact been prepared over more than a decade, and it was this position that Gandhi chastised Nehru for demolishing. In 1916 the Lucknow Pact between the Congress and the League, in which the two organizations were united in support of self-government and a parliamentary system for India, provided for separate electorates along with reserved seats for Muslims and 'weightage', granting a larger proportion of seats to the minority community than its share of the population. It had been the negotiating position for the reforms of 1918.

The Nehru Report of 1928, named for Motilal Nehru, the chairman of the All-Parties Conference committee, was drawn up in anticipation of the next step in the self-governing process. It called for dominion status but withdrew the Lucknow Pact's commitment to separate electorates and to 'weightage'. Instead of reserving one third of the seats in the central legislature as Jinnah, on behalf of the Muslim League, had requested, the Nehru Report limited Muslim representation to 25 per cent, roughly the Muslim community's share of the population. 'The atmosphere at the [All Parties] conference', Wells writes, 'was distinctly hostile to Jinnah .... The rejection of [Jinnah's] ... six points [the most important of which was that one-third of the elected representatives of both houses of the Central Legislature should be Mussalmans] was to be expected, considering the views of Jawaharlal Nehru and the younger nationalists in Congress, the high [Hindu] Mahasabha representation at the conference, as well as the number of Hindus from the Punjab present for the deliberation ... the Liberals under Sapru were prepared to concede many of the Muslim League's demands [but] the Congress was not'.[41]

Despite his treatment at the All Parties Conference that adopted the Nehru Report, 'Jinnah', Wells argues, 'still saw himself as a nationalist and continued to harbour a dream to unite the Hindu and Muslim communities to strive for a common political goal.' Throughout 1928 he persisted in his efforts to bring the two communities together. Like Gandhi but unlike

Nehru and the younger generation of nationalists, Jinnah saw the Hindu-Muslim question as 'a national problem, not a communal dispute'.[42] At the end of 1928, 'Jinnah still saw Hindu-Muslim unity as a byword for swaraj and he retained his faith in constitutional methods as the way it could be achieved.'[43]

Although Jawaharlal initially went along with the [Motilal] Nehru Report he soon found its acceptance of communal representation and commitment to dominion status unacceptable. As I have already remarked, he returned from his European tour a changed man. His Gandhian ideological commitments were overlaid, perhaps displaced, by, an anti-imperialist socialist ideology. His nationalist understanding changed too; he was now committed to an integral nationalism that was consistent with uniform citizenship and majoritarian democracy. Class replaced other social categories, notably religion, as his way of understanding the political process. In rejecting communal representation and dominion status[44] he was rejecting key aspects of a pluralist state and a multi-cultural society in India, for example, minority representation, safeguards, and a federalized state. It is important to remember that Nehru wrote to Gandhi that the very thought of dominion status 'suffocated and strangled' him.

'It was Nehru', A.G. Noorani writes, 'who insisted on "blindly" following "British practice and procedure" in India's plural society by refusing to recognize the need for safeguards for minorities, especially the Muslims.'[45] Safeguards [for example, reserved seats for Muslims] and weightage [allocating a higher proportion of legislative seats than a minority's share of the population] were not needed; Indian citizens, regardless of their religion or caste, would have constitutionally guaranteed uniform rights and that was good enough. In any case, safeguards played into the hands of Britain's divide and rule strategy.

At a deeper level the disagreement between Gandhi and Nehru in January 1928 involved a clash between two versions of India's identity as a nation. Amitav Ghosh has argued that an Indian identity, feeling and being Indian, was not a matter of language, religion or place. None of these coincided with 'India'. It was a state of mind. But what kind of state of mind? Was India, for example, to be imagined as a culturally homogeneous political community of equal but unmarked citizens or was it to be imagined as a culturally diverse political community of equal but marked citizens? Was India to be defined as a multi-cultural nation that knew how to live with difference or was India to be defined as a homogeneous nation that 'belongs to the majority'?[46]

Such questions draw their meaning and urgency from the existence and concerns of India's religious and social minorities,[47] 'minorities' who at this time began to feel endangered by the monopoly sovereignty claims of the Congress' majoritarian nationalism. In the 1920s, at the provincial as well as the all-India level, 'minorities' had acquired political consciousness and identities and began to seek a voice, representation, and rights. India's existence as one country depended on the willing support of its Muslim community for an independent Indian nation. As James Madison, an influential drafter of the US Constitution, argued in Federalist #10, governments can be oppressive when measures are decided 'not according to the rules of justice and the rights of the minor party, but by the superior force of an interested and overbearing majority'. In Federalist #51 he argued that 'the rights of the minority will be insecure ... if a majority [is] united by a common interest'.[48] Many Muslims feared that in an independent India they would face the tyranny of a permanent majority.[49]

In the event, the expectations of both Gandhi and Nehru were defeated by British domestic political developments beyond their control. The second Round Table Conference in September-November 1931, which Gandhi attended as the Congress's 'sole spokesman', revealed that British opinion, particularly ascendant Conservative Party opinion inside and outside Prime Minister Ramsay MacDonald's tottering national government, was too divided and too hostile to grant India the dominion status that Lord Irwin as Viceroy had tried for and that the 1928 [Motilal] Nehru Report had called for. In any case, the goal of dominion status had been rendered moot by Congress' December 1929 decision to demand 'full independence'.

The international context for negotiations too turned radically negative during the second Round Table conference. The collapse of the world economy with the onset of a world economic depression, particularly as the depression affected the two largest economies, the British and the US, precipitated the abandonment of the gold standard first in Britain [21 September 1931], later in the US [January 1933], rapidly rising unemployment, and sharp declines in national income. MacDonald's Labour government resigned on August 24. He then formed a national coalition government of Conservatives, Liberals, and Labourites. It resigned on 27 October 1931, two-thirds of the way through the second Round Table Conference. The general election of October 1931 returned MacDonald's coalition with a majority of 500 seats. His third government, dominated by Conservatives unsympathetic, even hostile, to Indian aspiration for self-government, continued until the next general election in June 1935.

The Failure of Dominion Status and the Transformation of Jinnah

The outbreak of World War II in September 1939 launched an endgame that produced Partition as well as Independence. Some argue that it was an intransigent, ambitious, envious Jinnah whose refusal to compromise, to give as well as take, forced partition on an unwilling country. Others argue that abstract forces such as imperialism's divide and rule strategy or communalism's ancient hatreds were responsible for partition. I read the record to show another dimension, Nehru's sovereignty monopolizing modernism overcoming Gandhi's sovereignty sharing postmodernism.

Jinnah's latter-day intransigence can be understood as being as much the result of the triumph of Nehruvian modernism as being the consequence of divide and rule imperialism or 'two-nation' Hindu and Muslim communalism. Between 1920, when he left the Congress, and 1940, when he declared for a Muslim homeland in India, Jinnah found that Nehru's ideologies of integral nationalism, majoritarian popular sovereignty, and high stateness had carried the day over Gandhi's conceptions of pluralist and inclusivist nationalism, a multi-layered federal state, reliance on self-help and civil society and sharing sovereignty through minority rights and representation.

Jinnah was transformed from a political liberal averse to popular politics and agitational means to a populist demagogue willing to exploit religious sentiments and rouse mass passions. He was transformed from a Congress nationalist working for Indian self-government to a Muslim nationalist whose conception of a Muslim 'homeland' ended up being a 'moth eaten' sovereign state. He became the kind of politician he denounced Gandhi for being when, in 1921–2, Gandhi took the lead in arousing and mobilizing India's Muslims in the Khilafat movement.[50] Known as the 'ambassador of Hindu–Muslim unity'[51] at the time of the Lucknow Pact in 1916, Jinnah became the author of a 'two-nation' doctrine whose implication of self-determination boomeranged when it led not only to the partition of India but also to the partition of the two great Muslim majority provinces, Bengal and Punjab.

On 16 August 1946, the erstwhile liberal constitutionalist abandoned negotiation over his Pakistan 'homeland' demand and called for 'direct action', in favour of a call that 'unloosed a communal frenzy of violence that opened the way to Partition.'

How did this happen? And how is it related to Nehru's commitment to modernity and to Gandhi's postmodern perspective? It may be well to start addressing these questions by asking another one, how did Mohammed Ali Jinnah, the anglicized liberal constitutionalist and Indian nationalist ambassador of Hindu–Muslim unity become over time a proponent of Muslim nationalism and the *Quaid-e-Azam* [great leader] of an independent and sovereign Pakistan? His aloofness, narcissism and enigmatic personality may have made him difficult to know and deal with but that isn't reason enough to explain this transformation. As suggested in these pages, the transformation seems to be related to Congress' retreat from its commitment in the Lucknow Pact to share sovereignty in a multi-cultural nation.

In the 1920s, as the Congress came under increasing pressure from the Hindu Mahasabha on the one hand and from secular nationalists on the other, to imagine a majoritarian India, it became less willing to entertain the idea of sharing sovereignty in an independent India. On three occasions between March 1927 and March 1929 Jinnah put on offer various measures for sharing sovereignty: the pre-Nehru Report 'Delhi Proposals'; the 'Six Points' offered by the Muslim League as amendments to the Nehru Report after the League had rejected the Report in December 1928; and the 'Fourteen Points' offered by Jinnah after the All Parties Conference rejected the 'Six Points' in an effort to restore political agreement within the Muslim community and to find common ground with those in support of the Nehru Report.

The proposals to share sovereignty put on offer by Jinnah with variable support from the Muslim League and other actors in the Muslim community can be grouped under three heads: reservations of seats in legislatures, an increase in the number of Muslim majority states and the 'communal veto'.[52] Jinnah agreed to drop the separate electorates for Muslim seats provided for in the Lucknow Pact in return for reservation of one third of the seats in the central legislature. According to Ian Wells, 'With one-third of the representation in the Central Legislature, Jinnah felt he could hold the balance of power in any government formed, satisfying two aims, namely sufficient representation for the Muslim community and the opportunity to take a leading part in a self-governing India. Gandhi's rise to power had

severely thwarted Jinnah's political ambitions and he eagerly sought a return
to the prominence he had enjoyed prior to 1918.'[53]

Although the principal authors of the Nehru Report, Motilal Nehru
and Tej Bahadur Sapru, like Jinnah, liberal constitutionalists, may have
been sympathetic to reserving one-third of the seats, the Hindu Mahasabha
representatives, M.S. Aney and M.R. Jayakar, and the Congress younger
nationalists led by Jawaharlal Nehru, were not. They welcomed the
elimination of separate electorates and reduction of Muslim representation
[which put an end to 'weightage' at the Centre] but rejected Jinnah's quid
pro quo, reserving enough seats to insure the sharing of sovereignty with
the Muslim community in the central legislature. Ignoring his de facto
collaboration with the communalists, Aney and Jayakar, in scuttling this
and other Jinnah proposals, Jawaharlal told the press that the Report had
put an end to communalism in India.[54]

A second way to share sovereignty was to increase the number of Muslim
majority states from two to five. In addition to the two great Muslim majority
provinces, Bengal and Punjab, Jinnah proposed to add Sind, Baluchistan,
and the North West Frontier Province [NWFP].[55] With five Muslim
majority provinces, almost half the total, Muslim India's voice would carry
a great deal more weight with the Government of India, the Indian National
Congress and the governments of Hindu majority provinces.[56]

A third way that Jinnah proposed to share sovereignty was by means of
a milllet-like[57] 'communal veto'. First introduced in the Lucknow Pact
[1916], Gandhi made a version of it Article XXIX of the Indian National
Congress' 1920 constitution. If Hindu or Mohammedan delegates 'as a
body' vote in super-majority proportions against the introduction of a
resolution or, once introduced, against its substance, 'such resolution shall
be dropped'.[58] Gandhi created another important sovereignty-sharing
provision in Congress' 1920 constitution, 20 language-based Pradesh
Congress Committees [PCCs] to serve as the basis of representation at
Congress' annual meetings. Gandhi's language-based PCCs legitimized the
linguistic states of independent India's federal system.[59]

A Modernist Road to Partition

The time has come to take stock of what we have learned about the meaning
and implications of 'the road not taken' after 1929. I start with the counter-
factual claim that the partition of India would have been less likely if

Jawaharlal Nehru had not successfully rebelled against Gandhi by replacing dominion status with complete independence as Congress' political goal. The effort is to avoid reading history backward, as most interpretations of partition have done. Knowing that partition happened, the question becomes, why did it happen? What are the causes of partition? The historiography of partition is replete with grand narratives.[60] It was the British divide and rule policy that created Muslims and Hindus and set them against each other. Jinnah's religious communalism, ambition, jealousy, and intransigence subverted the realization of an undivided Indian nation based on Nehru's conceptions of secularism and democracy. From time immemorial Hindus and Muslims have lived as races apart.

The effort has been to avoid anachronistic, teleological and functionalist analysis and explanation by thinking forward rather than backward. Go back in time, contextualize historical analysis, treat nothing as foreordained, assume that contingency and over and under determination limit but don't preclude analysis and explanation. What I want to avoid is the kind of thinking that is evident in the title of a book I read years ago in college, William M. McGovern's *From Luther to Hitler*.[61] An equivalent view for the partition story in India might be that its roots can be found in Warren Hastings' decision to have Muslims judged by the law found in the Koran and the Hindus by the law found in the *shastras*.[62]

In making the case for 'the road not taken' after 1929 I am not arguing that partition had to happen as a result of not taking the road to dominion status. There were other roads taken and not taken that might have avoided partition. If Nehru and the Congress had not gone back on their agreement after the 1937 provincial elections to include Muslim League ministers in the United Provinces [and Bengal] governments. If, somehow, the 1942 Cripps mission had succeeded rather than failed, allowing the Congress to enter a national government and participate in the war effort. If the Cabinet Mission had succeeded rather than failed. If Jinnah had been less resentful and Nehru less ideological.

My argument for the importance of the road not taken after 1929 turns on the importance of world view for shaping historical possibilities. I have invoked Nehru's high modernist world view and Gandhi's postmodern world view and operationalized the difference between them in terms of a willingness or unwillingness to share sovereignty; whether they imagined India as a unitary or as a multicultural nation; and whether they understood

India's democracy as majoritarian or as including minority representation and rights.[63]

The run up to, the writing of and the bargaining over the [Motilal] Nehru report marks a watershed for these questions. Along the way from the Lucknow Part in 1916 and to partition in 1947 Mohammed Ali Jinnah began to change from a liberal constitutionalist and Indian nationalist capable of trust and cooperation to a jealous, resentful, and distrustful communalist and demagogue. By the early 1920s he may have resented Gandhi displacing him at the head of the parade of national and Congress leaders but, as protégés of Gopal Krishna Gokhale, they did share for some time a liberal constitutionalist and multi-cultural outlook. Nehru's class perspective distinguished him not only from Gandhi but also from Jinnah and others like them who took religion and religious identity as meaningful categories of thought and action. In *The Discovery of India* Nehru tells us that 'The communal organizations, whether Hindu or Moslem, were closely associated with feudal and conservative elements and were opposed to revolutionary change. The real conflict had, therefore, nothing to do with religion, though religion often masked the issue, but was essentially between those who stood for a nationalist—democratic—socially revolutionary policy and those who were concerned with preserving the relics of a feudal regime.'[64]

The Muslim League's poor showing in the 1937 provincial elections in the United Provinces strengthened Nehru's conviction that the Muslims' claim to power sharing, to rights and representation, was both dangerous and hollow; dangerous because religion was the false knowledge of superstructure, and hollow because those vociferously seeking rights and representation in the name of Islam were *zamindar*s, feudal landlords, seeking to perpetuate their privileges and power. For Nehru the modern rationalist, 'Muslim' was a spurious category, an obfuscation designed to mask class interest and privilege.

At a personal level, Nehru found Jinnah exasperating and hard to take seriously. Wells contrasts 'Gandhi's high opinion of Jinnah's political importance' with Nehru's view that Jinnah didn't 'fit in' and talked nonsense. De facto Nehru joined forces with Hindu nationalists in the Congress to oppose consideration of Jinnah's 14 Points amending the Nehru report[65] and to restrain Gandhi and Motilal Nehru from accepting any of Jinnah's 'amendments' to it.[66] According to Wells, Jinnah at this time 'still saw himself as a nationalist and continued to harbour a dream to unite the Hindu and Muslim communities to strive for a common political goal ....'[67]

Wavell, the penultimate viceroy, 'spoke of Jinnah as the Frankenstein monster they had helped to create ....' Created as a liberal and nationalist Edwardian gentleman [he sported a monocle and a cigarette holder and wore three piece suits] who scorned the demos and embraced constitutional politics, he became a demagogue who aroused Muslim masses by telling them that their religion was in danger. Without minority rights and a share in sovereignty their cultural survival was at risk. Without a Muslim 'homeland' India's Muslims would be crushed by a permanent majority, whether a Hindu communalist majority who thought of Muslims as alien or a secular nationalist majority who thought of Muslims as obscurantist.

With the wisdom of hindsight and of counter-factual scenarios, Nehru's success in displacing dominion status with complete independence can be construed as a pyrrhic victory; it led the nationalists to subordinate the practice of pluralism and shared sovereignty which might have averted partition. Confrontational and polarizing, it emptied the middle ground that makes accommodation and compromise possible. As Gandhi anticipated in 1928, in the 1930s, and at the outset of, during and at the close of World War II, the Nehru instituted demand for complete independence seems to have strengthened the hand of Tory hardliners committed to empire in India and to have weakened the hand of Liberals and Labourites committed to responsible government for India.

Looking back from the perspective of 2005, it seems reasonable to ask whether India would have experienced the rupture, trauma, and violence of partition into two hostile successor states, four wars, the testing of nuclear weapons, and five decades of distrust, insecurity, if, in December 1927, the Congress had remained committed to a pluralist vision of dominion self-government. Can't we say of partition, as John Keegan has said of World War I, that it was both tragic and unnecessary?[68]

Notes

[1] I use the word 'Empire' rather than Commonwealth because it was not until December 1931 that Parliament passed the Statute of Westminster giving force of law to the changes in empire relations worked out at an Imperial Conference in 1926. The report of an Imperial Conference in October and November 1926 declared that Great Britain and the Dominions 'are autonomous communities within the British Empire, equal in status, in no way subordinate to one another in any aspect of their domestic or external affairs, though united by a common allegiance to the crown and freely associated as members of the British Commonwealth of Nations'.

² Gandhi's postmodernism has some affinity with Peter Steinfels' recently coined ironic term, 'postsecular'. 'If, for some years,' Steinfels writes, 'the big post has been postmodernism, the most glamorous new post on the intellectual block is postcolonialism .... The lesson is obvious. Those who study, articulate or propound the beliefs and practices by which most of humanity tries to place itself in relationship to the transcendent should post themselves. They should simply drop that old-fashioned word 'religion'. What they are about, they should announce, is 'postsecularism'. *The New York Times*, 3 August 2002.

³ The term, 'extremist', was a replay of the struggle in the Congress in the decade before World War I between the 'extremist', Bal Gangadhar Tilak, and the 'moderate' Gopal Krishna Gokhale, the latter Gandhi's 'political guru'.

⁴ The case is most forcefully made by Madhu Limaye in volume I [1916–31] of his *Mahatma Gandhi and Jawaharlal Nehru: A Historical Partnership, 1916–1948*, New Delhi: B.R. Publishing, 1989. Similar arguments are made by S. Gopal, Michael Brecher, and B.R. Nanda.

⁵ My re-telling of the partition story in terms of the high modernism of Nehru and the postmodernism of Gandhi suggests that Nehru is more 'to blame' for partition than the dominant nationalists discourse has recognized. However, there is plenty of blame to go around. Nehru is by means alone, just more culpable in my view than has hitherto been recognized by most scholars of the subject.

⁶ Beginning in 1995 with *Memory, history, and the question of violence: reflections on the reconstruction of partition*, Calcutta: Centre for Studies in Social Sciences, 1995, Gyanendra Pandey's work on the trauma of partition has generated a lot of attention to and scholarship about the trauma of partition: His *Remembering Partition: violence, nationalism, and history in India*, New York: Cambridge University Press, 2001, is a recent leading expression of the 'partition remembered' scholarship.

⁷ For the relationship between modernism and stateness I draw on James C. Scott, *Seeing Like a State: How Certain Schemes to Improve the Human Condition Have Failed*, New Haven, CT: Yale University Press, 1998, and 'High Modernist Social Engineering: The Case of the Tennessee Valley Authority', in Lloyd I. Rudolph and J.K. Jacobsen (eds), *Experiencing the State*, New Delhi: Oxford University Press, 2006.

'The gleam in Condorcet's eye', Scott writes, 'became, by the mid-nineteenth century, an active utopian project. Simplification and rationalization previously applied to forests, weights and measures, taxation, and factories were now applied to the design of society as a whole .... While factories and forests might be planned by private entrepreneurs, the ambition of engineering whole societies was almost exclusively a project of the nation state'. 'High Modernist Social Engineering ...' p. xx.

⁸ For a 'Gandhian' version of postmodernism relevant to smallness, pluralism and the local see E.F. Schumacher, *Small is Beautiful: Economics as if People Mattered*, New York: Harper & Row/Perennial Library, 1975, 1989.

[9] Mushirul Hasan, 'Introduction', in Mushirul Hasan (ed.), *India's Partition; Process, Strategy and Mobilization,* Delhi: Oxford University Press, 1993, 1994, 1996, p. 6. Hasan's introduction provides a masterful overview of the subject and of scholarship about it. His edited book contains thirteen essays by authoritative authors and texts relevant to the subject of Partition by Jinnah, Azad, Gandhi, and Nehru.

[10] Hasan, ibid., pp. 7–8. Hasan says that the Muslim League in the 1920s and 1930s 'was little more than a paper organization ... its membership had plummeted to 1,330 in 1927 .... The 1929 session was adjourned for lack of a quorum'.

[11] For the Quit India movement see Francis G. Hutchins, *India's Revolution: Gandhi and the Quit India Movement,* Cambridge, MA: Harvard University Press, 1973.

[12] According to Surjit Mansingh, 'the name "Pakistan" first appeared in a pamphlet authored at Cambridge, England, in 1933 to stand for Muslim-majority Punjab, Afghanistan or the North West Frontier Province, Kashmir and Sind ... Mohammed Ali Jinnah ... launched the demand for Pakistan [with ambiguous definition and motive] in 1940'. Surjit Mansingh, *Historical Dictionary of India,* New Delhi: Vision Books, 1998, p. 301.

Ayesha Jalal tells a similar story about the source of the idea and word, Pakistan. Mohammad Iqbal, she says, 'argued that the "life of Islam as a cultural force in this country very largely depends on its centralization in a specified territory."' Iqbal's speech at the 21st session of the Muslim League, 29 December 1930, as cited by Jalal in footnote 14, page 12 of her *The Sole Spokesman: Jinnah, the Muslim League and the Demand for Pakistan,* Cambridge, UK: Cambridge University Press, 1985.

Sometime later, Jalal doesn't say just when, Iqbal's speech inspired Chaudhuri Rahman Ali, a student at Cambridge, 'to coin the word "Pakistan"'. Ali, Jalal says, 'drew up a scheme for an independent Muslim state in north-western India for the Muslim delegates attending the Round Table Conference in London ...' Since there were three Round Table Conferences in London between 1930 and 1932 and Jalal doesn't say which one she has in mind, we can't be sure just when Ali invented his scheme. We are told that Ali's scheme stipulated that P is for Punjab, A for Afghanistan or the Northwest Frontier Province, K for Kashmir, S for Sind and 'tan' for Baluchistan. 'The literal translation', Jalal says, 'of Pakistan was "the land of pure or holy."' Since Ali's scheme envisaged massive transfers of Muslim populations from other parts of India, 'it was understandably dismissed by the delegates as a "student scheme" which was "chimerical" and "impractical"'. Jalal, *Sole Spokesman,* p. 12, footnote 14.

[13] The Muslim League won 1 of 86 seats in the Punjab; 3 out of 33 in Sind; 39 out of 117 in Bombay; 27 out of 64 in UP; 20 out of 29 seats in Bengal; 10 out of 28 in Madras; and 9 out of 34 in Assam. Surjit Mansingh, *Historical Dictionary of India,* p. 270.

[14] Jalal, *Sole Spokesman,* provides a detailed, analytic account of Muslim politics in the Punjab, Bengal, and Uttar Pradesh.

[15] Hasan, Introduction, p. 8.

[16] Hasan, Introduction, p. 10, n. 36.

[17] After the Muslim League's victory in Muslim seats in the 1946 election, when Jinnah called for Pakistan, 'a Muslim nation that had gained freedom Britain and from "Hindu" India', Wavell, the viceroy, 'spoke of Jinnah as the Frankenstein monster they had helped to create ....' Sucheta Mahajan, *Independence and Partition; The Erosion of Colonial Power in India*, New Delhi, Thousand Oaks, London: Sage Publications, 2000, p. 385. This fresh explanation of partition's endgame draws a particularly perceptive portrait of Gandhi in the final months before Independence and partition.

[18] Of the many works on Jinnah or that deal with Jinnah, I would like to mention Stanley Wolpert's Gandhi-centric *Jinnah of Pakistan*, Oxford: Oxford University Press, 1984; Ayesha Jalal's historically and politically insightful *The Sole Spokesman: Jinnah, the Muslim League and the Demand for Pakistan*, Cambridge, UK: Cambridge University Press, 1985 and Ian Bryant Wells psychologically insightful *Ambassador of Hindu-Muslim Unity: Jinnah's Early Politics*, New Delhi: Permanent Black, 2005. Wells' book has the great virtue of reading Jinnah forwards, that is, examining his ideas, thoughts and actions chronologically and contextually rather than backwards, i.e. constructing Jinnah from the perspective of the author's take on partition.

[19] In addition to the Mushirul Hasan edited book, *India's Partition*, and the Sucheta Mahajan book, *Independence and Partition*, both already cited, of the many fine books on or relevant to partition, I want to mention the solid contribution of B.B. Misra, *The Unification and Division of India*, Delhi: Oxford University Press, 1990 and the four books included in *The Partition Omnibus*, introduced and edited by Mushirul Hasan, David Page, *Prelude to Partition: The Indian Muslims and the Imperial System of Control 1920–1932*; Anita Inder Singh, *The Origins of the Partition of India 1936–1947*; Penderel Moon, *Divide and Quit*; and C.D. Khosla, *Stern Reckoning: A Survey of Events Leading Up To and Following the Partition of India*.

I found Ayesha Jalal's last two chapters of her magisterial *The Sole Spokesman; Jinnah, the Muslim League and the Demand for Pakistan*. Cambridge, UK: Cambridge University Press, 1985, 'The interim government: Jinnah in retreat', and 'The end game: Mountbatten and partition', engagingly written and persuasive. After it is all over except for the ceremonies, she concludes, *inter alia*, that '... until the bitter end the League continued to protest against Hindustan adopting the title "Union of India". A commentary perhaps that Jinnah never quite abandoned his strategy of bringing about an eventual union of India on the basis of Pakistan and Hindustan,' p. 293.

[20] According to Ian Bryant Wells 'In the late 1920s it became apparent to the Tory government [of Stanley Baldwin] that the strength of the Labour Party was

growing and it would soon be in a position to form a government. The Tories decided to convene a statutory commission to investigate political reform for India early to ensure the continuation of their own policies in India .... The government's motivation to exclude Indians from the statutory commission originated from within the Government of India. In 1926, the newly arrived viceroy, Lord Irwin, found himself surrounded by advisers from the Punjab branch of the service. These advisers, particularly Sir Malcolm Hailey and Geoffrey de Montmorency, were the driving force behind the all white commission.' Wells, *Ambassador of Hindu-Muslim Unity*, pp. 165–6.

[21] Wells, *Ambassador of Hindu-Muslim Unity*, pp. 167–8.

[22] Lord Irwin's effort to secure Dominion Status for India was supported by the Prime Minister, Ramsay MacDonald, and by Stanley Baldwin, the leader of the Conservative Party in Parliament, by far the largest component of MacDonald's National Government. The debate in the House of Commons on Irwin's declaration began on Friday, 8 November 1929. The Prime Minister spoke for Dominion Status and Baldwin announced that the Conservatives supported MacDonald. At least a third of the Conservative members were said to be prepared to vote against the declaration. 'They had listened glumly to their leader; their applause for him had been perfunctory ... The diehards were ... violently opposed to it .... Winston [Churchill] was almost demented with fury. ...' Baldwin won a pyrrhic victory by forcing Churchill to enter the political wilderness on the issue but Churchill ultimately won the battle for party and public opinion on the issue. Churchill's first attack came a week later in the pages of the *Daily Mail.* 'Britain', he said, 'had rescued India from ages of barbarism .... Self-government was unthinkable ... and it was absurd to contemplate [Dominion Status] .... If the viceregal proposal was adopted the British Raj would be replaced by a Gandhi Raj ...'. William Manchester, *Winston Spencer Churchill: The Last Lion. Vol. I: Visions of Glory, 1874–1932*, A Delta Book/ Dell Publishing, 1983. pp. 845–6.

[23] See Wells, *Ambassador of Hindu-Muslim Unity*, 'The Delhi Proposals', pp. 158–65. The key proposal as far as Jinnah was concerned was to reserve one-third representation for Muslims in the central government. '... [H]e saw this demand as vital for India's political future. With one-third of the seats in the central government, the Muslim community and consequently Jinnah himself could play a significant role in the government of an independent India. Further, it would not then be possible for the Government of India to be dominated by Hindus.' The Congress committee [Mahomed Ali, Srinivas Iyengar, Motilal Nehru, Sarojni Naidu] assigned to negotiate on the proposals was ready to accept them but then Pandit Madan Mohan Malaviya and the Hindu Mahasabha intervened and, de facto, vetoed the agreement. Wells, *Ambassador of Hindu-Muslim Unity*, p. 163.

[24] In a 25 June 1927 letter to Sarojini Naidu, Gandhi took the view that there was 'no other man than Dr Ansari who could be the Congress President in 1927 to pilot a Hindu–Muslim pact through the Congress'. K.P. Goswami, *Mahatma;*

A Chronology, New Delhi: Publications Division, Ministry of Information and Broadcasting, 1994, p. 121.

[25] Madhu Limaye, *Mahatma Gandhi*, vol. I, p. 191.

[26] The letter is in *Collected Works of Mahatma Gandhi*, New Delhi: Publications Division, Ministry of Information and Broadcasting, CD by Icon Softec, vol. 41: December 1927–1 May 1928, pp. 79–80, hereafter CWMG.

Gandhi's letter of 4 January 1928 being quoted here was published along with a Nehru note pointing out that 'I returned from Europe in December 1927 and went straight to the Madras Session of the Indian National Congress. A number of resolutions were passed at my instance. This letter [the one being quoted in the text] was written by Gandhiji because he did not approve of some of my activities at this session'. CWMG, vol. 41, p. 79, note 1.

[27] In his *Young India* article of the next day, 5 January 1928, Gandhi says that '... irresponsible talk and work were the order of the day [at the Committee meetings] .... Resolutions involving great consequences were sprung upon the Subjects Committee and readily accepted by that august body without much thought or discussion. The Independence Resolution that was rejected last year was passed without much thought or discussion .... it was hastily conceived and thoughtlessly passed.' CWMG, 'The National Congress', vol. 41, p. 84.

[28] Gandhi worked with Motilal Nehru to promote and support dominion status. Motilal chaired the committee on constitutional reform established by the 1928 All-Parties Conference that in August recommended dominion status. Both men had worked hard on establishing a consensus for dominion status which became the Conference's first recommendation.

In 31 December 1928, at the Calcutta Congress's annual session one year after the Madras session where Nehru's resolution for independence had carried, Gandhi moved the resolution that endorsed the Nehru Report's support for dominion status, a status that involved *inter alia* allegiance to the British crown and participation in imperial institutions and forums.

Gandhi seems to have tried to hold on to dominion status in part because he thought it a better framework for assuring Muslim participation in a sovereign India. It is in the light of these events and considerations that his remarks about Jawaharlal going 'too fast', taking a 'hasty step' and joining the 'republican army' can be understood.

[29] Gandhi's reference to a 'disciplined party', violence, and even to hooligans should be read in the context of Nehru's new-found revolutionary fervour and the formation two years earlier of the Communist Party of India (CPI) whose first demand was complete independence of British rule.

Gandhi may also have had in mind the formation of the Swaraj Party in December 1922 by C.R. Das, Motilal Nehru, and others. It broke away from the Indian National Congress because its adherents wanted the representative and responsible government promised by the Montagu–Chelmsford Reforms and opposed the Gandhi-led mass-based Non-Cooperation Movement of 1920–2. The Swarajists were willing to cooperate with the British government in elections and legislatures, hoping in this way to attain dominion status at an early date. The party split in 1926 with some members joining the Hindu Mahasabha and others rejoining the Congress.

Gandhi began his critical letter of 4 January 1928 to Nehru in his usual non ad hominem way by saying that 'I feel that you love me too well to resent what I am about to write. In any case I love you too well to restrain my pen when I feel I must write'. CWMG, vol. 41, 3 December–1 May 1928, p. 79.

[30] Possibly a reference to a day of the new moon and the first day of the month in the ancient Roman calendar. *The American Heritage College Dictionary*, Third Edition, p. 199.

[31] Gandhi's constructive work organizations survive 50 years after independence. Gandhi anticipated that the rush to power, patronage and pelf would undermine Congress when he recommended its dissolution as political party and conversion to a service organization a few months before his assassination on 30 December 1948.

[32] Over time Gandhi gave a variety of meanings to the term Ramaraj. As in the case of *Hind Swaraj*, Nehru was, at best, tone deaf to Gandhi's revitalized indigenous language. At worst he filters out rejects, speech that doesn't use the idiom of the modern, the scientific or the rational.

[33] We may surmise that the Nehru who wrote these words in early 1928 had in mind Fabian and/or Marxian socialist utopias and theories.

[34] Presumably by 'remedy' Nehru had in mind something like simple living, craft, and agricultural production in self-reliant village communities, the kind of activity suggested by *Hind Swaraj* and institutionalized in late 1934 when Gandhi retired from the Congress to launch the AIVIA (All-India Village Industries Association) whose goal was the economic, moral, and hygienic uplift of the rural population. These Gandhian rural voluntary organizations became models for the enormous proliferation of voluntary service organizations that now characterize the Indian social welfare scene.

[35] Limaye quotes and paraphrases Nehru's speech before a UP political conference on 13 October 1923 in *Mahatma Gandhi and Jawaharlal Nehru; A Historic Partnership 1916–1948*, Four Volumes, vol. I, 1916–31, Delhi: B.R. Publishing Corporation, 1989, p. 80.

[36] 'The National Congress', *Navijivan*, 5 January 1928 and 'Independence v. Swaraj', *Young India*, 12 January 1928, which criticize Nehru's independence resolution.

[37] CWMG, vol. 41, p. 139. 'Letter to Jawaharlal Nehru' pp. 120–2.

[38] Nehru's response to Gandhi's 17 January 1928 letter is given in S. Gopal (ed.), *Selected Works of Jawaharlal Nehru:*, New Delhi: Sangam Books/Orient Longman, 1972, vol. 3, 18–19.

Limaye glosses Nehru's response by saying that 'Jawaharlal was besides himself with anger at this unexpected blast from Gandhi .... [and thought] the outburst was wholly unjustified'. Limaye, *Mahatma*, vol. I, 1916–31, p. 195.

[39] The seven-member statutory commission landed in Bombay on 3 February 1928. Led by Sir John Simon, a barrister and a Liberal Party MP, it was composed of four Conservative Party and two Labour Party MPs. The Commission was asked to investigate the working of the Montagu–Chelmsford Reforms of 1919. Indian authors tend to believe it was constituted before the stipulated 10-year interval because of political pressure from Gandhi and the Congress for some form of self-government for India. As we have seen, above, the Baldwin government, anticipating a Labour Party government, acted early to prevent the appointment of a statutory commission favorable to Indian self-rule.

The argument that the Commission was appointed early because of nationalist pressure is contradicted by its composition; not one member was an Indian. The Congress at its annual session in Madras resolved to boycott the Simon Commission. Given the incipient break between Gandhi and Nehru we are examining here, it is significant that Jinnah agreed with the Congress about the Simon Commission; under his leadership the All-India Muslim League voted to boycott the Commission and Jinnah took the lead in organizing national resistance to it. See Wells, *Ambassador of Hindu-Muslim Unity*, 'Temporary Unity: Opposition to the Simon Commission', pp. 165–72.

The Commission was met with black flags; both Nehru and Subhas Chandra Bose were arrested and jailed for leading anti-Simon Commission protests.

The Simon Commission report to Parliament in May 1930 confirmed its opponents' worst fears; it rejected all ideas of transferring power and made no mention of dominion status, the anticipation of which may have contributed to Gandhi's movement in Nehru's direction, i.e. toward 'complete independence'.

Already in 1928 Gandhi helped to orchestrate and then endorsed the Motilal Nehru Report which outlined a Constitution for India as a self-governing dominion of the British Empire. On 31 December 1928, Gandhi successfully moved the adoption of the [Motilal] Nehru Report at the Congress's annual session in Calcutta. He began to explain his shift in an article published in the 29 December 1928 number of *Young India* entitled 'What Is In A Name?', that discussed 'Dominion Status vs Independence'.

[40] As I suggested above, Gandhi's take on dominion status and on British politics was shaped by his South African experience with the rights of citizens. It should be recalled that Gandhi spent about 25 years invoking the rights of 'citizens of the empire' and invoking the Empire's rule of law, 21 years in South Africa and almost five years in India. I take the massacre by British troops of non-violent protesters at Jallianwala Bagh in April 1919 to be the moment of disillusionment, when Gandhi stopped being a loyal citizen of the Empire and began to question its commitment

to a government of laws. Nevertheless, his continuing support for dominion status suggests that he continued to value the importance of India's British connection.

[41] Wells, *Ambassador of Hindu-Muslim Unity*, p. 181. For the intricacies of Jinnah's and the Muslim League's failed efforts to secure satisfaction at the All Parties Conference that adopted the Nehru Report see Wells' section, 'The End of Unity: Rejecting the Nehru Report', pp. 173–84.

[42] Jinnah to M.C. Chagla, 5 August 1929, *Chagla Papers*, as cited in Wells, *Ambassador of Hindu-Muslim Unity*, fn. 104, p. 184.

[43] Wells, *Ambassador of Hindu-Muslim Unity*, pp. 183–4.

[44] For Gandhi's views, see CWMG, vol. 41, 3 December–May 1928, p. 84. Gandhi subsequently discussed the meaning and implications of distinguishing between dominion self-government and independence in 'Independence v. Swaraj', 1 January 1928 and a year later in 'What Is In A Name?', *Young India*, 3 January 1929, CWMG, vol. 43, 3 January 1929, pp. 466–7.

[45] Quoted from A.G. Noorani's review of Basudev Chatterji (ed.), *Towards Freedom: Documents on the Movement for Independence in India 1938*, in three parts, New Delhi: Indian Council for Historical Research and Oxford University Press, 2000, *Economic and Political Weekly*, vol. XXXV, no. 14, 1–7 April 2000, p. 1166.

[46] The phrase 'belongs to the majority' was used at a public discussion in New Delhi on 13 April 2000 by Neera Chandhoke, professor of political science, Delhi University, to characterize BJP nationalism. The *Hindu*, 14 April 2000.

The Canadian model of plural national identity was formulated, for example, by Pierre Trudeau when he implemented a 'bi-lingual' Canadian identity that gave equal respect to English and French culture and language at the federal level. His success seems to have pre-empted Quebec's French Canadian secessionist efforts.

[47] Religious minorities include Muslims, Sikhs, Christians, Jains, Buddhists, Parsis, and Jews; social minorities include 'untouchables' (Scheduled Castes or SCs, also known as Dalits or oppressed and formerly as Harijans—Gandhi's term); 'tribals' (Scheduled Tribes or STs); and lower castes (Other Backward Classes or OBCs). Gandhi had addressed the question of linguistic minorities in his 1920 reorganization of the Indian National Congress into 20 language-based Pradesh [provincial] Congress Committees (PCCs). In line with their modern universalist-postmodern pluralist differences, Nehru, according to Selig Harrison in *India, The Most Dangerous Decades* (Princeton: Princeton University Press, 1956), almost drove the country to 'balkanization' by being politically tone deaf to what Gandhi in his time pre-empted, the politics of language. Nehru learned to hear in time, acceding between 1956 and 1962 to what became known as 'states' reorganization'.

[48] Alexander Hamilton, James Madison, and John Jay, *The Federalist Papers*, New York: A Mentor Book, 1961. Introduction by Clinton Rossitor, p. 77 and p. 323.

[49] Rule by a permanent majority in India could mean either the anti-Muslim 'Hindu' majority many Muslims alleged lay beneath the Congress' secularist claims, or, as became evident after Independence and Gandhi's assassination, a secularist, 'scientific temper' majority that devalued religion even while granting Muslims special rights in post-Partition India. The principal special right was protecting, some claimed privileging, Muslim personal law. For accounts that deal with the politics and constitutionality of Muslim personal law see Lloyd I. Rudolph and Susanne Hoeber Rudolph, 'Living With Difference; Legal Pluralism and Legal Universalism in Historical Context', in David Marquand and Ron Nettler (eds), *Religion and Democracy*, Oxford, Blackwell's, 2000, pp. 20–38.

[50] '... Jinnah's 1920 difference with Gandhi was not over Khilafat. In September 1920 Jinnah spoke of "the spoliation of the Ottoman empire and the Khilafat, a matter of life and death". What he was opposed to was the changing of Congress's goal from "Swaraj within the Empire" to just Swaraj and to Gandhi's willingness to experiment with mass defiance of laws.' Rajmohan Gandhi, *Revenge & Reconciliation; Understanding South Asian History*, New Delhi: Penguin Books, 1999, p. 267.

[51] The phrase is usually attributed to G.K. Gokhale, who, until his death in 1915, was construed as a political patron and guru by both Gandhi and Jinnah.

[52] The possibility that a super-majority of the members of any community in a legislative body can block a bill on the ground that it would be injurious to the interests of the community.

[53] Wells, *Ambassador of Hindu-Muslim Unity*, p. 189.

[54] Press interview, *The Tribune*, September 9, 1928, as cited in Wells, *Ambassador of Hindu-Muslim Unity*, in footnote 76, p. 176. In the same interview Nehru took the opportunity to reveal his disagreement with a principal recommendation of the Nehru Report, its call for dominion status. Nehru told the press that the nationalists' goal should be 'full independence out side the empire'. For an account of Nehru's de facto collaboration with the Hindu nationalists Aney and Jayakar see pp. 175–6 and ff.

[55] Three new Muslim majority provinces were to be created by separating Sind from Bombay and upgrading NWFP and Baluchistan to full provincial status.

[56] Jinnah would gain politically within Muslim India by the creation of three additional Muslim provinces by providing a counter-balance to the Punjabi Muslims who often challenged Jinnah's effort to be the 'sole spokesman' for Muslim India.

[57] The reference here is to the Ottoman Turkish term, millet system, the separate legal courts pertaining to personal law under which minorities were allowed to rule themselves with little interference from the Ottoman government.

[58] The text of Article XXIX of Gandhi's 1920 Congress constitution can be found in vol. 22, p. 178 of the *Collected Works*.

[59] Article XVIII of Gandhi's 1920 Congress constitution provided for 21 language based PCCs., one of which was Burma with Rangoon as its capital.

Article VVIII laid the basis for the states' reorganization between 1953 and 1960 that transformed India's federal system and made it safe for sharing sovereignty on the basis of language. For the text of Article XVIII and the schedule of language based PCCs, including the languages involved and PCC capital cities see vol. 22, pp. 175–6. In a letter to the Chairman of the All-India Congress Committee three months before the Nagpur annual session that adopted Gandhi's 1920 constitution, Gandhi wrote that 'we should re-divide India into provinces on a linguistic basis.' vol. 22, p. 239, *Collected Works.*

[60] For an excellent review and critique of the recent historiography of partition see Ayesha Jalal, 'Secularists, Subalterns and the Stigma of "Communalism"', *Modern Asian Studies*, 30, 3 [1996].pp. 681–736. Jalal notes inter alia that the subaltern school has not addressed the question of 'why partition'. Instead it has concerned itself with the violence and trauma of partition.

According to Surjit Mansingh 'Partition is probably the most controversial event in modern Indian history.' She finds three main explanations: 1. Partition is the culmination of British imperial tactics of 'divide and rule by pitting Muslim against Hindu at each stage of constitutional reform and delaying responsible government;' 2. Partition is portrayed '... as an inevitable consequence of Muslim separatism in India, an expression of belief that 'two nations'—Hindu and Muslim—could not live together in one state;' 3. The '... role of contingent or accidental factors in the period before Partition ...' including '... human failures among the main characters in the final drama—such as Jinnah's vanity, Jawaharlal Nehru's obstinacy, and Mountbatten's ambition.' Surjit Mansingh, *Historical Dictionary of India*, New Delhi: Vision Books, 1998, 2001, p. 315.

[61] William M. McGovern, *From Luther to Hitler: the history of fascist-nazi political philosophy*, Boston: Houghton Mifflin Co., 1941.

[62] For efforts to avoid anachronism by contextualizing historical change with respect to Hindus and Muslims as constructed categories over time, see Susanne Hoeber Rudolph and Lloyd I. Rudolph, 'Living with Difference in India: Legal Pluralism and Legal Universalism in Historical Context,' in Gerald James Larson (ed.), *Religion and Personal Law in Secular India: A Call to Judgment.* Bloomington, IN: Indiana University Press, 2001, and Lloyd I. Rudolph and Susanne Hoeber Rudolph, 'Occidentalism and Orientalism; Perspectives on Legal Pluralism', in Sally Humphrey (ed.), *Cultures of Scholarship*, Ann Arbor, MI: University of Michigan Press, 1997.

[63] Sugata Bose poses similar questions and concerns in his article 'Nation, Reason and Religion; India's Independence in International Perspective', *Economic and Political Weekly*, 1 August 1998. He speaks of the dangers of 'majoritarian triumphalism': and the 'conceits of unitary nationalism' as helping to embitter relations between religious communities. 'The territorial claims of a minority turned nation', he writes, 'heaped further confusion on the furious contest over sovereignty in the dying days

of the raj. Having failed to share sovereignty in the manner of their pre-colonial forbears, late-colonial nationalist worshippers of the centralized state ended up dividing the land. Surely godless nationalism linked to the colonial categories of religious majorities and minorities has much to answer for,' p. 2090.

[64] Jawaharlal Nehru, *The Discovery of India*, New Delhi: Oxford University Press, 1981, 2002, p. 394.

[65] 'Among the Hindus', Wells writes, 'the Fourteen Points were scorned, with Jawaharlal Nehru referring to them as "Jinnah's ridiculous 14 points,"' [Jawaharlal to Gandhi, October 4, 1931, in J.Nehru, *Selected Works*, vol. 5, 1972–4, p. 137, as cited by Wells, footnote 28, p. 194.] 'Jawaharlal Nehru', Wells continues, 'was president of the Congress and his ongoing hostility towards Jinnah was reflective of the attitude of the younger Congressmen'. Wells, *Ambassador of Hindu-Muslim Unity*, p. 194.

[66] See Wells, *Ambassador of Hindu-Muslim Unity*, p. 196. In early 1929 'Gandhi emerged as Jinnah's unlikely political saviour ... [by holding] private conversations with him on the communal question .... Gandhi saw Jinnah's branch of the Muslim League as the best possibility for an alliance with the Congress Party ... [But] Gandhi was restricted in the concessions he could make during negotiations with Jinnah [with respect to Jinnah's amendments to the Nehru Report] ...' by Hindu communalists within the Congress. Moonje advised Malaviya to '... tell Mahatmaji that if he were to yield on these points you would be painfully obliged to lead the opposition on behalf of the Hindus against him, Jinnah and Motilal combined.' Moonje to Malaviya, July 31, 1928, *Jayakar Papers*, F. 442, as cited by Wells, *Ambassador of Hindu-Muslim Unity*, footnote 32, p. 185. The quotations from Wells' text are from p. 185.

[67] Wells, *Ambassador of Hindu-Muslim Unity*, pp. 183–4.

[68] See John Keegan, *The First World War*, New York: Alfred Knopf, 1999, xx.

3

Gandhi in the Mind of America*

My title is figurative, not literal; Gandhi never set foot on American soil. His presence is the result of American responses to his person, ideas, and practice. For most Americans, they were exotic, often alien, fascinating for some, threatening or subversive to others. This chapter analyses America's reception and understanding of Gandhi by pursuing two questions: Is he credible? Is he intelligible?

For a person to be credible, it must be possible to believe that this seemingly quixotic individual is someone like 'us': someone who makes sense in terms of America's cultural paradigms and historical experience. From the beginning many thought that Gandhi was putting 'us' on, that he was fooling us while fooling around. Was he for real or was he a fraud?

Even if 'we' are prepared to accept an alien 'other' like Gandhi as believable and authentic, the problem of intelligibility remains. What language, what images, what metaphors, what myths can be used to talk about him? How can we think about and talk about an alien other? In thinking and talking about Gandhi in America we are faced with an epistemological as well as ontological problem.

Americans have been conscious of Gandhi since about 1920, when his first non-cooperation campaign almost toppled British rule in India. He has been revered and reviled since then. In 1921, John Haynes Holmes told his Community Church congregation in New York that Gandhi was 'the greatest man in the world', greater even than Lenin and Woodrow Wilson. 'When I think of Mahatma Gandhi, I think of Jesus Christ'. In 1930, the year of Gandhi's second great non-cooperation campaign against the British Empire in India, Winston Churchill, the Empire's great exponent, coined the epithet 'the half-naked fakir', a phrase that spoke for Americans and Britons who identified Gandhi with what they believed was India's self-inflicted poverty and with fraudulent spirituality.

Gandhi's presence in American consciousness has varied with historical circumstance and his public image. There is the anti-imperialist, a nationalist leader who challenged the British Empire in India; the *guru*, a world historical teacher whose ethic of non-violent collective action in pursuit of truth and justice offers a new way to think, believe, and live; the *mahatma*, the great soul, saint, and *homo religioso*, whose meaning is translated in terms commensurable with or found in America's religious perceptions and beliefs; and the fraud, an oriental 'other' whose alien and subversive ideas and practices threaten American religion, morality, and politics. Each of these Gandhis, the anti-imperialist, the guru, the mahatma and the fraud, provide text and context for a roughly chronological examination of Gandhi's meaning in and for America.

The Anti-Imperialist

Gandhi's first public career in South Africa (1893–1915), although not visible in the US, became an important part of the Gandhi myth.[1] A failure in India as an England-returned barrister-at-law, he left at 24 to try again in a distant, alien country whose oppressed and exploited Indian minority of indentured labourers and poor cultivators needed him. In time, he found an answer to his search for himself and for their needs in a method of collective action, satyagraha, non-violence, non-cooperation, and civil disobedience. By the time he returned to India in 1915, *The Story of My Experiments with Truth* (the title of his 1927 autobiography) had preceded him. Rabindranath Tagore, Nobel laureate in 1913, welcomed him as a 'mahatma' and Gopal Krishna Gokhale, leader of Indian nationalism, as his political heir. Four years later, in 1919 at 46, he assumed the leadership of the national movement against British rule. The stage was set for Gandhi's reception in America.

In his invaluable *The Americanization of Gandhi; Images of the Mahatma*, Charles Chatfield identifies four periods when national attention to Gandhi was most intense: 1919–24, the period of Gandhi's first and most momentous non-cooperation campaign against British rule; 1929–34, when Gandhi led a march to the sea to make salt, launched the second non-cooperation campaign, and travelled to London as the sole representative of the Indian National Congress at the second Round Table Conference; 1939–44, the era of World War II when Gandhi attempted to secure Indian independence while not opposing the war against fascism; and 1947, the year of Partition, communal violence, and Independence.[2]

Chatfield describes Gandhi as 'our lens on India'. What Americans saw was his 'enigmatic personality, his ideas on religious and economic questions, and the tactical and philosophic meaning of non-violence'.[3] He first appears on the American horizon in 1919, in the immediate aftermath of World War I. The war had dealt a devastating blow to the promise of technological and moral progress in the Western world. American consciousness was radically transformed. The fervid patriotism and lofty idealism that led millions to offer their lives for their country faded from view. For a time, war was discredited as a test of national greatness and as an instrument of policy. In the new anti-war climate, pacifism achieved a greater measure of credibility and public standing, a circumstance that helped to open the way to Gandhi's ideas and practice.

In Europe, where Romain Rolland's 'critical attitude toward the great butchery of 1914–18 had elevated him to the status of keeper of the conscience of the world, in the manner of Tolstoy', his 1923 volume, *Mahatma Gandhi*, linked Europe's eager tilt toward pacifism to Gandhi's project:

There was nothing to expect from the triumphant Western imperialisms who were intent on enjoying the spoils and, in their stupid state of bloated satisfaction were not even cautious enough to properly keep watch on those spoils. I thought I had found [the] rampart [of sovereign reason] ... in the little Saint Francis of India, Gandhi. Did he bring, in the folds of his sackcloth, the word which would free us of the murders to come, the heroic non-violence which does not flee but resists, 'Ahimsa'? ... I believed in it passionately for many years.[4]

His success in using non-violent collective action to challenge the world's mightiest empire in India intersected with political and ideological currents in the US. Gandhi's successful use of non-violence justified pacifists, some of whom opposed the great war. Woodrow Wilson, a broken man after his paralytic stroke on 2 October 1919, had failed to convince the Senate to ratify the League of Nations treaty. His vision of the US' allies and of idealistic internationalism lay shattered. Warren Harding's election in 1920 purported to return the country to 'normalcy'.

Three varieties of pro- and anti-imperialism now shaped American notions of national interest, preparing the ground for negative and positive receptions of Gandhi in America. One variety of American imperialism enthusiastically and unselfconsciously assumed the white man's civilizing mission and world order politics. Another, viewing Britain as a rival imperial power, opposed British imperialism and favoured American. A third opposed all imperialisms in world politics.

Enthusiastic, unselfconscious US imperialism dates from the 1890s. By 1890 Americans had conquered the continent, closed the frontier, and begun to build a navy. It was the year in which the last armed conflict between Indians and whites took place at Wounded Knee, the Census Bureau declared there was no longer a land frontier, and Congress authorized the building of the US' first three battleships that would provide the global military reach of a world power. It was in 1890 too that Alfred Thayer Mahan launched his career as the preeminent theorist of US imperialism with the publication of his immensely influential *The Influence of Sea Power on History*. He told his fellow Americans that 'whether they will or not Americans must begin to look outward', a theme that Rudyard Kipling embellished for America's reading public with his poetic call to 'Take up the White Man's burden/Send forth the best ye breed/Go bind your sons to exile/To serve your captives' need ....' By 1898, the US had joined the competition for empire, going to war with Spain, seizing and annexing the Philippines, Puerto Rico, and Hawaii, 'liberating' Cuba, and, in 1900, sending 5000 troops to China, ostensibly to help put down the Boxer rebellion.

Admirers of British imperialism in the US accepted the mission of the white races, Britain and America, to bring order and civilization to the benighted. Among the admirers were Presidents Theodore Roosevelt and William Howard Taft. In 1908, Roosevelt was concerned with Britain's ability to deal with Indian unrest and 'hold down any revolt',[5] and in 1909 he described the British role in India as 'the greatest feat of the kind that has been performed since the break-up of the Roman empire ... [and] one of the most notable and the most admirable achievements of the white race during the past centuries'.[6] Echoing Roosevelt's sentiments, Taft in 1914 told the Toronto Empire Club that '... the debt the world owes England ought to be acknowledged in no grudging manner'. And President Woodrow Wilson, an admirer and emulator of the English form of government as well as an advocate of self-determination, resisted the demands of Indian nationalists that the Government of India be represented in the League of Nations. 'Under no circumstances', he told Colonel House, 'would he consent to the admission of a delegate from India because it was not self-governing'.[7] This American imperialism did not respond to Gandhi.

The second perspective on American imperialism included proponents of it who were also arch-enemies of British imperialism, such as press baron

William Randolph Hearst. By 1922, Hearst had become an early advocate of Gandhi's cause. Seizing the opportunity to twist the lion's tail that Gandhi's challenge to the British Empire offered, he authored a signed article in the *Washington Times* that inveighed against British rule in Indian. 'On what basis of justice, or general good will, or public benefit, or individual advantage, or liberty, or democracy, or self-determination, or anything that is recognized as right, is India kept in bondage by England?' The principle of self-determination should be applied to India. How could the United States, he asked, 'support England in her domination of India against the will of her three hundred million people?' America should scrap the 'unnatural alliance' with England that 'stultifies all our principles of liberty and nullifies the whole inspiring spirit of our history'.[8]

Ironically, it was the jingoist voice of the US' 'manifest destiny', a voice that supported expansion of US power across the North American continent and into South America, the Pacific, and Asia, that brought Gandhi to the attention of US public opinion. Colonel Robert R. McCormick, publisher of the *Chicago Tribune*, joined Hearst in publicizing Gandhi's challenge to British rule in India. It suited both publishers' purposes to use Gandhi's challenge to British rule in India to discredit and attack those who benefited from and admired Britain and its empire. Hearst and McCormick spoke for US nationalism and expansionist imperialism that had taken shape in the generations preceding the great war.

Those opposed to imperialism, American as well as British, and who identified with those oppressed by colonial masters, also contributed to Gandhi's positive reception in the US after World War I. Their first manifestation was the Anti-Imperialist League. Founded in Boston at Faneuil Hall in June 1898, it was led by Harvard luminaries Charles Eliot Norton and William James, ex-president Grover Cleveland, president Jordan of Stanford and Angell of Michigan, Andrew Carnegie for capital and Samuel Gompers for labour, and spoken for by E.L. Godkin's *Evening Post* and *Nation*, and Mark Twain. The League tried but failed to ensure that the Spanish-American war would result in liberation, not conquest.

William Jennings Bryan, the standard-bearer of populism and progressivism, and three-time presidential candidate, very nearly succeeded in 1896.[9] From the great plains of America's West, he spoke for the farmer and working man in an era dominated by Eastern industrial and financial capital. He vehemently opposed war, including the war against Spain and the war against Germany. After visiting India in 1905–6, Bryan became a forceful opponent of imperialism and the standing armies, big navies, and European entanglements it seemed to entail. 'Let no one', Bryan wrote after his visit to India, 'cite India as an argument in defense of colonialism'. The Briton '... has conferred some benefits upon India, but he has extorted a tremendous price for them .... [He] has demonstrated, as many before, man's inability to exercise with wisdom and justice, irresponsible power over the helpless people'.[10] When Woodrow Wilson broke his campaign pledge to keep the US out of Europe's war, Bryan resigned his post as Secretary of State in Wilson's Cabinet. In challenging apologists of imperialism, war and British rule in India such as Theodore Roosevelt and William Howard Taft, Bryan contributed to the post-World War I anti-imperialism and pacificism that helped make Gandhi credible and intelligible in the US.

The sea change that occurred after World War I in the US' outlook toward war, imperialism and orientalism helped make the dhoti-clad, bare-chested Gandhi a hero of pacifists whose opposition to the war now seemed justified. It also made him a hero of those opposed to British imperialism in India and to the US' special relationship with England. American opinion was ready to celebrate a nationalist leader who was Asian, non-violent, and 'spiritual' if he was capable of challenging the British Empire. In the early 1920s, Gandhi became a celebrity in American consciousness. What manner of person was he? Were Americans to admire, learn from, even believe in him, or had they let a spiritual and political disruptor into their midst?

The Guru

Although it is a Hindi word, I use guru rather than 'teacher' to discuss Gandhi's influence on important public figures in the US. The English word 'teacher' strongly suggests the Hindi word, *adhyapak*, a teacher in a school or college, and only weakly, if at all, guru. A guru is a mentor or a master with respect to knowledge or skill, and a spiritual guide, often but not always in a religious sense. A guru is not only at a higher plane of accomplishment but also at a higher plane of being than those who recognize or learn from him or her.

Gandhi was a guru for two prominent Americans, John Haynes Holmes and Martin Luther King, Jr, for most of their adult lives. He was a guru too for a third prominent American, Reinhold Niebuhr, but only for a short but important period (1930–2) when, in the face of economic collapse, rising fascism, and aggressive war, he was seeking moral, non-violent forms of collective action to realize 'equal justice'.

Culturally, the ground for Gandhi in the US was prepared by the US version of an 'oriental renaissance'. Reading Indian texts led Emerson to his transcendentalist essays such as 'The Oversoul' and 'Brahma'. Emerson's essays and his own reading of the Bhagavad Gita helped shape Whitman's orientalism, most evident in his poem 'Passage to India'. Emerson's lavish praise for Whitman's *Leaves of Grass* when it first appeared in 1855 helped Whitman on his way to becoming America's greatest poet. The orientalism of Emerson's Concord friend, Henry David Thoreau, took several forms. For a time he shared with Emerson the editorship of the transcendentalist magazine, *The Dial*. His meditative withdrawal to Walden Pond and subsequent de facto renunciation of society and celebration of nature and solitude owed much to familiarity with the Bhagavad Gita and the ideas and practices of Indian ascetics.[11]

Conversely, Gandhi's positive reception in the US owes something to his multifaceted occidentalism; of the twenty books that shaped Gandhi's thinking in his seminal 1909 text, *Hind Swaraj*, eighteen were written by occidental authors, including six by Tolstoy, two by Ruskin and Thoreau, one of which was *On the Duty of Civil Disobedience*.[12]

Later, from an entirely different quarter of America's cultural landscape and without benefit of oriental text, the outspokenly anti-imperialist Mark Twain helped to translate India to the US. After visiting that distant and exotic land in 1893, he wrote the widely read and frequently reprinted *Following the Equator; A Journey Around the World (1897)*. Twenty-four chapters were devoted to 'the most extraordinary country on earth'. The master of fantastic realism, 'the tall tales' about fabulous doings and beings, and the satirist and critic of middle class pieties and conventions, found India a land to his liking. 'In the sixth decade of Victoria's reign', Justin Kaplan writes of Twain, 'he had completed an equatorial tour of empire and imperialism, had seen the white man's secure dominion over alien races, black, brown, and yellow, and the accompanying victory of what he would soon be calling, as his indignation boiled to the surface, the "Blessings-of-Civilization Trust".'[13]

It was on ground prepared by these oriental themes that Holmes, King, and Niebuhr receive Gandhi's words and political morality.

John Haynes Holmes

John Haynes Holmes was the earliest, longest-serving, and arguably the most loyal and zealous of Gandhi's followers in the US. Minister of the Community Church of New York from 1919 until 1949, editor of *Unity*, which spoke for a liberal Christianity that was pacifist, internationally and socially concerned, and politically radical, Holmes announced his 'discovery' of Gandhi in 1921, and remained, until his death in 1964, his most ardent admirer and advocate in the US.[14] Between the wars particularly, Holmes' voice from the pulpit, the press (he wrote frequently for the *New York Herald Tribune*) and his and other journals of opinion was heard in New York, the East Coast, and beyond in support of radical reform at home, and peace and anti-colonialism abroad.

When, in 1927, Gandhi became correspondent from India for Holmes' journal, *Unity*, it published his autobiography (*The Story of my Experiments with Truth*) in the serial form in which it had recently appeared in India. This was the autobiography's first publication abroad. Holmes corresponded with Gandhi over many years and met him twice, once in England when Gandhi travelled to London to attend the second Round Table Conference in 1931, and a second time, more briefly, soon after Indian independence on 15 August 1947, when Holmes and his son Roger Holmes travelled to India by air to meet Gandhi in Delhi.[15] Gandhi was 78 and would be assassinated a few months later, on 30 January 1948.

Holmes announced in April 1921 that he would deliver a sermon on 'Who is the Greatest Man in the World?' By his own retrospective account, 'I climbed tremulously into my pulpit on Sunday morning to answer my own question'. The answer he gave was M.K. Gandhi. 'In the light of what was known, and not known, at that time about Gandhi here in our Western world', the audacity of his declaration, Holmes tells us 32 years later in *My Gandhi*, 'seems now incredible'.[16]

Holmes found Gandhi credible as a 'mahatma' (translated to his attentive congregation not as 'great soul' but as 'the Saint') and intelligible in Christian terms. 'When I think of Lenin, I think of Napoleon. But when I think of Gandhi', Holmes told his congregation, 'I think of Jesus Christ. He lives his life; he speaks his word; he suffers, strives, and will some day nobly die, for his kingdom upon earth'.[17] Holmes had prepared his audience for this encomium by considering but rejecting several other contemporary great men and by telling what he knew of Gandhi's life and views. 'I wonder how many of you ... know the story of his life. Listen while I tell this story, and see if I am right in calling its hero the greatest man in the world today!' It was a novel assertion but one to which Holmes remained committed for the rest of his life.

'The drama of this experience of discovery', Holmes wrote, looking back to 1921 from 1953, 'was terrific. Here was our world rent to ruin by mad resort to force and violence. Out of this vast convulsion (following World War I) there emerged this single man who put all his trust in truth and love. While the world gave itself over to self-destruction, Gandhi found the way of life and triumphantly walked therein. History has known nothing like it since Christ and Caesar'.[18]

Holmes' sermon in April 1921 seems to have affected the formation of public opinion. Until mid-1921, news about India in US papers relied on Reuters, the British-owned news service whose imperial bias was evident from its failure to provide copy to the US about the Jallianwala Bagh massacre at Amritsar in 1919 and Gandhi's first non-cooperation campaign. It did provide extensive coverage of the visit of the Prince of Wales in 1921 without mention of the hostility, boycotts, and violence with which it was met. Soon after Holmes' sermon, by mid-1921, news about India and Gandhi independent of British sources and views improved markedly. On 13 March 1922, when Holmes gave a second sermon about Gandhi, 'Gandhi, His World Significance', it was reported in the *New York Times.* So too was a luncheon meeting a day earlier of the Foreign Press Association that discussed Gandhi's arrest on 10 March 1922. These were the first news reports about Gandhi that originated in the US. The shift was no doubt determined by the huge extent and newsworthiness of the mass satyagraha of 1922. By the spring of 1922, Gandhi had become news inside as well as outside the US.

A decade after Holmes had declared Gandhi 'the greatest man in the world today', *Time* featured him on its cover as 'Man of the Year' for 1930. It was the year of the Salt March, Gandhi's most effective challenge to the legitimacy of British rule in India. World attention and concern had moved from the prospect of prosperity and peace in 1921 to deepening depression and intimations of war in 1931. Gandhi's ingenious strategy and dramatic execution of the Salt March in March and April of 1930 had revitalized Indian nationalism and led Britain's new Labour government to call negotiations at a second Round Table Conference in London in September 1931. Gandhi was to be the sole representative of the Indian National Congress.

The prospect of Gandhi, now the Mahatma for some and for many a world historical figure, leaving for London stirred Holmes and Niebuhr to dash to London in the hope of a meeting with the man who both believed held the key to Christian conduct on behalf of social justice. Holmes was then a leading figure in the East Coast liberal reform establishment, Niebuhr on the verge of becoming one.[19] Despite the resemblance between their careers and their commitments and their ostensible friendship, by 1931 the younger, ambitious Niebuhr had come to regard the more senior and established Holmes not only as the faithful publicist for Gandhi in the US but also as the 'ultimate symbol of the sentimental liberal pacifist',[20] who failed to recognize that, 'the human capacity for love is always tainted by the inclination to be self-serving and even destructive'.[21] Nevertheless, in late August 1931, Holmes and Niebuhr embarked on competitive missions to meet, learn from, and speak for Gandhi in the US.

Holmes, of course, had every advantage, not least a personal invitation from Gandhi to meet him in London should he attend a conference there. Nevertheless, twenty-two years later, in his 1953 book, *My Gandhi*, Holmes adopts a tone of great humility and self-effacement; he tells the story of his encounter with Gandhi as if he was nobody who became somebody by virtue of Gandhi's grace.

As Holmes tells the story, he was touring in Switzerland when he happened to see a newspaper with a dispatch from Bombay telling of Gandhi's embarkation for the Round Table Conference:

I was appalled at the spectacle of my own audacity in seeking intrusion upon so important, even historic [an] occasion ... would not [the Mahatma] ... be troubled by my unheralded appearance and my insistent expectation of an interview? ... When I reached London, the first thing I did was to hunt out Miss Lester [Muriel Lester, head of Kingsley Hall, the East End settlement house at which Gandhi would stay] and state my case. 'I will be a busboy,' I said, 'a dishwasher, a garbage man, if only you let me in to see and talk with Gandhi.' She not only gave me entrance, but managed, in kind and clever ways, to bring the Mahatma and me together. So hoped I was not over-reaching myself, nor exacting attention to which I was not entitled.[22]

Gandhi, of course, expected to see Holmes; he had corresponded with him for a decade and on 30 July 1931 wrote to Holmes from the Sabarmati ashram that 'if I do succeed in going to London we must meet'.[23] Gandhi was not surprised to find Holmes among those who greeted him at Folkestone when his boat-train arrived from Boulogne on 12 September 1931. They met on four subsequent occasions over the next five days, the last time being Thursday, 17 September, when Holmes advised Gandhi not to accept any of the several invitations he had to visit the US.

This proved to be the most significant aspect of Holmes' encounter with Gandhi. Holmes was determined to prevent Gandhi from being exposed to what he believed would be an exploitative and uncomprehending America. The preliminary to one of the invitations was to be an interview with Jimmy Walker, the Mayor of New York, who was then in London. Webb Miller, a well-known correspondent who had covered Gandhi's Salt March and was currently representing the United Press, tried to arrange the interview. According to Holmes' account of his five days in London, he not only prevented Miller from arranging an interview between Gandhi and the charming but corrupt Mayor of New York but also dissuaded him from accepting any invitations to visit the US.

Miller's report of Gandhi's Salt March (12 March to 6 April 1931) had caught world attention at the time, subsequently became a classical account of the practice of non-violent resistance, and was seen by millions in 1982 and 1983 as recreated in the film, *Gandhi*.[24] Miller apparently wanted to capitalize on the world personality that he thought he had had a hand in creating.[25] Holmes was 'disgusted, even frightened', by 'such tricks for making news' and by 'a deliberate attempt to exploit [Gandhi] for cheap and vulgar ends'. Later, when Gandhi asked Holmes, 'Do you know Mayor Walker?' Holmes told him that 'I am acquainted with [his] ... record because I helped to write it .... Mr Walker is ... now under serious charges of misconduct in office, and is pretty certain to be removed. His administration had become a municipal scandal. I should hate to see you in company with the Mayor, and my sober judgement is that you should not receive him'. The meeting did not take place, nor did Gandhi, after consultation with Holmes, accept any of several invitations to visit the US.

Invitations for Gandhi to visit the US at the conclusion of the Round Table Conference were at hand when he arrived in London. Many of them, according to Holmes, were from 'more or less designing persons' who 'counted shrewdly on the prestige which he would bring to movements or interests they represented'. At least one, Holmes conceded, was signed by more or less influential names [Holmes did not give them but they included Adolph Ochs, publisher of the *New York Times*, Alfred P. Sloan, chairman of General Motors Corporation, Robert M. Hutchins, president of the University of Chicago, John Dewey, the philosopher, Jane Addams, the social worker, and Rabbi Stephen S. Wise], and 'showed some appreciation ... of the problems involved'. On 9 October 1931, under a two-column headline on page 1 that read 'Gandhi to visit US if we take him seriously; Holmes' warning of ridicule deters him', the *New York Times* quotes Gandhi as saying, 'If [the invitors] can convince Holmes I ought to go to America I shall be glad to reconsider my decision'. But Holmes was not satisfied; he could see no real 'evidence of preparation for Gandhi's coming'. A reception committee, itinerary, speaking engagements, care for the Mahatma's comfort and safety, an informed and sympathetic press, and interviews with the President and other leading citizens were all required yet, 'so far as I could see, no responsible organization was at hand or in prospect to take over as difficult and important a piece of business as the people of this country have ever attempted'.

Holmes' objections, it turned out, were more fundamental than the inadequacy of preparations for the visit. From the beginning, Holmes writes, 'I was opposed to the whole proposition'. Gandhi's place after the conference was India 'in this hour of continuing crisis'. Besides, Holmes wrote in 1953, America in 1931 'was by no means that international center which in recent years it has become'. Holmes confesses, 'there was the question ... as to whether the American people as a whole were ready [in 1931] to receive the Mahatma in true appreciation of his character and work. He had not yet won independence for India from Britain nor world recognition and reverence ... His policies were still regarded as fantastic, and his personality as queer ... What I dreaded in 1931 ... was a vast explosion of vulgar curiosity and ribald jesting'.

Having said this much, Holmes admitted: 'I was perhaps ignoring Gandhi's supreme power and influence over men. His simplicity and grace, to say nothing of his courage, were passports to human favour'. Had not Gandhi been 'rapturously received and applauded' by the Lancashire weavers who had been all but ruined by his non-cooperation boycott in India of cotton goods imported from England? Holmes remained unsure of Gandhi's reception in the US, 'especially when time was so short and preparations so scant. I think now [in 1953]', Holmes concludes, 'as I thought then, that I was right in disfavouring the whole American proposal'.[26]

Before rushing to judgement about Holmes' advice to Gandhi, we should bear in mind the circumstances surrounding Gandhi's reception in Britain. London in September 1931 was at the epicentre of a worldwide economic earthquake that began with the October 1929 stock market crash in the US: the world and domestic economies were collapsing. In retrospect it seems that the British lion, 'hegemon' of world trade, finance, and security, was a dying beast.[27]

Ramsay MacDonald's first national coalition government, formed on 25 August 1931 to deal with the 'national emergency' just two weeks before the Round Table Conference opened, was already on its last legs, and in no position to bargain about independence for India, the issue that Gandhi insisted had to be settled before the problem of India's minorities could be tackled. A hostile British press mocked and belittled him. When Gandhi made his opening remarks at the Round Table Conference, a speech *Chicago Tribune* correspondent William L. Shirer considered 'the greatest of his long political life', the conference secretariat refused to make a verbatim record, the popular press largely ignored it, and *The Times* buried it. Most papers revelled in the prospect that the Conference would fail and Gandhi with it.[28]

The mood of uncertainty and fear generated by Britain's economic and political disintegration deepened Holmes' doubts. Holmes may have asked himself if a reception similar to the British establishment's hostile and uncomprehending one awaited Gandhi on the other side of the Atlantic. On balance, Gandhi's most ardent admirer and most forceful advocate in the US seemed to fear that, once on American soil, Gandhi would lose credibility and find it difficult to explain himself in terms that Americans would understand. Did Holmes, Gandhi's self-appointed vicar in the US, underestimate the Mahatma and misread American opinion? Niebuhr's response to Gandhi suggested that he may have.

Reinhold Niebuhr

Holmes, when faced with the prospect of an earthly Gandhi on American soil, was overcome by doubts about Gandhi's credibility and intelligibility. Reinhold Niebuhr seems to have come to opposite conclusions. True, he did not have to advise Gandhi about a trip to the US. But his account of 'seeing' Gandhi in London suggests a different conclusion than Holmes'. Gandhi's 'innate dignity' did not allow the charge of being a 'ridiculous figure'. By declaring Gandhi a 'prophet' and 'statesman', Niebuhr seemed to reveal that Gandhi in 1931 may have been what he, Niebuhr, hoped to become in the US, 'the prophet to Politicians', 'father of us all', 'establishment theologian', and aspiring politician.[29]

When Niebuhr sailed for England in August 1931, his head was full of questions he wanted to put to Gandhi. They were the key questions for his book on social change: What was the difference between violent and non-violent resistance to evil, and between non-resistance and any form of resistance? But interrogating Gandhi was not the only thing on Niebuhr's mind. True to his realist commitment to mixed motives, he eagerly looked forward to being with Ursula Keppel-Compton, an intelligent, religious, and stunningly attractive English postgraduate student at the Union Theological Seminary in 1930–1, to whom Niebuhr, a 38-year-old bachelor professor living with his widowed mother, became engaged in June and married in December.

Niebuhr at this time was still in his pacifist and socialist phase. He had helped to establish the pacifist Fellowship of Reconciliation, supported in 1928 the non-Marxist Socialist Party led by ex-Presbyterian minister Norman Thomas, and had visited the Soviet Union in the summer of 1930. Niebuhr spoke of the centrality of 'social intelligence'[30] for social action. In an article on 'The Religion of Communism' in the *Atlantic* [April 1931] he linked 'social intelligence' to 'some kind of religion' which is 'the basis of every potent social program. Those who fear too much fanaticism which is the inevitable by-product of religiously created energy are consigned to social impotence by the multitude of their scruples'. Religiously-created energy was dangerous—it bordered on fanaticism—but essential. These were Niebuhr's expectations as he hastened to London to meet Gandhi, a man who seemed to be providing the religious energy needed for national and social liberation.

Unlike Holmes, Niebuhr did not meet and talk to Gandhi in London. Along with a bevy of reporters, he was left standing outside Kingsley Hall, the East End settlement house where Gandhi was staying, while Holmes, Niebuhr's 'ultimate symbol of the sentimental liberal pacifist ..., went inside for a personal appointment'.[31] Niebuhr, the budding political realist, did not find Gandhi bizarre or absurd: 'Since it is Gandhi's day of silence, the crowd outside and several dozen of us inside the hall who hope for an interview get no more than a smile from him. It is a very engaging and charming smile and one begins to regret the charges of sentimentality one has brought against friends who have insisted that the homeliness of the man is soon forgotten, once he reveals his personality. Nor is there anything ridiculous about him, in spite of the loincloth [that article of apparel looks like what boys call track pants] and the homespun Indian shawl. There is too much innate dignity about the man to allow the impression of a ridiculous figure, which London newspapers try to assiduously to cultivate, to remain'.[32]

In the key chapter of *Moral Man and Immoral Society*, 'The Preservation of Moral Values in Politics', Niebuhr elaborates and refines his interpretations of Gandhi in 'What Chance Has Gandhi?', the article he wrote soon after his return from London. The 1931 article and the 1932 chapter constitute Niebuhr's considered estimate of Gandhi. It was of a world historical, even transcendent, figure. In the decaying and desperate world of failed capitalism and failing democracy, Gandhi's ideas and practices as Niebuhr interpreted them provided a religiously meaningful and politically effective way to pursue 'equal justice, the most rational ultimate objective of society'. He wondered 'whether there has ever been a more historic moment in the centuries than this visit of Gandhi to London'.[33]

After this almost hagiographic estimate of December 1931, Niebuhr became more ambivalent about Gandhi. As he proceeded to write *Moral Man and Immoral Society*, he made 'a conscious declaration of independence from the pacifistic circle—liberal and Socialist—in which (he) had worked in the previous decade'.[34] In his December 1931 article, Gandhi, the unique 'prophet' and 'statesman', combined 'translucent honesty' and 'spiritual self-discipline' with 'necessary opportunism' and 'patient application of general principles to detailed situations'.[35]

In *Moral Man*, Niebuhr arrived at the view that the responsible Christian should accept the use of force and that the use of force implied the use of violence in certain situations. He came to this position in part through an at best superficial and at worst perverse interpretation of Gandhi's use of *satyagraha* [truth-force], militant non-violent collective action or resistance. Gandhi, according to Niebuhr, used non-violence as a pragmatist; he was not committed to non-violence absolutely. 'Beginning with the idea that social injustice could be ... resisted by ... truth force and soul force ... [Gandhi] came finally to realize the necessity of some type of physical coercion upon the foes of his people's freedom, as every political leader must.'[36] For weak collectives such as Indian nationalists or weak minorities such as American Negroes, non-violence was the best tactic. Having made Gandhi intelligible in realist terms, Niebuhr held that he, not Gandhi's self-appointed champion in the United States, John Haynes Holmes, was 'a true Gandhian'.[37]

Niebuhr broke with his liberal Protestant and political reformist past in *Moral Man* by arguing that coercion, even violent coercion, that liberates 'oppressed nationalities' or the 'working classes' in the name of equal justice is 'placed in a different moral category from the use of power for the perpetuation of imperial rule or class dominance'. Conflicts involving oppressed nationalities and classes could not, as Gandhi thought they could, be resolved through non-violent collective action that made mutual understanding and accommodation possible. They had to be resolved by force in struggles that eventuated in victory for one side and defeat for the other. By 1932, Niebuhr had come to believe that victory over imperialists, capitalists, and fascists required physical force, not truth force.

But Niebuhr could not so easily repudiate his past self, a self which he found Gandhi's satyagraha exemplified, a *homo religiosus* as prophet and statesman, a self to which, in modified form, he gradually returned. Towards the end of Chapter IX of *Moral Man*, 'The Preservation of Moral Values in Politics', he presented another Gandhi, one more in keeping with the Gandhi both Niebuhr and Holmes saw in London at Kingsley Hall.

'The advantage of non-violence as a method of expressing goodwill', he wrote, 'lies in the fact that it protects the agent against the resentments which violent conflict always creates in both parties to a conflict, and that it proves this freedom of resentment and ill-will to the contending party in the dispute by enduring more suffering then it causes'. Again affirming Gandhi's view of conflict resolution based on non-violence and the mutual pursuit of truth, he observed, 'One of the most important results of a spiritual discipline against resentment in a social dispute is that it leads to an effort to discriminate between the evils of a social system and situation and the individuals who are involved in it ... Mr Gandhi never tires of making a distinction between individual Englishmen and the system of imperialism which they maintain'.

Niebuhr concludes his 'Gandhi chapter' in *Moral Man* with a powerful endorsement of Gandhi's perspective,

There is no problem of political life to which religious imagination can make a larger contribution than this problem of developing non-violent resistance. The discovery of elements of common human frailty in the foe and, concomitantly, the appreciation of all human life as possessing transcendent worth, creates attitudes which transcend social conflict and thus mitigate its cruelties ... These attitudes ... require a sublime madness which disregards immediate appearances and emphasizes profound and ultimate unities.

So, can Gandhi's 'sublime madness' be made available to the Western world? Niebuhr turns orientalism on its head to explain why, in his view, Gandhi's way can't be made available to the crisis-ridden Western world: 'it is no accident of history that the spirit of non-violence has been introduced into contemporary politics by a religious leader of the orient'. Because occidental man lacks the spirit of non-violence he is 'incapable of engaging in non-violent social conflict'. Western man's spiritual bankruptcy is the result of being 'deprived of religion'. Lacking a meaningful religious life, 'the white Man' has become a 'beast of prey'. Niebuhr is particularly concerned about the disappearance of the religious inheritance of the disinherited for whom the spirit required for non-violent resistance is most important. The religious heritage of the disinherited white man '... has been dissipated by the mechanical character of his civilization' and by the sentimentality and moral confusions introduced by the 'comfortable and privileged classes' into the Christian religion. Because the insights of Christianity 'are not immediately available for the social struggle in the Western world .... Western civilization ... will suffer from cruelties and be harassed by animosities which destroy the beauty of human life'. 'Even if', he concludes, 'justice should be achieved by social conflicts which lack the spiritual elements of non-violence, something will be lacking in the character of the society so constructed'.[38]

In the final paragraph of 'The Preservation of Moral Values in Politics', Niebuhr attempts to resuscitate his 'realistic' account of 'moral man and immoral society' by denying the Gandhi he has just so eloquently affirmed. 'The perennial tragedy of human history', he alleges, 'is that those who cultivate the spiritual elements usually do so by divorcing themselves from or misunderstanding the problem of collective man where the brutal elements are most obvious ....' With Gandhi now standing accused of 'divorcing [himself] from or misunderstanding the problem of collective man', Niebuhr feels free to sweepingly conclude that 'to the end of history the peace of the world, as Augustine observed, must be gained by strife'.[39]

Niebuhr's pacifist [both secular and Christian] and Socialist friends and allies felt shocked, dismayed, and some betrayed, by *Moral Man's* 'cynicism' and 'unrelieved pessimism'. Niebuhr answered his critics who included Norman Thomas and John Haynes Holmes by charging them with being 'immersed in the sentimentalities of a dying culture'.[40] Addressing his critics from the columns of his own *World Tomorrow*, Niebuhr '... for the first time labelled himself a "Marxian" as well as a "Christian"—the better to distinguish himself from the likes of Holmes, with whom he had now come to verbal blows and who was 'now his chief nemesis on the religious left'.[41]

If Niebuhr lost friends and allies he gained recognition and fame as a 'Christian realist.' *Moral Man and Immoral Society*'s 'uncommon brilliance',

Fox argues, vaulted Niebuhr into the front ranks of the US' public intellectuals. Its 'historic significance ... lay in Niebuhr's biting repudiation ... of the historic liberal Protestant quest for the Kingdom of God'. Ignoring Niebuhr's affirmation of Gandhi in his chapter on 'The Preservation of Moral Values in Politics', Fox reads *Moral Man* to say that Niebuhr 'dismissed with utter derision the deepest hope that animated thousands of radical and liberal Christians ...: the hope that human history would eventually see the inauguration of a community of love'. What's love? It was an ideal that was central to the heritage of American social thought. Most American thinkers between 1880 and 1930 'yearned for a future cooperative commonwealth that would transcend the brutal confines of industrial society'.[42] Niebuhr's German Lutheran roots distanced him from an Anglo-Saxon Protestant tradition that placed a quest for the Kingdom of God and a cooperative commonwealth rather than original sin at the centre of its concerns. It was the legacy of Puritan America, of those who, in the face of persecution and intolerance, fled to a wilderness where they pledged to establish a community of Christian brothers.

Yet, as Richard Fox concludes, Niebuhr was trying to have it both ways: idealism and realism. On the one hand, coercion, even force, had to be used, to oppose and defeat immoral 'collectives' in the domestic and international arenas. Unlike his theologian brother, Richard, Reinhold's faith did not involve abandoning himself to God's will. On the other, 'he held to the old liberal dream of transforming human society ....' Despite his fulminations against sentimental liberalism, against complacent faith in the redemptive character of human goodwill, Reinhold remained a thoroughgoing liberal.[43] It was the liberal Niebuhr, the Niebuhr who glimpsed the redemptive power of non-violence and sought greater equality and justice in society, who allowed himself to admire, even to identify with Gandhi the prophet and statesman who could command a nation and humble an empire.[44]

Martin Luther King

Gandhi's greatest and most enduring success as a guru in America was the influence he had on Martin Luther King, Jr. Through King, Gandhi affected the conduct of the civil rights movement that began in the mid-1950s and crested in the mid-1960s. King discovered Gandhi early in his career, made Gandhi's ideas and practice his own, and remained faithful to them when, in what turned out to be the last years of his life, many of those whom he had previously influenced and led abandoned satyagraha and non-violence.

King, the preeminent leader of the civil rights movement in the US, played a central role in moving the country toward a resolution of what Gunnar Myrdal called 'An American Dilemma', the contradiction between the equality promised in the Declaration of Independence and the reality of inequality found in slavery, segregation, discrimination, and poverty. In 1950, King had heard Dr Mordecai Johnson, then President of Howard University, speak about Gandhi. Johnson, who admired Gandhi, had just returned from India. King found Johnson's account of Gandhi 'so profound and electrifying that I left the meeting and bought a half dozen books on Gandhi's life and works'.[45]

King began reading about ahimsa (non-violence) and satyagraha (collective action in pursuit of truth), terms that have been subject to extensive interpretation in American and Indian scholarly, intellectual, and religious circles.[46]

I came to see (King wrote): that the Christian doctrine of love operating through the Gandhian method of non-violence was one of the most potent weapons available to the Negro in his struggle for freedom .... Prior to reading Gandhi, I had about concluded that the ethics of Jesus were only effective in individual relationships .... Gandhi was probably the first person in history to lift the love ethic of Jesus above mere interaction between individuals to a powerful and effective social force on a large scale.[47]

The Montgomery bus boycott in 1955 has been read as launching the on-going civil rights movement in the US. In the medium term, the boycott led to the desegregation of public facilities in the Southern US. A Gandhian version of globalization played a critical role in launching the civil rights movement; on 1 December 1955, Rosa Parks, a Black seamstress, teacher and NAACP activist, refused to move to the back of the bus. She broke the law by violating a local segregation ordinance that allocated the front of the bus for White passengers and the rear for Black passengers.[48]

Rosa Parks had participated in a workshop on Gandhian methods of non-violent resistance at the Highlander Folk School in Monteagle, Tennessee. Ram Manohar Lohia, the charismatic Gandhian Socialist from India had visited the School in 1951 at the suggestion of Harris Wofford, himself already a civil rights activist. Lohia had familiarized Highlander Folk School leaders with Gandhi's ideas and practices about non-violent civil disobedience and urged them to use them. According to Wofford's account of Rosa Park's historic refusal to move to the back of the bus, 'She had thought about Gandhi, and discussed the idea of civil disobedience at an earlier seminar at the Highlander Folk School in Monteagle, Tennessee'.

On the Sunday following Rosa Parks' arrest a dozen Montgomery pulpits and the Women's Political Council in Montgomery called for a boycott of the bus service. The twenty-six-year-old minister of the Dexter Ave. Baptist Church, Martin Luther King, who was soon to be elected President of the Montgomery Improvement Association, was astonished by the response; 'instead of the 60 per cent cooperation [that he] ... had hoped for, it was almost 100 per cent .... It would have been a one-day boycott', King subsequently told Harris Wofford, 'but for the surprising popular response ....' That evening King told the thousands who came to hear him that 'There comes a time that people get tired. We are here this evening to say to those who have mistreated us so long that we are tired—tired of being segregated and humiliated.'[49]

But how would Montgomery's Black community approach the community that created and enforced segregation laws? It fell to King to articulate what that approach would be. Addressing a public meeting to endorse the bus boycott five days after Rosa Parks' arrest and $14 fine, Martin Luther King said:

There will be no white persons pulled out of their homes and taken on some distant road and murdered. There will be nobody among us who will stand up and defy the Constitution of this nation. Our method will be that of persuasion, not coercion. Our actions must by guided by the deepest principle of our Christian faith. Love must be our regulating ideal. Once again we must hear the words of Jesus echoing across the centuries: 'Love your enemies' ... we must not become bitter and end by hating our white brothers. As Booker T. Washington said, 'Let no man pull you so low as to make you hate him.'[50]

In retrospect King made clear that his thinking about adversarial relationships in Montgomery and beyond was deeply influenced by Gandhi. *In Stride toward Freedom*, an account of the Montgomery Bus Boycott, King wrote:

As the days unfolded ... the inspiration of Mahatma Gandhi began to exert its influence. I had come to see early that the Christian doctrine of love operating through the Gandhian method of non-violence was one of the most potent weapons available to the Negro in his struggle for freedom ... in the summer of 1957 the name of Mahatma Gandhi was well known in Montgomery. People who had never heard of the little brown saint of India were now saying his name with an air of familiarity. Non-violent resistance had emerged as the technique of the movement ...[51]

King and Gandhi diverged in their paths as men of faith. American Baptism did not require or even recommend a holistic self-dedication to the life of the *homo religiosus*. Its preachers did not walk the narrow road of the ascetic nor were they likely to become the spiritual leaders of a dedicated commune [ashram] that combined cultivation of the moral self with worldly activity. The cultures of Vaishnavite Hinduism and of American Southern Baptism provided different models of religiously toned leadership. More worldly than Gandhi, King was a Baptist preacher guiding at first a congregation on how to transform the difficult political and social world of Alabama and Georgia and then mobilizing large parts of an entire nation, both black and white, both the segregated and the the segregators, to reject a deeply entrenched institution of humiliation and oppression. King and Gandhi not only shared political skill, a mastery of symbolic and moral politics and the intuition to identify strategies that would mobilize political voice and participation. They also shared the gospel of love and non-violence found in both Christian and Hindu, especially *Bhakti*, traditions.

In the dozen years between King's launching the civil rights movement in 1956 and his murder in 1968, the mood and vocabulary of the country changed. Negroes became 'Blacks' and blacks called for black power. Some advocated violent means to achieve liberation and ethnic identity. Frantz Fanon replaced Jesus and Gandhi as the teacher of black power extremists. King objected less to the idea of black power than he did to two ideas frequently associated with it: retaliatory violence and separatism. Both violated his Gandhian values.[52]

Other disappointments and failures followed. Like Gandhi, who near the end of his life faced the carnage of Partition riots, King towards the end of his life faced the violence of city race riots and escalation of the war in Vietnam. King and Gandhi were despised and opposed form 'within', Gandhi by militant Hindu fundamentalists, King by extremist blacks, and from 'without', Gandhi by 'two-nation' Muslims, King by J. Edgar Hoover and white racists and segregationists. Both were murdered and martyred. These affinities and parallels between King's and Gandhi's lives made Gandhi a familiar figure in other wise unlikely American households.[53]

Gandhi's presence in American popular consciousness as a person to respect or to vilify is partially linked to Martin Luther King's reputation and standing. They were at their nadir in the years immediately following King's death in 1968. His growing significance for Americans, whites as well as blacks, was evident when a King bust joined representations of other American statesmen and heroes in the rotunda of the Capitol on 20 January 1996 and the US for the first time celebrated the birthday of Martin Luther King, Jr as a national holiday.

The Mahatma

One of Gandhi's images in America was that of the mahatma. Its meaning was determined in part by longstanding attitudes and beliefs about India and the Orient and about Christianity that structured perceptions and evaluation.

Since the late renaissance and certainly since the mid-18th century the occident has found it difficult to regard the orient in any other light than backward, inferior, and benighted. Gandhi, the *homo religiosus*, the man of religion, whether as a mahatma, a saint or a teacher of a way of life like Buddha or Jesus, quickly became a source of both controversy and inspiration.

Until Gandhi became America's 'lens on India', American views on Indian religion, society and politics were largely filtered through British sources. They include those of the missionary, Alexander Duff, who held that 'of all the systems of false religion ever fabricated by the perverse ingenuity of fallen men, Hinduism is surely the most stupendous'. Charles Grant could not '... avoid recognizing in the people of Indostan a race of men lamentably degenerate and base', and John Stuart Mill, echoing the view of his father, James Mill, regretted that 'in truth, the Hindu, like the eunuch, excels in the qualities of the slave'.[54] More generally, the West's cultural hegemony and superiority made it difficult to accept an Indian, an oriental such as Gandhi, as a teacher of the good life.[55] The conquering West equated the superiority of its power and wealth with the superiority of its civilization and beliefs. Gandhi made a dent in this sense of superiority. The notion that the East could teach the West, that the US had something to learn from Gandhi, was strongly, sometimes hysterically, resisted. Gandhi's reception as a religious figure reveals a great deal about how American attitudes about India and the orient structured his presence in the US.

'Charlie' Andrews, the Anglican missionary who early on became one of the principal interpreters of Gandhi to the West, first met Gandhi in

Durban on 1 January 1914.[56] He bent to touch his feet. It was an act of canonization. Mark Juergensmeyer, a leading contemporary interpreter of Gandhi in the US, traces the origins of the Western propensity to construct Gandhi as a saint to C.F. Andrews' accounts of his initial encounters with Gandhi[57] and to Rabindranath Tagore's use of the term 'mahatma' in 1915 when Gandhi returned to India.[58]

'Saint', a culturally available category for an otherwise anomalous being, was not an Indian term.[59] Saint in Western parlance can refer to persons canonized by the Church for pre-eminent holiness (official saints) or to one of a Christian God's chosen people, a person in whom grace had triumphed and who was, as a consequence, eminent for piety or virtue. The aura of Christian holiness and transcendent power associated with the term 'saint' quickly melded with English versions of Indian terms loosely translated as saint. In 1915, Tagore, the recent Nobel laureate, used an Indian term, mahatma (great soul), to welcome Gandhi on his return to India from South Africa. Mahatma was taken to be an Indian version of a saint and the two terms became hard to distinguish in Western usage. Mohandas Gandhi came to be referred to and known as Mahatma Gandhi (as if this were his proper name), a designation that nevertheless suggested his saintly meaning and provenance. But was Gandhi a 'saint' by his own lights? Could he have meant to be a saint in India, much less in the US? What does his construction as a saint tell us about Gandhi in the US?

Saintliness, like charisma, is the fruit of a collaboration between viewer and viewed. Mark Juergensmeyer argues that although Gandhi's canonization as a saint was largely at the initiative of his English and American admirers, he collaborated in the result: 'What made Gandhi truly a Christ figure for Westerners from Andrews through Attenborough ... was not just that he looked the part. He acted the part too—or at least his actions were amenable to that interpretation. He was regarded as a man who exhibited saintly qualities'. Gandhi, it seems, wanted it that way, wanted his Western admirers to believe he was a saint. His capabilities, Juergensmeyer reasons, revealed his intentions. The fact that 'he ... appeared unclad but for a loin cloth made him look like what many Americans expected in a Messiah .... [B]ehind his wizened appearance was the awesome cultural backdrop of India, which seemed to Gandhi's American admirers as distant from the modern age as Jesus' Galilee.'

Ultimately Gandhi himself becomes responsible, holds Juergensmeyer, for the cultural noise that accompanied his translation from the world of the Indian orient, the world of *sanyasi*s, *sadhu*s, gurus, and *swami*s, to the world of the American occident, the world of saints. It begs the question to hold that 'saintliness, like beauty, exists largely in the eye of the beholder ...' if Gandhi meant to play the saint to his occidental admirers. They may have 'extravagantly revered' him but Gandhi becomes culpable if they were gullible. An authentic modern saint had a powerful appeal: more 'adequate' than Jesus to the 'global, rational, modern point of view .... Gandhi, the English speaking, London trained, Hindu is intercultural in his appeal—"a universal saint" as [John Haynes] Holmes put it .... Many Christians, especially those of a liberal theological bent who shy away from an other worldly view of Christ, feel that Gandhi fills the role as adequately as Jesus did'.

According to Juergensmeyer, 'the point of view is as interesting as the object of attention'. It is the authenticity of the believers, not the authenticity of the saint that 'shows that sainthood is far from dead, even in the present day'. Gandhi seems to have become a saint by pretence and enticement. For Juergensmeyer there is a touch of manipulation and a hint of fraud in the emergence of Gandhi the saint.[60]

Gandhi himself had trouble coping with his 'saintly' image, what he called his '*darshan* dilemma'. To take darshan is to profit spiritually from the sight of an auspicious person or icon. Soon after Gandhi returned from South Africa in 1915 he attended the Kumbha Mela, a vast religious assemblage of pilgrims and sadhus. Darshan-seekers did not allow him a minute to call his own. 'The darshanvalas' blind *love* has often made me angry, and ... sore at heart.' At the same time, 'the unique faith of India and the frankness and generosity of our people enchant me'. Yet the people do not 'profit in any way by having darshan'; he knew nothing in himself, he said, that made him 'worthy of giving darshan'. 'It is not possible', he said, 'simultaneously to work and to give darshan.' 'I do', he protested, '... make every effort to extricate myself from this dilemma.' His solution ultimately was not to choose between darshan and work but to try to do both: 'At present, even when people come for darshan, I continue to write and do other work.'[61]

The second difficulty that Juergensmeyer encounters with 'St Gandhi' is one endemic to saints. Those who bracket Gandhi with Jesus as a saint encounter the same difficulty with respect to Jesus. We ordinary mortals cannot be like such saints. According to Juergensmeyer, Gandhi '... is portrayed as essentially different from us, endowed with a spiritual power to which ordinary mortals are not privy .... We can laud his moral achievements without felling the necessity to live up to all of them ourselves'. Reinhold Niebuhr, Juergensmeyer's teacher, found Jesus' virtues 'dazzling precisely because they are not emulable: they are extremes of selfless love that provide ordinary Christians with a noble but ultimately unobtainable goal'. For Juergensmeyer Gandhi's saintliness is similar; 'We cannot live up to the standard that he achieved'.[62] Saint Gandhi may be a credible construction for some like John Haynes Holmes but for grudging admirers like Niebuhr and Juergensmeyer his sainthood did not provide a satisfactory guide to the religious life.

Gandhi neither wanted to be nor claimed to be a saint. A guru, yes, perhaps a sanyasi or sadhu, even a mahatma, but not a saint. The lives of saints are indeed unlike those of ordinary mortals. Gandhi's confessional autobiography was meant to show just how ordinary and mortal a creature he was. It showed too that he managed to realize in his daily life and public actions cultural ideals that many Indians honoured in their own lives and actions but found difficult though not necessarily impossible to enact. Gandhi did not, like a saint is said to do, mediate for or empower others. If he meant to be anything, he meant to be a guru, to teach through example, action, and precept. Margaret Chatterjee in her superb book on *Gandhi's Religious Thought* observes that 'The guru idea has been explored in recent years by Christian theologians in India, but not too successfully, for the guru in Hindu traditions is a preceptor, not a mediator. The tables can be turned and guru and disciple reverse their roles'.[63]

If I am right in believing that those who, for good or ill, assimilated Gandhi to the essentially Christian concept of saint misread the historical text, their 'mistake' does not remove the image of 'St Gandhi' from the meaning of Gandhi in the US. It continues to play an important and controversial role.

Beyond the image of Gandhi, the universal saint, and incorporating it lay the possibility that Gandhi was a world historical teacher of transcendent ethics comparable to Buddha, Mohammed, and, particularly for Christians, Jesus. During Pope John Paul II's widely reported visit to India in February 1986 he told inquiring reporters on his return to Rome, 'I was there to evangelize .... I have evangelized the Indian people through the works of Mahatma Gandhi'. 'Gandhi', according to the Pope, 'was much more of a Christian than many people who say they are Christians'.[64] Other Christians have viewed Gandhi in this framework. Kenneth Scott Latourette in his

1953 *A History of Christianity* argued that through Gandhi 'the influence of Christ ... became more dominant in ... [India] than at any previous time. Through Gandhi the teaching and example of Jesus made for non-violent resistance, greater opportunity to the depressed classes, and the positive meanings of unselfish service'. Jaroslav Pelikan, another distinguished Yale historian of Christianity, in his 1985 *Jesus Through the Centuries; His Place in the History of Culture*, compares Gandhi to Jesus in his chapter on 'The Liberator.'[65] John Haynes Holmes, a Protestant, and Thomas Merton, a Catholic, treat Gandhi as a redeemer and a liberator.[66]

Pope John Paul II's 'recognition' of Gandhi in 1986 was foreshadowed by Pope John XXIII in *Pacem in Terris* and by the Church's *Declaration on the Relationship of the Church to Non-Christian Religions* (*Nostra Aetate*) of the Second Vatican Council 28 October 1965. This *Declaration* recognized Hinduism, Buddhism, Islam, and other faiths as religions and said of them, 'The Catholic Church rejects nothing which is true and holy in these religions, [they] often reflect a ray of that Truth which enlightens all men (John 1:9)'.

Gandhi as world historical teacher of transcendent ethics revived issues first raised in the fifth century by the English (or Irish) theologian, Pelagius, in his dispute with Augustine of Hippo over Adam's fall, original sin, and God's grace. Pelagius disputed Augustine's doctrine that the consequence of Adam's fall entailed original sin and restricted to Christians only the possibility of knowing God and of God's grace. The doctrine carved a deep divide between Christians and non-Christian believers. Pelagius took the view that God's grace gave man free will, that subsequently it was 'helpful but not necessary and that the heirs of Adam were not stained with original sin'. Consequently, non-Christians could act righteously and know God. Pelagius' doctrine narrowed the space between Christian and non-Christian believers.

Pelagius' dispute with Augustine did not end in the fifth century, 'semi-Pelagianism' has survived as a recurrent mentality in Christianity.[67] It is the mentality that made it possible to write *Nostra Aetate* in 1965 and for Pope John Paul II to evangelize in Gandhi's name in 1986.

We have seen that 'Saint Gandhi,' while an image of Gandhi in the US, was not an image Gandhi meant to convey. At the same time, Gandhi thought about Christianity in terms not unlike those used by liberal Protestants and neo-Pelagian Catholics about him. There was, at this level but not at others, mutual admiration and an elective affinity that facilitated

Gandhi's reception in the US. In words that might have pleased Pelagius and no doubt did please John Haynes Holmes, Gandhi said in 1941, '... because the life of Jesus has the significance and the transcendency to which I have alluded, I believe He belongs not solely to Christianity, but to the entire world, to all races and people'.[68] 'But this is not to say', Margaret Chatterjee adds to her gloss of Gandhi's views, 'that those who have not heard the name of Jesus Christ cannot do the will of the Lord'. For Gandhi, Jesus was 'a great world teacher among others'. 'Jesus,' Gandhi continued, 'preached not a new religion but a new life'.[69]

Catholic Christians were not as quick to respond to Gandhi as were some liberal Protestant Christians. Pope Pius XI twice refused Gandhi's requests to call on him when, in his only trip abroad as India's national leader, he passed through Rome in December 1931 on his way back from the second Round Table Conference. On the other hand, Pope John Paul II's first act on his visit to India 55 years later was to visit the site of Gandhi's cremation on the bank of the Yamuna river. Removing his shoes, the Pope knelt in silent prayer at the memorial to the 'apostle of non-violence' and then spoke of humanity's debt to 'this man so marked by his noble devotion to God and his respect for every living being ....' 'It is entirely fitting', he said, 'that this pilgrimage should begin here. Today we still hear him pleading with the world, "Conquer hate by love, untruth by truth, violence by suffering".'[70]

The Pope's ten-day tour of India was widely reported in US electronic and print media. His tasks were manifold, complex, and delicate. Unlike his visits to other Third World countries, in India he was a Christian pontiff appealing to a predominantly Hindu country. The Pope prepared for his trip to India by immersing himself in the teachings of Gandhi. In India he quoted Gandhi often and at length. It was on his return to Rome that he uttered the sentence already cited, 'I have evangelized the Indian people through the words of Mahatma Gandhi.'[71] Was this good tactics in a poor, Hindu country or the revitalized neo-Pelagianism and the ecumenism of Vatican II's *Nostra Aetate*? At the beginning of his tour, the Pope appealed to Gandhi when he said, 'I want to show respect, esteem, and encouragement to all those who search for God, who commit themselves to search for perfection, who work in the service of their brothers to construct peace and justice'. Joaquin Navarro Valls, the chief Vatican spokesman accompanying the Pope, characterized the Pope's invocation of Gandhi as part of a '... broader effort to link Roman Catholic teaching to Gandhi's objectives'.[72]

Gandhi the saint, mahatma, and possible redeemer had been heard and seen in the US for three decades to mixed reviews, contested evaluations, and ambiguous understandings. His presence in American consciousness was mediated by shifting and intersecting historical currents and by meta-thought, the mentality that selects and colours contemporary events and experience.

The Fraud

Gandhi, Charles Chatfield found, was America's lens on India. He was also its lightning rod for images of India and the orient, a particularly powerful, pervasive, and intrusive version of the 'other'. Xenophiles find themselves attracted by the other, xenophobes repelled; but what comes first, the experience of thinking and feeling about the other or the cultural paradigms, the meta-ideas, that distinguish and define 'them' and 'us'?

The British images of India depicted earlier, the India of 'false religion', a 'lamentably degenerate' people, and a 'slave' mentality, were common in an America that, until after World War I, got most of its news and views from British sources. There were exceptions to the European and British image of India and the orient, contributors to the integral humanism of the 'oriental renaissance' who learned in India as well as about India. Such were the Frenchman Anquetil-Duperron and the Englishman Sir William Jones. So too were there American exceptions, Ralph Waldo Emerson, Henry David Thoreau, Walt Whitman, and Mark Twain. But when Gandhi, the Indian and the oriental, appears in the press and quarterlies of the early 1920s, he is constructed and interpreted not only in terms of the imperialist politics of that era, but also in terms of deeprooted meta-ideas and cultural paradigms about India and the East. The residues of such paradigms persist into the 1980s, perhaps into the millennium.

The film *Gandhi* provided a particularly effective lightning rod for the view of Gandhi as Fraud. Released in 1982 but seen for the most part in 1983, it won an unprecedented eight Academy Awards, topped the list for viewers, and made a lot of money. It presented Gandhi as an epic hero: a myth for our time, perhaps for all time. In a world in which entertainment and news construct each other, and history is made as well as represented on the screen, illusion and reality can merge. *Gandhi* was great entertainment and great box office but it was also a message and a worldview. An Indian saint became a transcendent figure. Although America was neither seen nor mentioned in the film, the visual language of the film—the film as text—was taken by some to legitimize and justify ideas and actions at issue in the US. More than ever before, Gandhi became a popular concept in the US, a brand name that could be deployed for an array of causes from environment to health to diet to peace.

The film generated a neo-conservative backlash, what Hendrick Hertzberg in a brilliant riposte to two such attacks labelled a 'nasty outbreak of Mahatma-bashing'.[73] Principal spokesman of the backlash was Richard Grenier, film critic for *Commentary* and sometime novelist. In the March 1983 number of *Commentary* Grenier engaged in 'Deflating the Gandhi Myth' by depicting 'the Gandhi Nobody Knows' as a fraud. In particular, he asserts the 'St Gandhi presented in the film was really a lecher, racist, hypocrite, fool, and faddist'. The film's director, Sir Richard Attenborough, 'Dickie' to Grenier, is depicted as a paid political propagandist for the Government of India (it financed one-third of the film's cost) who surreptitiously, even subliminally, slipped in his pacifist, socialist, environmentalist, and anti-imperialist views.[74]

'We are dealing', Grenier says, 'with two strangenesses here, Indians and Gandhi himself'. His principal authority for the claim of strangeness is V.S. Naipaul, 'a Hindu and a Brahmin, born in Trinidad' and the author of two 'quite brilliant' books, *An Area of Darkness* and *India: A Wounded Civilization*. It is not the literary quality of Naipaul's books that Grenier admires but their depiction of Indian orientalism, the alien other that Grenier feels is so repellent.

India, according to the Naipaul quoted in Grenier, 'has little to offer the world except its Gandhian concept of holy poverty and the recurring crooked comedy of its holy men'. Hinduism, as Naipaul understands it, 'has given men no idea of a contract with other men .... It has enslaved one-quarter of the population [the untouchables] and has left the whole fragmented and vulnerable ... Through centuries of conquest the civilization declined into an apparatus for survival, turning away from the mind ... and creativity ... stripping itself down, like all decaying civilizations, to its magical practices and imprisoning social forms'.

Naipaul says that Gandhi's autobiography reveals that he was headed for 'lunacy'. He was rescued by his response to external events, a response—presumably satyagraha—that was determined in part by 'his experience of the democratic ways of South Africa'. It was in South Africa that Gandhi caught a glimmer of that strange institution, that is, democracy, 'of which he would never have seen even a reflection within Hindu society'. Gandhi, like India more generally, is 'dependent in every practical way on other, imperfectly understood civilizations'. Grenier and Naipaul are building not only on 19th century British orientalist views of India but also on more recent orientalist constructions of India and Gandhi, among which Katherine Mayo's *Mother India* is paradigmatic.

Katherine Mayo's Diseased Continent

Gandhi-bashing, like India-bashing, has a history. One of its first transnational statements was Katherine Mayo's *Mother India*. First published in 1927, it was written in the context of official and unofficial British efforts to generate support in the US for British rule in India. *Mother India* appeared on the eve of the Simon Commission's visit to make inquiries about the viability and propriety of further measures of statutory reform. The book added contemporary and lurid detail to the image of Hindu India as irredeemably and hopelessly impoverished, degraded, depraved, and corrupt. Mayo's *Mother India* echoed not only the views of men such as Alexander Duff, Charles Grant, and John Stuart Mill but also those of Theodore Roosevelt who gloried in bearing the white man's burden in Asia and celebrated the accomplishments of imperialism.[75]

Mayo's enthusiastic and detailed chronicling of a diseased and unhygienic India—Gandhi referred to it as a 'Drain Inspector's Report'— was particularly painful for Gandhi, whose notorious concern for cleanliness made him vulnerable and perversely sympathetic to her critique even while rejecting its gross reductionism. Mayo took special aim at Gandhi, whose success in challenging British rule deeply troubled her British friends and patrons. They took considerable trouble to provide information, facilitate train travel, and interviews in India and publicize her book after its publication. Gandhi agreed to her request for an interview and spent a good deal of time answering her queries about the state of India and giving his views about the causes of and remedies for India's ills. Her selective and truncated account of Gandhi's views made them appear 'thoroughly ridiculous'.[76]

Mayo was obsessed by two evils, Hinduism and disease. The two seemed to be linked in some kind of ontological nexus. In an article in the *Atlantic* soon after Gandhi's widely reported Salt March in 1930, she returned to the task of denigrating his image in the US. After charging him with sedition, she alleged that a smallpox epidemic in an area where Gandhi had walked on his way to Dandi was due to the contagion carried by his followers. They in turn had been contaminated before their departure on 12 March 1930 because Gandhi's ashram was a 'smallpox pest center'. Mayo succeeded in adding a new dimension to the litany of the ills of Hindu India. Many years later, Daniel Patrick Moynihan, who served as US ambassador to India under Presidents Nixon and Ford, demonstrated the persistence of Mayo's vision when he publicly remarked that the only thing India had to export was communicable diseases.

Mayo made sense to Americans: health was better than disease, monotheist Muslims better than idolatrous Hindus; enslaved, dehumanized, but underdog and potentially Christian untouchables better then their upper-caste Hindu oppressors who were, in any case, incapacitated physically and morally by their horror of pollution. The obvious and moral conclusion was that British rule, which helped and protected Muslims, untouchables, and Christians, must and should continue. Gandhi's teaching that all religions approached truth and his doctrinal and practical efforts to realize national and religious brotherhood and to purify Hinduism by ridding it of untouchability were spurious, politically inspired deceptions designed to unite India behind his ill-fated demand for independence.

Arthur Koestler's 'Naked Fakir'

We move back in time in our selective review of pre-Grenier versions of Gandhi-bashing. It is the late 1950s. World War II has been fought and won, decolonization is almost complete. Freud's perspective on human nature has become conventional wisdom. A jaded, disillusioned Arthur Koestler, whose *Darkness at Noon* (1940) brilliantly and starkly conveyed the horror of Stalin's 1930s purge trials, sets out for Asia to find the answer to Europe's 'deadly predicament': 'the exhaustion of the old ideologies ... [and] a hunger for new ones'[77] and the 'coca-colonization of Western Europe' under the impact of American mass culture and materialistic civilization. Alarmed 40 years before the disruptions in 1999 and 2000 of WTO meetings in Seattle and Genoa that 'A global civilization with a standardized style of living ... is beginning to emerge all over the world', Koestler hastened to Asia to find answers at mid-century to the pernicious effects on European civilization of US-driven globalization before it was too late.[78]

'I travelled in India and Japan [in 1958–9]', Koestler tells us in the preface to *The Lotus and the Robot*, 'in the mood of the pilgrim' seeking answers to 'our perplexities and dead-locked problems' from 'a different spiritual latitude'. Four 'saints' and some Zen masters later, he concludes that Asian mysticism has no 'significant advice to offer'. His encounter with the Asian 'other' convinced him that his 'place was in Europe' whose 'unique history', 'organic coherence', and 'distinct identity' stood in marked contrast to their absence in Asia. In Asia, there was 'continuity without change'; 'conceptual thinking could not develop' in face of the 'irrationality, subjective, mystical, logic-rejecting' modes of being. Having begun his journey 'in sackcloth and ashes', he returned 'rather proud of being a European ... and with a new confidence and affection for that small figure [Europe] riding on the back of the Asian bull'.[79]

It was not Europe but India that faced a 'tragic predicament'. The heart of the predicament lay in family relations, specially 'the need to submit oneself unreservedly to one's father's authority, to treat him as a god .... He stands for ... disciplining of the passions ... to yield to spontaneous emotion or sensual appetite is felt to be both wrong and dangerous: this is especially the case with sexual satisfaction, which is always felt to be illicit and somehow impious'.[80]

As he warms to his subject, Koestler, in extended psychological and cultural language, echoes John Stuart Mill's succinct characterization: 'in truth the Hindu, like the eunuch, excels in the qualities of a slave'. Hindu India's 'religious-social ideal [produced] something like a Hindu national character .... The young male's unconditional submission to the will of his father ... [was] designed to ... undermine his initiative and independence; the family household was a school of conformity, obedience and resignation .... The result was an ingrained reluctance to make decisions, a lack of self-reliance and independence; a tendency to evade responsibilities ... Indians give that curious impression of never having grown up, of a rather moving child-like quality ... which seems somehow blurred, soft ... without proper contour and individuality'. Some '... seem to have no will and no personality of their own—eager for praise, over-sensitive to criticism, smilingly irresponsible .... [Yet] underneath the meek and gentle manner there may be a furnace of repressed passions, leading to unexpected outbursts ....'[81]

Koestler then links India's slave mentality to Gandhi. In India, while he was alive, Gandhi was known as 'Bapu' or father; it was a more common designation than Mahatma. India, a democracy 'in name only ...' is in fact ruled by bapus, father figures, who put 'a premium on uncritical obedience ....' How could a citizen be expected to elect a government when he was not allowed to elect his own bride? '... Out of the sacred womb of the Indian family only political yes-men could emerge'.[82]

At a less grand level of discourse than civilizational *angst* or national character but one equally important for locating Gandhi in the mind of America, Koestler found that most Asians are either frauds or deeply troubled neurotics. Gandhi was no exception. Here is Koestler's summing up of Gandhi:

Gandhi was an extremist in every respect. The secret of his genius, of his power over the nation's imagination, lies perhaps in his unique gift to exaggerate [sometimes to grotesque proportions] and to dramatize [sometimes to the degree of showmanship] precisely those elements in Hindu tradition which had the deepest emotional appeal. This is true for the whole range of his activities: his vegetarian and fruitarian apostolate; his [sometimes fatal] activities as a nature healer; the loin-clothed appearance of the 'naked fakir' in Buckingham Palace; the Stakhanovite cult of *khadi*; the principles of tolerance and non-violence carried to Jacobin extremes; the martyrdom of the fasts; the prayer meetings in the patriarchal ashram; the rejection of sex, even among married couples, as a source of spiritual debility; the inhuman 'detachment' from his family in the interest of public service; and the belief in the life-long absolute right of the father to rule over his sons.

We have here an amalgam of 'queerness' and 'wackiness' with extremism and obsessiveness that, in popular parlance, translate into 'sick' and 'sickening', and in social scientific language into psychologically disturbed and culturally deviant. At the same time Gandhi's exaggeration and showmanship suggest that he is a trickster or magician, that is, a fraud. 'Naked fakir' becomes an irresistible *double entendre*. Once the great issue of British rule over India was removed and psychological language captured discourse, Gandhi the saint or mahatma could be treated as a celebrity and at the same time unmasked as a neurotic and a fraud whom only the gullible could revere.

Erik Erikson and Clifford Geertz: Gandhi's Truth or Gandhi's Malaise?

Erik Erikson's *Gandhi's Truth: On the Origins of Militant Nonviolence* appeared in 1969, about a decade after Koestler's *The Lotus and the Robot* announced that a sick and dying traditional Asia had nothing of value to say to the Western world. Erikson, an eminent neo-Freudian whose theory of the stages of life and concept of identity spoke particularly to the civil rights and Vietnam generations, used his examination of Gandhi's life to suggest that there was a convergence between Freud's psychoanalysis and Gandhi's satyagraha. Both were therapeutic methods of pursuing and realizing truth, one in the individual, the other in society. The result, Erikson held, was 'a correspondence in method and convergence in human values which may well be of historical, if not of evolutionary significance'.[83] In this sense Erikson's book contributed to Gandhi's 'Mahatma' image in the mind of America. But this section is about Gandhi as 'fraud', not Gandhi as social therapist. It is Clifford Geertz's reading of Gandhi through the medium of Erikson's book rather than Erikson's *Gandhi's Truth* that interests us here.

Suggesting that Gandhi, like Freud, provided a way to pursue and realize truth was too much for Clifford Geertz. In the late 1960s he was a rising star, in the 1980 one of the brightest stars, in America's social science firmament. By the 1990s, Geertz had become '... a kind of demigod' of academic anthropology.[84] In the 20 November 1969 number of *The New York Review of Books*, Geertz did not attack Erikson directly or Gandhi head-on. Yet his interpretation of Gandhi left no doubt that he thought of him as a poseur and a sham. Confused, muddled, contradictory, in life Gandhi had been a danger to India as well as to himself, in death as an icon, he could join the Koestler pantheon as a 'god that failed'. The unstated message of the review was that Erikson, guide to the concerned and perplexed, was himself gullible and foolish in his admiration for Gandhi.

Geertz says that Erikson is like the little girl who visited the dinosaur in the museum only after she had decided the dinosaur was 'good' rather than 'bad'. Erikson chose to study Gandhi because, 'for twenty years, since his *Childhood and Society* announced the Freudian vocation to be the empowerment of the ego, Erikson has been asking the same question ... whence does hope arise'. In Gandhi, Erikson found an 'appropriate' but 'most refractory' subject.

Gandhi claimed to be a saint, Geertz argues, 'if not in so many words, certainly in almost every action he took ...' because a saint 'demands a moral response'. 'It is the triumph of Erikson's book', Geertz tells us, to uncover Gandhi's 'inherent moral ambiguity', the 'admiration and outrage, awe and disgust, trust and suspicion', that accompany the career of 'a man who recommends his character to the world as a saving revelation'.

After taking from Erikson's account of Gandhi that he is 'an obsessive tease', a person 'with an extraordinary capacity to make others feel furious and foolish at the same time', Geertz proceeds to explain satyagraha as a form of teasing. 'He is always taunting, testing limits, playing with other's emotions .... Forged into a political instrument this becomes the famous *Satyagraha* ....' Geertz renders satyagraha as 'mass taunting' or 'collective needling'. What in the end Gandhi did to colonial India was to 'drive it to distraction'. In his conduct during 'the event', the Ahmedabad textile strike of 1917, which is the centrepiece of Erikson's book, Gandhi's teasing 'was openly exposed, and with it the fact that shaming men into virtue was a complex and treacherous business, both less selfish and less pacific than it looked'.

Geertz pictures Gandhi's thinking about non-violence as 'moral double talk' and hypocrisy. Non-violence, as Geertz understands Gandhi, derives its 'moral grandeur' from the violence it contains. In a remarkable trans-valuation of values, Geertz argues that the practitioner of non-violence must be powerful in the sense that he must be 'competent to strike back, even to kill ...'. If one has such competence, not to strike back or kill is 'an assertion of moral superiority which an aggressor ... must necessarily acknowledge. The road to true non-violence passes then through the attainment of power, that is, the means of violence ...'. Because Gandhi the thinker was 'stymied by the paradox that non-violence is the reciprocal of strength' his philosophy 'dissolved into a collection of colliding homilies and Indian eccentricities'.

Geertz concludes his essay on Erikson's *Gandhi's Truth* by observing that the book was 'more convincing in describing the dinosaur than in judging him'. This gets to the heart of the problem. Can a subject be intelligible if it lacks credibility, 'the power to inspire belief'? The little girl was not sure she could learn anything about the dinosaur in the museum because she was not sure she believed in dinosaurs. Ten years after attacking Gandhi as a poseur and sham, Geertz published the brilliantly convincing *Negara*,[85] a tale about an erstwhile Balinese kingdom. In *Negara* we learn about the 'theater state' where the represented—symbols, ceremonies, rituals—is the real; in Geertz's words, 'all there is'. But Geertz has trouble making sense of Gandhi because he doesn't find Gandhi's representations credible; his peasant dress, like his saintliness, were unconvincing affectation.[86] For Geertz, Gandhi isn't for real. Lacking credibility, Gandhi lacks intelligibility.

Who Goes There, Friend or Foe?

Gandhi first entered American public consciousness in 1921 when John Haynes Holmes declared him to be the greatest man in the world. Eighty years later, at the turn of the 21st century, Holmes' claim seems far less far-fetched than when it was first made. *Time's* 31 December 1999 end-of-the-century issue named Gandhi (along with Albert Einstein and Franklin Roosevelt) as Person of the Century. His prospects for the coming century look good.

In June 1983 *Firing Line* host William Buckley asked Richard Grenier, *Commentary's* film critic, 'what was it about the movie *Gandhi* that struck [you] as historically offensive?' 'Above all', Grenier replied, 'Gandhi has been on the back burner for 30 years, he's been completely off the stove, he's been down in the cellar. What brought him back was ... the new wave of pacifism—a new pacifism. Otherwise they would not be making the movie today'.[87] These words were spoken in 1983, the high noon of the cold war. MAD [mutually assured destruction] was the prevailing nuclear doctrine, Ronald Reagan's metaphor, the 'evil empire', was the prevailing signifier. Grenier was attacking Gandhi, the film and the man, because they legitimized non-violent politics and morality.

But was he right in claiming that Gandhi had disappeared from view after Indian independence. Could he be so potent a symbol of non-violence if he had been on the back burner for thirty years? I have tried to show why and how Gandhi has been an active presence in American consciousness since at least 1921, and not least in the post-World War era of decolonization.

Let us recall that Gandhi began his career in the US as an anti-imperialist, an intrepid opponent of the British Empire in India who appealed to William Randolph Hearst, an American press baron jealous of and virulently opposed to British power and prestige. Gandhi's meaning quickly moved from the realm of history, of factuality and positive truth, to encompass the realm of myth, of belief and imaginative truth. A guru for some, a mahatma for others, in time he became a world historical figure whose life and message taught a new way of thinking, living and acting that inspired and legitimized the peace, environmental, and self-help movements.

John Haynes Holmes, a liberal Protestant, told his parishioners in 1921 that when he thought of Gandhi he thought of Jesus. For Holmes, a social reformer, Gandhi was a universal saint, a person who could show the way to realizing the Kingdom of God on earth. Reinhold Niebuhr, an incipient Christian realist, scorned such claims. Yet, confronted in 1932 with the collapse of capitalist economies and liberal democracies, he identified for a time with Gandhi, the 'prophet' and the 'statesman', a leader whose religious energy could inspire the disinherited and disenfranchised to achieve justice.

In the 1950s Martin Luther King 'came to see that the Christian doctrine of love operating through the Gandhian method of non-violence [was] ... one of the most potent weapons available to the Negro in his struggle for freedom'. Erik Erikson's *Gandhi's Truth* spoke to civil rights and Vietnam generations in search of meaning and identity. Nelson Mandela credits 'the Gandhian influence' with dominating 'freedom struggles on the African continent up to the 1960s because of the power it generated and the unity it forged among the apparently powerless'.[88] In the early 1980s Richard Attenborough and Ben Kingsley's film *Gandhi* served as counter-poise to the threat of nuclear war in what proved to be the closing decade of the Cold War. In 1986, Pope John Paul II chose to evangelize in India through the word of Mahatma Gandhi.

But there was a powerful countercurrent that challenged the view that the US had anything to learn from Gandhi. Some held that Americans were being deceived; Gandhi was a fraud, not saint. As Franky A. Schaefer, the evangelical fundamentalist who introduced Richard Grenier's denigrating book, *The Gandhi Nobody Knows*, put it, 'it is time that Westerners— Christians and Jews—adopt a little more self-confidence in answering the challenge of Hinduism. Christians in particular need to affirm the fact that there is only one Christ and Savior and his name is Jesus, not Gandhi.'[89] The persistence and intensity of efforts to denigrate and unmask Gandhi are measures of the threat that some feel from his acceptance in much of the West. Gandhi's 'contradictions' weigh heavy on Geertz and Niebuhr— saint in era of saintlessness, 'otherworldly' Mahatma acting in the world, non-violent advocate of militancy, Hindu with a Christ-like ethic of love, homo religiosus believing in many paths to God, votary of truth who takes an experimental view of truth. It may be that it is these very 'contradictions' that have made him a world historical figure in a globalizing twenty-first century whose denizens, caught in a maelstrom of change and uncertainty, have difficulty answering Tolstoy's question, how should we live?

Notes

* An earlier version of this chapter appeared in Sulochana Glazer and Nathan Glazer (eds), *Conflicting Images: India and the United States*, Glenn Dale, Maryland: Riverdale Company Publishers, 1990.

[1] See Mohandas K. Gandhi, *Satyagraha in South Africa*, Ahmedabad: Navajivan Publishing House, 1950, 1928, and Robert A. Huttenback, *Gandhi in South Africa; British Imperialism and the Indian Question*, Ithaca: Cornell University Press, 1971.

[2] Charles Chatfield (ed.), *The Americanization of Gandhi; Images of the Mahatma*, New York and London: Garland Publishing, 1976.

[3] Chatfield, pp. 24–5.

[4] Claude Markovits, *The Un-Gandhian Gandhi: the Life and Afterlife of the Mahatma*, Delhi: Permanent Black, 2003, pp. 17–18.

[5] Roosevelt to Whitlaw Reid, ambassador to London, 26 November 1908, in Elting E. Morrison, *The Letters of Theodore Roosevelt*, Cambridge: Harvard University Press, 1952, vol. 6, pp. 1383–4.

[6] 'Some American Opinions on the Indian Empire', London, n.d., pp. 1–2, as quoted in Manoranjan Jha, *Civil Disobedience and After: The American Reaction*, Meerut and Delhi: Meenakshi Prakashan, 1973, p. 10.

[7] David Miller, *The Drafting of the Covenant*, New York: G.P. Putnam's Sons, 1928, p. 492, n. 56, and Charles Seymour, *The Intimate Papers of Colonel House: The Ending of the War*, Boston: Houghton Mifflin Co., 1928, p. 311. Only after General Smuts pointed out that India as a signatory power 'would automatically have a right to a delegate' did Wilson 'acquiesce' to Government of India membership.

[8] Reproduced in the *Hindu* (Madras), 27 February 1922, as quoted in Manoranjan Jha, *Civil Disobedience and After: The American Reaction*, Meerut and Delhi: Meenakshi Prakashan, 1973.

[9] But for Mark Hanna's shrewd and expensive management of William McKinley's nomination and campaign, Bryan might have become president in 1896. And Bryan is sometimes pictured as a yokel rather than a progressive and statesman. As a boy wonder orator his speeches were sometimes mocked as being like the great Platte river, a thousand miles long three inches deep. His 'Cross of Gold' speech became a myth in his time and the inspiration for Frank Baum's compelling and enduring Wizard of Oz story. He ended his career as Clarence Darrow's fundamentalist foil in the Scopes 'monkey trial' where, in the name of the literal truth of Genesis, he opposed the teaching of Darwinian evolutionary biology.

[10] *The Old World and Its Ways*, St Louis: The Thompson Publishing Co., 1907, ch. XXVI, 'British Rule in India', p. 308.

[11] See the late Barbara Stoller Miller's Introduction and Afterward, 'Why Did Henry David Thoreau Take the Bhagavad-Gita to Walden Pond?' in her *Bhagavad-Gita: Krishna's Counsel in Time of War*, Toronto, New York: Bantam Books, 1986, 1988.

[12] For the text and a brilliant framing essay see Anthony Parel, editor, *Hind Swaraj and Other Writings*, Cambridge, UK: Cambridge University Press, 1997. Gandhi's *Hind Swaraj* was the first text to appear in John Dunn and Geoffrey Hawthorn (eds), 'Cambridge Texts in Modern Politics'.

[13] Justin Kaplan, *Mark Twain and His World*, New York: Simon and Shuster, 1974, p. 163.

[14] The Holmes papers are in the Library of Congress, Washington, DC. Holmes left his extensive collection of books by and about Gandhi to Harvard where they are now housed in the university library.

[15] He was a professor of philosophy at Mount Holyoke College for most of his career.

[16] John Haynes Holmes, *My Gandhi*, New York: Harper and Brothers, 1953 p. 29. The sermon was delivered on 10 April 1921 at the Lyric theatre to an overflow congregation 'who expected to hear Woodrow Wilson or Sun Yat-Sen, Lloyd George, or Lenin!' Carl Hermann Voss, 'John Haynes Holmes: Discoverer of Gandhi', *Christian Century*, 6 May 1964, in Chatfield, pp. 589–98.

[17] 'Who is the Greatest Man in the World', New York: The Community Church, 61 East 34th Street, New York, 1921, in Chatfield, pp. 599–621. Quote on p. 620.

[18] Holmes, *My Gandhi*, p. 33. Holmes told his audience that he first came across Gandhi's name in 1918 in an article by the Oxford classicist Gilbert Murray in the *Hibbert Journal*. Murray's article on the concept of the soul went on to discuss saints including recent ones such as Gandhi. Murray warned Great Britain in connection with Gandhi that a nation whose government prosecuted saints is neither wise, generous, nor high-minded. Voss, 'Discoverer of Gandhi', in Chatfield, p. 589.

As we shall see below, the Anglican missionary in South Africa and India, Charles F. Andrews, 'discovered' and 'canonized' Gandhi four years earlier in 1914 when he met him for the first time in South Africa but no public word of Andrews' experience seems to have reached Europe or the US until after Murray's article.

The discovery in 1986 of 260 letters written between February 1909 and 5 December 1944 by Gandhi 'to his close friend and disciple, the Jewish-Polish-German architect Hermann Kallenbach', forcefully reminds us that Kallenbach should be recognized as the first non-Indian to acknowledge Gandhi. In May 1910 Kallenbach, 'mesmerized by Gandhi', donated to him the 1100-acre farm near Lawley, 20 miles from Johannesburg, that became Tolstoy Farm. 'In 1914, he [Gandhi] compared Kallenbach with C.F. Andrews, and wrote: "Though I love, almost adore, Andrews so, I would not exchange you for him"'. In a letter to another friend in 1946, the year of Kallenbach's death, Gandhi spoke movingly of his 'old friend'. Ramesh Chandra, 'The Mahatma's Letters,' *India Today*, 31 December 1986, pp. 52–3.

[19] Both were important members of the pacifist Fellowship of Reconciliation and active supporters of Norman Thomas, who had abandoned his ministerial career in 1917 to lead the Socialist Party in New York. Holmes' younger colleague, friend, and incipient rival, Niebuhr, had recently left his well-publicized socially concerned pastorate of Detroit's comfortable Bethel Evangelical Church to become a professor at the Union Theological Seminary in New York where, in November 1930, his candidacy for a State Senate seat attracted more publicity than votes. Richard W. Fox, *Reinhold Niebuhr—A Biography*, New York: Pantheon Books, 1985, pp. 129–30.

[20] Fox, *Niebuhr*, p. 130.

[21] Mark Juergensmeyer, *Fighting with Gandhi*, San Francisco: Harper & Row, 1984, p. 127.

[22] Holmes, *My Gandhi*, pp. 35–6.

[23] John Haynes Holmes Paper, Box 3, Autograph Collection, A-1 folder (Gandhi), Library of Congress, Washington DC. As at Sabarmati, 30 July 1931. [Typewritten] 'There is no certainty about my going to London as yet. There are difficulties which may prove insuperable. I feel I must not leave India unless some glaring breaches of the Settlement are repaired. I am straining every nerve to avoid a conflict, but the result is in God's hands. But if I do succeed in going to London we must meet'.

[24] Gandhi broke the law by taking salt—protected by government monopoly—from the area at the government's Dharsana Salt Works 150 north of Bombay near Dandi; 400 policemen brutally assaulted the non-violent marchers who remained courageously steadfast in their commitment. Miller's account is reproduced *inter alia* in Homer Jack (ed.), *The Gandhi Reader: A Source Book of his Life and Writings*, Bloomington: Indiana University Press, 1958. William L. Shirer in his *Gandhi, a Memoir*, New York: Simon and Schuster/Touchstone, 1979, described Miller four decades after the Salt March as 'one of the great American foreign correspondents'. His story, Shirer says, 'was flashed around the world' and 'published in more than a thousand newspapers at home and abroad', pp. 97–9.

[25] Webb Miller, *I Found No Peace: The Journal of a Foreign Correspondent*, New York: Simon and Schuster, 1936. See Chapters 16 through 19 and 21 for Miller's coverage of India and Gandhi.

[26] The account of Holmes' advice to Gandhi on the Walker interview and invitations to the US is given in his *My Gandhi*, pp. 48–51, and in Manoranjan Jha, *Civil Disobedience and After*, pp. 181–3.

[27] Britain was afflicted with social unrest, vast and growing unemployment, a stagnant economy, an unbalanced budget, a slipping pound, and a sense of mounting financial and political crisis. Britain, leader of the financial and trading world, abandoned the gold standard on 21 September 1931, a move which had the effect of devaluing the pound by 25 per cent.

[28] J.L. Garvin, editor of the *Observer*, described Gandhi's call for Indian independence as 'a vain dream' and warned that without strong British rule, anarchy, worse than that in China, would follow. 'Though Gandhi is a gifted and fascinating agitator, his exalted but unconstructive ideology suggests the breaking and not the making of India'. Lord Beaverbrook's *Sunday Express* ran a lead editorial entitled 'The Failure of Gandhi'. 'Gandhi',—it opened, 'is out of his depth in England. He has gained publicity which a film star might envy, but he has been a complete failure in solving Indian problems. Unless he provides a miracle, the Conference will break up in two or three days and the last remnants of his prestige will disappear', Shirer, *Gandhi*, pp. 168, 177, 191–2.

[29] Soon after World War II, Niebuhr became a 'prophet to politicians', the 'Establishment theologian' and a 'celebrity intellectual', Fox, p. 273. The phrase, 'prophet to politicians', was used as the subtitle of Ronald Stone's 1972 biography, *Reinhold Niebuhr*. The often quoted phrase, 'father of us all', has been attributed to George F. Kennan but Richard Fox reports that in 1980 Kennan 'did not recall' describing Niebuhr in these terms, Fox, p. 238.

[30] The term, 'social intelligence', may have been a 'translation' into American political vocabulary of British Fabian Socialist and Labour Party views. Labour under the leadership of Ramsey MacDonald, then a much-admired figure in Niebuhr's circle, won power in Britain in the May 1929 election. American socialists were encouraged and influenced by the Labour victory.

[31] Fox, *Niebuhr*, p. 130.

[32] 'What Chance Has Gandhi', *Christian Century*, 16 December 1931, in Chatfield, *Americanization of Gandhi*, p. 705.

[33] Reinhold Niebuhr, *Moral Man and Immoral Society*, New York: Scribner's Sons, 1953, p. 234; Chatfield, *Americanization of Gandhi*, p. 705.

[34] Fox, *Niebuhr*, p. 136.

[35] Chatfield, *Americanization of Gandhi*, p. 706.

[36] *Moral Man,* p. 242.

[37] Fox, *Niebuhr*, p. 138.

[38] *Moral Man,* pp. 234, 247–9, 255–6.

[39] Ibid., p. 256.

[40] Fox, *Niebuhr*, pp. 142–3.

[41] Ibid., pp. 136, 143, 152–3.

[42] Ibid., p. 140.

[43] Ibid., p. 134.

[44] If Niebuhr had understood Hannah Arendt's distinction between power and coercion, the first based on willing, voluntary choice and action, on shared understandings, values, purpose or interest, the second on unwilling, forced choice and action, choice and action that arise out of intimidation, fear of physical and other forms of harm, threats to life and well-being, he might have re-thought his sweeping commitment to force, i.e., that to do good one must do evil. For Hannah Arendt on the distinction between coercion and power, see her *On Violence* plus other writings.

[45] Among those he read while a divinity student at Boston University was Holmes' book on Gandhi. King told Stanley Katz, Holmes' grandson-in-law, that the book had been a factor in his move toward Gandhi. Personal letter, 20 July 1988.

William Stuart Nelson in 'Gandhian Values and the American Civil Rights Movement', in Paul F. Power (ed.), *The Meaning of Gandhi*, Honolulu: University of Hawaii Press, 1971, reminds us that the first known contact between Gandhi and American blacks (then Negroes) occurred when Howard Thurman, a Negro minister and philosopher and dean of the chapel at Howard University, and the Reverend Edward Carrol, and their wives, met Gandhi in India on 28 February 1936. Among other things, Gandhi told his guests that 'one cannot be passively non-violent', p. 155.

[46] See, for example, Joan Bondurant, *Conquest of Violence; The Gandhian Philosophy of Conflict*, Princeton: Princeton University Press, 1958, reprint Berkeley and Los Angeles: University of California Press, 1967; Gene Sharp, *The Politics of Nonviolent Action*, Boston: Poster Sargent Publishers, 1973; Richard Gregg, *The Power of Nonviolence*, New York: Schocken Books, second revised edition, 1971; Staughton Lynd (ed.), *Nonviolence in America: A Documentary History*, Indianapolis: Bobbs-Merrill, 1966; Karl Potter, 'Explorations in Gandhi's Theory of Nonviolence', and William Stuart Nelson, 'Gandhian Values and the American Civil Rights Movement', in Power (ed.), *The Meanings of Gandhi*; Mulford Sibley (ed.), *The Quiet Battle; Writings on the Theory and Practice of Non-violent Resistance*, Garden City: Anchor Books, 1963; Sudarshan Kapur, *To Raise a Prophet: The African-American Encounter With Gandhi*, Delhi: Oxford University Press, 1993; Dennis Dalton, *Mahatma Gandhi: Non-violent Power in Action*, New York: Columbia University Press, 1993. *Gandhi Marg*, New Delhi, and *The Journal of Conflict Resolution* have published over the years many articles on non-violent civil resistance and collective action.

[47] Martin Luther King, *Stride Toward Freedom; the Montgomery Story*, New York: Harper & Row, 1958, pp. 85, 97. See also Bhikhu Parekh, *Gandhi*, Oxford: Oxford University Press, 1997, p. 61.

[48] Rosa Parks with Gregory J. Reed, *Quiet Strength ... Grand Rapids*, Michigan: Zondervan Publishing House, 1994. Rosa Parks with Jim Haskins, *My Story*, New York: Dial, 1992 . For the Monteagle and Lohia connections see Harris Wofford, *Of Kennedys and Kings; Making Sense of the Sixties*, Pittsburgh: University of Pittsburgh Press, 1980, pp. 112 and 191. For more on the Highlander Folk School and its director Myles Horton, and on Rosa Parks and her fellow activists in the context of the Montgomery bus boycott, see Diane McWhorter, *Carry Me Home: Birmingham, Alabama, the Climatic Battle of the Civil Rights Revolution*, New York: Simon & Shuster, 2001, pp. 90–5.

[49] Harris Wofford, *Of Kennedys and Kings*, pp. 113–14.

[50] Dennis Dalton, *Gandhi's Power: Non-Violence in Action*, New Delhi: Oxford, 1999, p. 180; see also 'Letter from Birmingham City Jail', the most powerful of King's rhetorical efforts, cited in David Hardiman, *Gandhi in his Time and Ours*, Delhi: Permanent Black, 2003, p. 263.

[51] In James M. Washington (ed.), *A Testament of Hope: The Essential Writings and Speeches of Martin Luther King, Jr*, San Francisco: Harper, 1991, p. 447.

[52] For King's views on these matters see his *Where Do We Go from Here: Chaos or Community*, New York: Harper and Row, 1967, particularly Chapter 2, 'Black Power', where he remarks *inter alia* that the bible of Black Plower advocates such as Stokely Carmichael is Frantz Fanon's *The Wretched of the Earth*. 'They don't quote Gandhi or Tolstoy'.

[53] For a vivid, insightful, and detailed firsthand account of these troubled and turbulent years that attends to the Gandhian dimension, see Harris Wofford, *Of Kennedys and Kings: Making Sense of the Sixties*, See also William Stuart Nelson, 'Gandhian Values and the Civil Rights Movement,' in Power (ed.), *Gandhi*, ibid., pp. 153–4. Nelson reminds us that Gandhi's influence on the civil rights movement among American blacks precedes King's. James Farmer was founding director of the Congress of Racial Equality (CORE), programme director of the National Association for the Advancement of Colored People (NAACP), and an assistant secretary in the Department of Health, Education, and Welfare in the Nixon Administration. His book *Freedom When?*, New York: Harper, 1965, gives an account of his understanding of Gandhi, Gandhi's relevance to American blacks, and Farmer's use of Gandhi's ideas and practice in the civil rights movement. See also James Farmer, *Lay Bare the Heart: An Autobiography of the Civil Rights Movement*, New York: Plume, 1986.

[54] These familiar quotes are drawn from a letter to the *Times of India*, 2 March 1988 by Sita Ram Goel.

[55] Raymond Schwab, *The Oriental Renaissance; Europe's Rediscovery of India and the East* 1680–1880, New York: Columbia University Press, 1984, translated by Gene Patterson-Black and Victor Reinking from the original 1936 French publication, shows how much Europe in the 18th and 19th centuries learned about and from the Orient. In the US leading figures such as Ralph Waldo Emerson and Walt Whitman were carriers of what might be called the 'oriental renaissance'. For orientalism with reference to India, see Ronald Inden, 'Orientalist Constructions of India', *Modern Asia Studies*, 20:3, July 1986, pp. 401–40.

[56] His *Mahatma Gandhi's Ideas, Including Selections from his Writings*, New York: Macmillan, 1930, and subsequent writing about Gandhi were among the earliest and certainly among the most read in the US. Romain Rolland's 1924 biography in English was probably the first account of Gandhi available in the US.

[57] Charles Andrews' first encounter with Gandhi is narrated by Hugh Tinker in his book *The Ordeal of Love; C.F. Andrews and India*, Delhi: Oxford University Press, 1979, 1998 pbk. The *S.S. Umtali* reached Durban on 2 January 1914. Charles Andrews and William Pearson were on board. They had sailed from Calcutta on 5 December. From Colombo he wrote on 12 December to his friend, Munshi Ram, 'I have a great happiness and blessing in store for me—to see Mohandas Gandhi. No life lived in our day could be more moving than his. My Journey will be a pilgrimage to touch his feet', p. 79. 'Andrews was expecting to encounter another superbly impressive spiritual presence, like [Rabindranath] Tagore or Mahatma Munshi Ram;

he looked in vain among the waiting group .... Hastily, he asked [Henry] Polak [whom he had met in Delhi] whether Gandhi was present, and was surprised to be taken to meet someone whose appearance was insignificant ....', p. 84.

Andrews, writing two weeks later, says that 'He [Polak] pointed to an ascetic figure with shaven head [probably a result of Gandhi's recent stint in prison], dressed in white dhoti and kurta of such coarse material as an indentured labourer might wear, looking as though in mourning, and said: "Here is Mr Gandhi." I stooped at once instinctively and touched his feet, and he said in a low tone, "Pray do not do that, it is a humiliation to me".' Charles Andrews, *Modern Review*, 14 March 'Letter from Natal,' as quoted on p. 14 in Tinker and cited in chapter endnote 1, p. 113.

[58] See his 'Saint Gandhi,' in John S. Hawley (ed.), *Saints and Virtues*, Berkeley and Los Angeles: University of California Press, 1986, for a more detailed account of these early formative events. While I learned a great deal from this important paper, his essay is in part a rejoinder to George Orwell's 1949 *Partisan Review* essay, 'Reflections on Gandhi' which articulates a similar grudging and sceptical admiration. Republished in Sonia Orwell and Ian Angus (eds), *In Front of Your Nose, 1945–50*, New York: Harcourt Brace Jovanovich, 1968, vol. IV, *The Collected Essays, Journalism and Letters of George Orwell*. Juergensmeyer's earlier *Fighting with Gandhi*, San Francisco: Harper and Row, 1984, provided a 'step-by-step strategy for resolving everyday conflicts' at home and in public life by translating Gandhi's method of satyagraha into a language familiar to Americans and constructed dialogues between Gandhi and Marx, Freud, Niebuhr, and the Mahatma himself that were not always to Gandhi's advantage.

[59] The absence of an equivalent term to 'saint' may be discerned from the meanings of Hindu terms loosely translated as saint: *sant*, in 'proper' Hindu usage an adjective (rather than a noun) indicating devotion to a guru or his text, has under the influence of English usage come to be used for 'saintly' and as an equivalent for the noun 'saint'; sadhu, a person who practices asceticism (mental and spiritual control), more loosely a religious mendicant, a holy man, or simply a good man but often translated as a saint; sanyasi, a monk or ascetic, he has taken the vows of sanyas, i.e., to leave all worldly things, including wealth and property, a state often identified with the fourth and final stage of life; guru, teacher, mentor, or spiritual guide, it can be applied to any teacher of any subject but is usually used specifically for religious teachers; *rishi*, a sage or seer who expounds or comments on the vedas, the oldest Hindu scriptures; and swami, master or lord, usually used for a religious ascetic but can be used to refer to a master in any context, i.e., proprietor of land, a craft, or a trade, a husband.

Karine Schomer, in the introduction to *The Sants: Studies in a Devotional Tradition*, a book that she and W.H. McLeod co-edited (Delhi: Motilal Banarsidass for Berkeley Religious Studies Series, 1987), refers to sants as '... those who sincerely seek enlightenment .... [C]onceptually as well as etymologically, it [*sant*] differs from the false cognate "saint" which is often used to translate it', p. 3.

[60] Mark Juergensmeyer, in John Stratton Hawley (ed.), *Saints and Virtues*, pp. 188, 194, 201.

[61] New York, Harper and Brothers, 1953, p. 1442; New Haven: Yale University Press, 1985. For these quotations and a more extended discussion of this dilemma, see Susanne Hoeber Rudolph and Lloyd I. Rudolph, 'This Worblly Asceticism and Political Modernization', in this volume, pp. 242–3. Diane L. Eck has dealt with darshan in the context of religious worship in *Darshan: Seeing the Divine Image in India*, second edition, Chambersburg: Penn, Anima Publications, 1985.

[62] Juergensmeyer, 'Saint Gandhi', p. 202. In 1962, when he was 70, Susanne Rudolph and I talked to Reinhold Niebuhr about Gandhi. He was living in Quincy House while teaching part-time at Harvard. He told us that Gandhi was too clever, too calculating to be a saint, a remark that presumably distinguished Gandhi's from Jesus' 'dazzling', non-emulatable qualities of selfless love. Saints were innocent of the strategy and tactics that distinguished Gandhi's conduct and message. Niebuhr's remark in 1962 was consistent with his characterization of Gandhi, after he saw him in London in 1931, as a 'prophet' and 'statesman'. In assimilating 'St Gandhi' to Jesus in the context of Niebuhr's remark about Jesus, Juergensmeyer was, presumably, constructing an argument rather than representing Niebuhr's view of Gandhi.

[63] Margaret Chatterjee, *Gandhi's Religious Thought*, London: Macmillan, 1983, 1 p. 49.

[64] *The New York Times*, 2 and 12 February 1986.

[65] New York: Harper and Brothers, 1953, p. 1442; New Haven: Yale University Press, 1985.

[66] For Merton's view, see his introduction, 'Gandhi and the One-Eyed Giant', in his *Gandhi on Non-violence*, New York: New Directions, 1964.

[67] This account draws on and quotes from p. 50 of Mary T. Clark's introduction to *Augustine of Hippo: Selected Writings*, New York: Paulist Press, 1984, and Kenneth Scoff Lattoure, *A History of Christianity*, New York: Harper and Brothers, 1953, 'Augustine and Pelagius', pp. 173–81, and 'Semi Pelagianism', pp. 181–2. Peter N. Brown's 'Pelagius and His Supporters: Aims and Environment', *Journal of Theological Studies*, 19, pt. 1, April 1968, and 'The Patrons of Pelagius: The Roman Aristocracy Between East and West', *Journal of Theological Studies*, 21, pt. 1, April 1970, have been very helpful. Also relevant to the Pelagius-Augustine struggle are aspects of Peter Brown's *The Body and Society: Men, Women and Sexual Renunciation in Early Christianity*, New York: Columbia University Press, 1988, and Elaine Pagel's *Adam, Eve, and the Serpent*, New York: Random House, 1988.

[68] *The Modern Review*, October 1941, p. 400, as quoted in Chatterjee, p. 55.

[69] *Harijan*, 18 April 1936 and 12 June 1937, as quoted in Chatterjee, p. 55.

[70] *The New York Times*, 2 February 1986.

[71] Ibid., 12 February 1986.

[72] *The New York Times*, 2 and 9 February 1986. For a Catholic commentary on Gandhi, see also John Chathanatt, S.J., 'In Pursuit of Truth: The Gandhian Experiment', unpublished paper, Divinity School, University of Chicago, 1986.

[73] Hertzberg's reply to Richard Grenier, to be dealt with below, and to Elie Kedourie's 'False Gandhi', in *The New Republic*, 21 March 1983, appeared in *The New Republic*, 25 April 1983 under the title 'True Gandhi'.

[74] For an account of the controversy over the film and the man see my 'The Gandhi Controversy in America', in Robert M. Crunden (ed.), *Traffic of Ideas Between India and America*, Delhi: Chanakya, 1985. This article, and one by me and Susanne Hoeber Rudolph, 'Gandhi Critic's Article Distorts History', in *Views*, Sunday *Sun-Times*, 1983 April 3, deal in some detail with Grenier's many errors and distortions. Also relevant to the controversy raised by Grenier's attack on Gandhi is the television programme on *Firing Line*, hosted by William F. Buckley, Jr, during which Richard Grenier and I spent an unrehearsed hour contesting facts and interpretations. The programme was taped in New York on 9 June 1983, and appeared subsequently on Public Broadcasting Service (PBS) stations in July and August. Video cassettes, audio cassettes, and published transcripts are available from Firing Line, P.O. Box 5966, Columbia, South Carolina 29250. Another response to Grenier-inspired attacks on Gandhi was by B.R. Nanda, author of a distinguished biography of Gandhi, *Mahatma Gandhi*, London: Allen and Unwin, 1958. His *Gandhi and His Critics* appeared in 1985, Delhi and New York: Oxford University Press.

[75] One of Mayo's earlier books, *The Isles of Fear: An Evaluation of America's Task in the Philippines*, helped to block the Wilson administration's efforts to move toward self-government in the Philippines by 'showing' that the Filipinos were neither ready nor desirous of independence. The message of *Isles of Fear* led the British to believe that they could count on a book supportive of British rule in India, a belief in which they were not disappointed. Here and below I rely primarily on the late Manoranjan Jha's careful and detailed research in *Katherine Mayo and India*, New Delhi: People's Publishing House, 1971. Jha's account of Mayo on the Philippines is on p. 20 and elsewhere.

[76] These are Manoranjan Jha's words on p. 69 in *Katherine Mayo*. Jha reproduces as Appendix I a six-page version of a typescript that Mayo had sent to Gandhi (pp. 106–11) and that Gandhi in turn had 'taken pains to fill in the gaps and amplify some of her statements' (p. 88). He also sent her long quotations from W.W. Hunter and Romesh Chunder Dutt on the causes of India's poverty. A reading of Mayo's account of Gandhi's views when compared to these texts supports Jha's characterizations.

[77] These are Daniel Bell's, not Arthur Koestler's, words but I use them because they capture the spirit of Koestler's odyssey to Asia. Bell used these words in his *The Coming of Post-Industrial Society*, New Delhi: Arnold-Heinemann, 1974, to speak about his 1960 book, *The End of Ideology*. He used them to warn readers about

surmising the thesis of a book from its title rather than from reading its argument, p. 34, fn. 39.

[78] *The Lotus and the Robot*, New York: Macmillan, 1961, and London: Hutchinson, 1960, p. 277.

[79] Koestler, *Lotus*, pp. 282–5.

[80] Koestler, quoting with approval Morris Carstairs, *The Twice Born*, London: Hogarth Press, 1957, pp. 71–2, on p. 148. Earlier quotations in this paragraph are on pp. 142 and 155.

[81] Koestler, *Lotus*, pp. 153–4.

[82] Koestler, *Lotus*, pp. 156–7.

[83] Erik H. Erikson, *Gandhi's Truth; On the Origins of Militant Non-violence*, New York: W.W. Norton, 1969, p. 245.

[84] 'A kind of demigod' modified by 'within the academy' is taken from Tanya Luhrmann's review, 'The touch of the real; At once cold and concerned: the exemplary eye of Clifford Geertz', in *The Times Literary Supplement* for 12 January 2001, of three books by or about Geertz, Sherry B. Ortner (ed.), *The Fate of 'Culture'; Geertz and Beyond*, Berkeley, CA: The University of California Press, 2000; Clifford Geertz, *Available Light*, Princeton, NJ: Princeton University Press, 2000; Fred Inglis, *Clifford Geertz: Culture, Custom and Ethics*, Cambridge UK: Polity, 2000.

[85] Clifford Geertz, *Negara: The Theatre State in Nineteenth Century Bali*, Princeton: Princeton University Press, 1980.

[86] In her prize-winning book *Clothing Matters: Dress and Identity in India*, Chicago: University of Chicago Press, 1996, particularly Chapter 3, 'Gandhi and the Recreation of Indian Dress', pp. 62–93, Emma Tarlo convincingly shows that Gandhi's peasant dress was symbolically constitutive for most Indians and many foreigners of Gandhi's time and since.

As suggested above, Mark Juergensmeyer, who found Gandhi's 'saintliness', while possibly unintended, deceptive, would probably agree with Geertz that the saintliness, like his peasant dress, were unconvincing affectations.

We have seen how in 1931 Reinhold Niebuhr, the budding political realist, did not find Gandhi bizarre or absurd: 'Nor is there anything ridiculous about him, in spite of the loincloth (that article of apparel looks like what boys call track pants) and the homespun Indian shawl. There is too much innate dignity about the man to allow the impression of a ridiculous figure, which London newspapers try so assiduously to cultivate, to remain'. 'What Chance Has Gandhi', p. 705. Like the budding realist Niebuhr, George Orwell, also a realist on guard against being taken in or put on, was of an age to have directly experienced the Gandhi phenomenon. Geertz, having served in the Navy during World War II, was in college when Gandhi was assassinated on 30 January 1948. Orwell concludes his essay, 'Reflections on Gandhi', by observing: 'One may feel, as I do, a sort of aesthetic distaste for Gandhi, one may reject the claims of sainthood made on his behalf [he never made any such claim himself, by the way] ... regarded simply as a politician, and compared with the other leading political figures of our time, how clean a smell he has managed to leave behind!' Sonia Orwell and Ian Angus, *The Collected Essays, Journalism and Letters of George Orwell. IV. In Front of Your Nose, 1945–50*, London: Secker and Warburg, 1968, p. 470.

[87] *Firing Line* program, 'Is Gandhi for Real?' appeared on PBS stations over the 1983 summer season.

[88] Nelson Mandela, 'the sacred warrior', *Time*, 31 December 1999, p. 74. Mandela continues: 'Nonviolence was the official stance of all major African coalitions, and the South African ANC [African National Congress] remained implacable, opposed to violence for most of its existence .... I followed the Gandhian strategy for as long as I could .... Even then (after adding "a military dimension to our struggle") we chose sabotage because it did not involve the loss of life, and it offered the best hope for future race relations', p. 74.

[89] Richard Grenier, *The Gandhi That Nobody Knows*, Nashville, Tennessee: Thomas Nelson, 1983, p. 4. Diana L. Eck's 'New Age Hinduism in America' in Sulochana Glazer and Nathan Glazer, (eds), *Conflicting Images; India and the United States*, Glen Dale, Maryland: Riverdale, 1990 provides a keen analysis of recent American responses to what is perceived as Hinduism.

4

The Coffee House and the Ashram Revisited

How Gandhi Democratized Habermas' Public Sphere *

Gandhi and Civil Society

Twenty-four hours before his death on 30 January 1948 at the hands of Nathuram Godse, Gandhi proposed in his 'last will and testament' that the Indian National Congress be dissolved and be replaced by a Lok Sevak Sangh, a people's service organization. For 62 years, since its founding in 1885, the Indian National Congress or Congress as it is known colloquially today had been the vehicle of the nationalist movement. It was about to become the ruling party of a new Indian nation-state. As such its leaders would seek, use, and desire power. Gandhi foresaw members of a Lok Sevak Sangh serving others in organizations like those he had launched in the 1920s and 1930s to transform village India, the All-India Spinners Association, which promoted the production of khadi [hand-spun and woven cloth] at the village level; the All-India Village Industries Association,

* This essay is called 'The Coffee House and the Ashram Revisited: How Gandhi Democratized Habermas' Public Sphere', because it is a revised and expanded version of previously published essays with similar titles, 'The Coffee House and the Ashram: Gandhi, Civil Society and Public Spheres', in *Heidelberg Papers in South Asian and Comparative Politics*, Working Paper No. 15, June 2003. URL: http://www.sai.uni-heidelberg.de/abt/sapol/hpsacp.htm and 'The Coffee House and the Ashram: Gandhi and the Public Sphere', in Carolyn M. Elliott (ed.), *Civil Society and Democracy: A Reader*, New Delhi and New York: Oxford University Press, 2003.

devoted to promoting village-level craft production and the technology appropriate to it; the Hindustani Talimi Sangh, for promoting literacy in Hindustani, Gandhi's preferred national language; the Harijan Sevak Sangh, designed to promote the material and social betterment of 'untouchables'; the *Go Seva Sangh*, a cow welfare society.[1]

From his early days in South Africa, Gandhi was a tireless creator of civil society. Wherever he went, whatever he did, he created voluntary self-help organizations and journals of opinion. In 1894, a year after his arrival in South Africa, Gandhi founded the Natal Indian Congress to give disenfranchised and discriminated-against Indian immigrants a voice and a means for collective action. In 1904 he took over the publication of *Indian Opinion*, a weekly journal of news and opinion.

Gandhi's ashrams were energizing centres for associational life and for civil disobedience, non-cooperation, and satyagraha campaigns.[2] In December 1904, half-way through his South African years [1893–1914], he established what, in retrospect, can be regarded as his first ashram. After reading John Ruskin's *Unto This Last* on an overnight train from Johannesburg to Durban, he resolved the next morning 'to change my life in accordance with the ideals of this book'.[3] He changed his life by establishing an agriculture settlement on 100 acres 14 miles from Durban, Natal's largest city and its principal port. The settlement became known as the Phoenix Settlement. As Martin Green suggests, Phoenix 'marked an important stage in Gandhi's progressive self–disentanglement from city life and from the ordinary circumstances of secular life'.[4]

In 1910, Gandhi founded Tolstoy Farm, an ashram in the first instance for satyagrahis. Located in the Transvaal 21 miles from Johannesburg, near Lawley, its 1,100 lush acres were donated by Herman Kallenbach. Like Henry Polak, Kallenbach was a young Jewish intellectual who had immigrated to escape an oppressive European country, Polak from England, Kallenbach from Germany. Both began a new life on the South African 'frontier'. Still in their twenties when they met, the three young men quickly became intimate friends. Although rarely remarked upon in accounts of Gandhi, the influence of Jewish immigrant intellectuals like Polak and Kallenbach, *kibbutzim* before their time, on the thinking and action of his formative South African years may have been as great as that of the non–conformist Protestant clergymen such as Joseph Doke who are frequently credited with deeply influencing Gandhi's early thinking and practice.[5]

We move from Gandhi in his twenties to Gandhi in his seventies, from the beginning of his public life to near its end, in order to raise the question, why did Gandhi urge Jawaharalal Nehru [whom he had chosen as his political heir] and other Congress leaders to disband the Congress as a political party and reconstitute it as a Lok Sevak Sangh? He seems to have foreseen that, like political parties elsewhere in the world, Congress leaders would pursue, exercise, and desire power. From opponents of the colonial state in India, they would, in Gandhi's view, become its advocates.

As early as 1909, in his seminal text, *Hind Swaraj*, Gandhi had warned against this possibility. Speaking as 'Editor' in *Hind Swaraj's* dialogue format, Gandhi asks his interlocutor, 'Reader': 'Supposing we get self-government similar to what the Canadians and the South Africans have. Will that be good enough?' 'Reader' replies: 'when we have the same powers, we shall hoist our flag. As in Japan [which had destroyed the Russian Tsar's fleet in 1905], so must India. We must have our own navy, our army, and we must have our own splendour, and then India's voice will ring in the world'. Editor replies: 'You have well drawn the picture. In effect it means this: that we want English rule without the Englishmen. You want the tiger's nature, but not the tiger ... This is not the Swaraj [self-rule] I want'.[6]

At a more mundane level, Gandhi as a person of civil society sees the statist face of party. In 1920 Gandhi had transformed the Congress from a talking shop for the English-speaking elite into an instrument capable of resisting, then ending British rule. Now it had done so. What kind of a creature should it be in independent India?

Parties can be viewed as amphibious creatures; sometimes they can be found in the sea of civil society, sometimes on the high ground of state dominion. Opposition parties resemble the associations of civil society that operate outside of and in opposition to the state. At the same time, their role as 'shadow governments', governments-in-waiting, and as recognized participants in the arena of state power, positions opposition parties to share the state's habitat. But when opposition parties gain power and command the state's apparatus and symbols, they shed their affinities with civil society and become state-like creatures. Why did Gandhi attempt to prevent the Congress from becoming the governing political party in a newly-independent India?

Gandhi's proposal that the Congress become a people's service organization follows from his view of political swaraj as self-government and individual swaraj as self-mastery. At the individual level, the desire for power, like other forms of desire, removes the possibility of self-mastery by enslaving those in its grip. Political power in the public arena was ephemeral and mercurial because its existence depends on the willing cooperation of the people. Without the people's cooperation state power loses potency and legitimacy, as Gandhi showed of the British Raj in India in 1920–2 during his first non-cooperation campaign and again in April 1930 during the civil disobedience of the great Salt March. Gandhi's view of power as based on willing cooperation and loss of power on the withdrawal of cooperation or obedience parallels Hannah Arendt's view of power.

Both start by distinguishing power from coercion, the first based on willing action, the second on unwilling compliance based on fear, intimidation or the threat of violence. Arendt tells us that 'power corresponds to the human ability not just to act but to act in concert'. If humans find themselves oppressed, it is because they have allowed themselves to become so; they are complicit in their own oppression. Gandhi asks in Chapter VII of *Hind Swaraj*, 'why was India lost?' He answers, 'The English have not taken India; we have given it to them. They are not in India because of their strength, but because we keep them'.[7] Arendt tells us that 'when we say of somebody that he is "in power" we actually refer to his being empowered by a certain number of people to act in their name. The moment the group, from which the power originated to begin with disappears, [*potestas in populo*, without a people or group there is no power] "his power" also vanishes'.[8]

Gandhi associated centralization with coercion, decentralization with power. Power was located in the voluntary associations of civil society and in the political communities of local governments,[9] coercion in the modern state and industrial enterprise. Gandhi would not have agreed with Max Weber that the 'concentration of the means of management' was inevitable.[10] His concept of swaraj read as self-rule and as self-government provided an alternative to the modernist view of the objectified, disempowered individual and bureaucratized state and economy. In the contest between structure and agency, Gandhi showed in action that moral agency can change the world. 'Independence must begin at the bottom', he said. 'My idea of village *swaraj* is that it is a complete republic, independent of its neighbours for its own vital wants, and yet interdependent for many others for which dependence is a necessity ....'[11]

Having made the case for Gandhi as a person of civil society and of moral agency, we turn to the question: What light do the ashram and satyagraha shed on the meaning that Jurgen Habermas has given to civil society and the public sphere? To what extent do time, place, and context matter? As John Keane remarks, 'reflexive, self-organizing non-governmental organizations that some call civil society can and do live by other names in other linguistic and cultural milieux.'[12] How did Gandhi's 'Indian' variant accord with, modify, or challenge the Habermasian concepts of civil society and the public sphere?

Civil Society and Public Sphere as Bourgeois Rationality

The discourse and practice of civil society have had a lively career both before and after Jurgen Habermas launched his version into academic discourse in 1962.[13] Civil society, Charles Taylor tells us, refers to a space that exists 'over against the state, in partial independence from it. It includes those dimensions of social life which cannot be confounded with or swallowed up in the state'.[14] Taylor stresses the obstreperous, challenging aspect of civil society, the aspect that showed its face in Medha Patkar's Narmada *Bachao Andolan* resisting the building of big dams on the Narmada river in India; in the global protests against the policies and actions of the WTO manifest in Seattle, Genoa, and Washington; in the movements for democracy and against corruption in South Korea; and in worldwide efforts to protect the environment, not least of which is the Gandhian-inspired non-violent efforts by the Chipko movement to save the Himalayan forests of the Garhwal. But there are other ways to read the term, civil society.[15]

An intimation of civil society's early history can be found in its *Oxford English Dictionary* etymology. In the seventeenth century, civil society has a more gentle, friendly tone, stressing its mutuality and *douceur*: 'having a proper social order,' keeping 'a certain civile iustice and friendly love to one another' [Hooker, 1600], or 'reformed, civill, full of good' [Shakespeare, 1591, in the Two Gentlemen of Verona].[16] The *OED* sounds rather like a text for Robert Putnam's or James Coleman's idea of social capital—the capacity to trust and habits of collaboration.[17] It is a view of civil society that finds expression in Rotary and soccer clubs, Parent-Teacher Association, *Lok Sevak Sanghs*, humanitarian and charitable associations to help the illiterate, the poor and the homeless.

Our late colleague, Edward Shils, took a more conservative view of civil society by choosing to read civility into the modifying adjective 'civil'.

Manners and mores were what mattered, not popular participation or policy activism. Civility for Shils referred *inter alia* to 'a solicitude for the interest of the whole society, a concern for the common good', and underlined obligations to rather than claims against the state, individual conduct rather than brotherly solidarity.

Transplanting concepts such as civil society and public sphere, born and used in Anglo-American liberal contexts, requires recalibrating the concept for use in the context of other histories and social structures. When talking about India, we have the excuse that so much of the liberal tradition was transplanted in the course of 19th century nationalist discourse and practice, as also in the Constitution of 1950, that the concept of civil society can claim a comfortable home in India. But definitions of political categories are often captive to their point of first use, in this case in a European historical context.[18] As the concept of civil society travels out of its quintessential 18th century European origin point to new temporal locations in the late 19th and the 20th century and to new cultural locations outside the West, it expresses itself through different cultural forms and takes on different meanings. Indeed, it was one of Gandhi's unique talents to give new shape to institutional forms and meanings associated with liberal and democratic spheres.

The version of civil society advanced in Jurgen Habermas' earliest ideas about a public sphere will serve as the theoretical grounding for our examination of why and how Gandhi reconfigured western conceptions of civil society, associational life, and the public sphere.[19] In his early work Habermas appears as a defender of the Enlightenment project of modernity against the critics of the modern. No doubt unknown to Habermas, Gandhi's critique of 'modern civilization' in his 1909 work, *Hind Swaraj*, was an early example of modernity critique. Habermas' seminal early work on civil society and the public sphere creates and employs categories and representations that we find best highlight the contrast between Gandhian and European variants of those concepts.

Habermas bases his early conceptualization of civil society and the public sphere an examination of political life in 18th-century England, France, and Germany. He finds a public sphere embedded in the activities of coffee houses, literary and cultural societies, political clubs, and literary journals and journals of opinion.[20]

There sprang from the midst of the private sphere a relatively dense network of public communication. The growing number of readers ... was complemented by a considerable expansion in the production of books, journals and papers .... The societies for enlightenment, cultural associations, secret freemasonry lodges and orders of illuminati were associations constituted by the free, that is, private decisions of their founding members, based on voluntary membership and characterized internally by egalitarian practices of sociability, free discussion, decision by majority, etc.[21]

In these locations and through these activities educated urban persons who previously led separate lives in private spaces become a public, transcending private preoccupations and addressing common purposes. As Habermas would have it, the communicative process directed at common questions creates shared discourses. Communicating with each other through conversation and print, certain urban persons came to share information, ideas and attitudes, practiced rationality and disinterestedness, and ignored or transcended the relevance of inherited identities. As Anil Seal showed in his path-breaking book about modern forms of associational life in late 19th-century India, *The Emergence of Indian Nationalism,*[22] one can find an Indian bourgeoisie, the English-educated urban middle classes. From Seal we learn how and why an Indian bourgeoisie formed and populated the kinds of clubs, associations and journals Habermas posited in Poona, Bombay, Calcutta, and Madras. An array of canonical nationalist names— Gokhale, Ranade, Tilak, Aurobindo, Surendra Nath Banerjee—is associated with the formation of literary clubs and journals, scholarly societies, and reform and service organizations.

Habermas, whose volume projected a downward-sliding historical trajectory, argues that associational life productive of a public sphere was limited to the places and times he had investigated. In this he articulates a pessimism of the 1960s common to conservative American sociologists and to those identified with the 'critical theory' of the Frankfurt School. Both expected to be overwhelmed by the deluge of mass culture, commodity fetishism, and the vulgar tastes of rampant consumerism.

Habermas' rationalist proclivity causes him to draw a sharp line between different sorts of opinion in terms of how it is formed, received and made habitual, on the one hand; considered and made reflective on the other. According to Habermas, opinion which has always been there differs from 'public' opinion which is the product of deliberation.

Whereas mere opinions (things taken for granted as part of a culture, normative convictions, collective prejudices and judgments) seem to persist unchanged in their quasi-natural structure as a kind of sediment of history, public opinion, in terms of its very idea, can be formed only if a public that engages in rational discourse exists.[23]

There is much in Habermas' discourse that implies the public interest can only be arrived at through acts of reasoning that conform to formal notions of rationality. He imagines public intellectuals engaged in deliberation with each other. As Eley suggests: 'The faculty of publicness begins with reading, thought, and discussion, with reasonable exchange among equals, and it is this ideal which really focuses Habermas' interest.'[24] Habermas' faith in the power of communicative action makes him a descendant of that German tradition, leading back to Hegel, which imagined that the philosopher could, by words and thought, speech acts and reason, break out of the objectification of human consciousness wrought by social forces. Naturalizing the historical stages characteristic of theories of modernity, Habermas assigns the condition conducive of the formation of public spheres to a specific historical moment:

> They [public spheres] developed only in a specific phase of bourgeois society, and only by virtue of a specific constellation of interests could they be incorporated in the order of the bourgeois constitutional state.[25]

Human scale associations marked by 'convivial social intercourse and by a relatively high standard of education' engage in rational consideration of public issues only for a brief, transitional 18th-century moment. Then begins the decline. The public sphere is superceded when the bourgeoisie loses its short-lived monopoly of opinion. That monopoly begins to be broken by a widening democratization of the public. Habermas speaks of a 'weakening of the public sphere'; of the public sphere becoming 'a field for competition among interests in the cruder form of forcible confrontations ... Laws that have obviously originated under the 'pressure of the streets' can scarcely continue to be understood in terms of a consensus achieved by private persons in public discussion'.[26]

Habermas' narrative of when and why the politics of the public sphere succumbed to democratization is governed by his privileging of the 'rational' over the democratic. The rationality of a proper 'public sphere' will be crowded out by the non-rationalities and irrationalities of democratic mobilization. Deliberation conducive to formulations of the common good will be subverted by the clamour of the media and of the parochial, self-interested, and well-heeled voices of organized pressure groups.

There is now a propensity among theorists to recognize that part of the problem with Habermas' conception of the public good is that it is too narrowly rationalist and too exclusively bourgeois. Habermas was troubled by the idea of a plebeian public sphere and ultimately rejected the possibility just as he had rejected the clash of interests even when it was dressed up as the 'marketplace of ideas'. A sympathetic critic, Geoff Eley, counters with the view that 'The liberal desideratum of reasoned exchange also became available for non-bourgeois, subaltern groups, whether the radical intelligentsia of Jacobinism and its successors or wide sections of social classes like the peasantry or the working class'. 'In particular', he continues, 'Habermas' oppositions of "educated/uneducated" and "literate/illiterate" simply don't work because ... the liberal public sphere was faced at the very moment of its appearance by ... a radical [public] that was combative and highly literate'.[27]

Eley's friendly modification may not go far enough, yielding as it does to the literacy-centrism of elite conceptions of the public sphere. The print media, the bookshop, the coffee houses, do not suffice to locate where publics may be found. In the era of mass media, communicative action takes different forms and creates different publics. 'The virtue of publicness could materialize other than by the intellectual transactions of a polite and literate bourgeois milieu.'[28] Ben Lee suggests an alternative conceptualization: 'In many contemporary societies the political public is coextensive with the mass media audience which may be mostly illiterate.'[29] In societies of the South, levels of literacy and forms of social organization need not deter but may reshape the forms that civil society takes.

Habermas' 'ideal' version of civil society envisions a unified process by which the public's deliberations via communicative actions produce a common conception of a general interest.[30] He does not imagine a variety of differently constituted associations, each with its own discursive formations rallying behind different visions of the public interest. Presumably, a multiplicity of publics is a sign of the articulation and assertion of private interest. Habermas names this a process of re-feudalization, invoking the negative valuation that enlightenment thought imprinted on the feudal.[31] It is a process that leaves behind the Habermas model of the public sphere, a model manifest in the political life of 18th-century Germany, France, and England.

Ben Lee's more historically and culturally insightful contextualization of the public sphere challenges Habermas' theory of its decline and subversion. 'Instead of the degradation of a pre-existing bourgeois public sphere ... what we see is the coeval emergence of different publics, public spheres, and public spaces, each with their own form of communicative organization'.[32] John Keane goes further:

The ideal of a unified public sphere and its corresponding vision of a territorially bounded republic of citizens striving to live up to their definition of the public good are obsolete. In their place ... public life is today subject to 'refeudalization', not in the sense in which Habermas' *Strukturwandel der Offentlichkeit* used the term, but in the different sense of modularization, of the development of a complex mosaic of differently sized, overlapping and interconnected public spheres ....[33]

To summarize, the civil society associations instanced in *Structural Transformations* have a number of attributes which will anchor our discussion of Gandhi's variants of civil society and public sphere. They are voluntary, not coerced; they are located in public spaces—the 'coffee house'—that are explicitly separated from the (private) sphere of house and home; they are marked by an opposition between private and public that impugns the private as the realm of personal interests, disruptive to the public interest; they are skewed toward the literate intelligentsia, not non-literate plebeians; they are grounded in rationalist forms of deliberation which implicitly exclude the effects of emotion [only 'minds' in the duo, 'hearts and minds']; and they are unmarked by identities—ethnicity, religion, language, place— which are seen to live in the arena of divisive and debilitating private interest.[34]

Gandhi's Transformation of the Public Sphere: Making the Private Public

How well does the concept of a public sphere travel through cultural space and time? What happens to it when it is placed in an Indian environment during the Gandhian era? What transferred to pre-Gandhi India were liberal assumptions. The bourgeois public sphere would provide 'the liberation and transparency that would follow from undistorted communication and the triumph of better arguments ...'[35] We will argue below that Gandhi's method of satyagraha extended these assumptions and consequences beyond the bourgeois public sphere to the plebeian world of non-literate villagers.

Earlier, when Partha Chatterjee asked what happened when the concept of civil society migrated to India, he gave a different answer. The concept of civil society, Chatterjee says, 'is best used to describe those institutions of modern associational life set up by nationalist elites in the era of colonial modernity, ... often as part of the colonial struggle'.[36] And indeed, the 19th-century specimens of voluntary associations, the Deccan Educational Society, the Brahmo Samaj, the Indian Association, the Prarthana Samaj, the Poona

Sarvajanik Sabha, fit rather well with the 18th-century rationalist, voluntary, bourgeois, public sphere imagery that Habermas offers. But the nationalist movement, after its transformation by Gandhi post 1920 into a village-and bazaar-based people's movement, spawned many social movements and collective actions that are not easily contained within the sober, rationalist, descriptors of the public sphere. English-educated parliamentary liberals such as Ranade and Gokhale were one thing, plebeian populist reformers such as E.V. Ramaswami Naiker ['Periyar'] in Tamil Nadu, J.G. Phule in Maharashtra, Shri Narayana Guru in Kerala, and Gandhi himself were another. Social movements were in fact deeply infiltrated by the symbolism, relationships, and practices of a society that was rural, religious, corporately organized, and largely non-literate.

C.A. Bayly's work on 18th-century India makes a case for something like a pre-modern public sphere. His discussion of 'an indigenous public sphere' suggests that there was a search for what might be called a public philosophy in the ubiquitous arena of religious discourses, a highly visible site for ethical reflection and normative practice.[37] Associational life in the pre-nationalist era did not sharply differentiate realms of life into private/ public, religious/secular, inherited/voluntary. A pre-modern indigenous public sphere shared features of a modern public sphere but felt and looked different.

One problem in asking how well the civil society/public sphere concepts travel to India is that one is moved by their 18th-century European genealogies to look to urban contexts. This is what Partha Chatterjee did. The rural arena does not appear on the radar screen, or only marginally so. A coffee house in a paddy field? Marx spoke for a general theoretical perspective among modernists when he supposed that peasants did not enter 'into manifold relations with one another'. They were homologous units; like so many potatoes in a sack, they made nothing more cohesive than a sackful of potatoes.[38] They could not speak for or represent themselves.

But Marx's metaphor for village India as a 'sackful of potatoes' overlooked strong and pervasive mechanisms of public life, the village and caste '*panchayats*' that provided local government and settled conflicts. It became conventional among India's colonial masters to mock the extravagant claims of nationalist historians who perceived an isomorphism between what they identified as India's ancient 'little republics' and Greek or Roman republican forms of rule. However vague the historicity of such social forms, recent anthropological knowledge suggests that panchayat forms of local and regional governments sustained arenas for informed and reasonable public deliberation based on consensual processes.

Susan Wadley put it this way:

Gatherings of respected men ... [are] commonly used to settle disputes in Karimpur ... those affected by the dispute call together a group of men to act as mediators in the conflict and arrange a settlement. These men should be aware of the complicated social relationships in which the case is embedded and should aim at a compromise acceptable to all.[39]

How about urban contexts? Was there a pre-modern version of a public sphere in India's cities and towns? Did they have the kind of print-dependent communicative action that characterized the 18th-century coffee house, political journal, and literary society in England and on the continent? We know that well into the 1830s and 1840s, lithography had not yet penetrated India. Was this absence significant? C.A. Bayly has explored the consequences of the absence of print media for the nature of publics in 18th-and 19th-century urban India. He speaks of the creation of an 'ecumene', a community of written discourse consisting of 'Hindustani-writing literati, Indo-Islamic notables and officers of state' who 'represented the views of bazaar people and artisans when urban communities came under pressure'.[40] Such exchanges and debates often revolved around religiously set agendas but 'they were much more than religious polemic ... the issue related to religion but in its public manifestations'.[41] Bayly attributes the late rise of print media in India to an abundance rather than a paucity of communication forms. News and views were speedily propelled across the subcontinent from the North-West to Banaras by news-writers, mail-runners, and public recitations.

Indians had created a highly effective information order in which strategically placed written communications reinforced a powerful culture of oral communication ... Oral exposition, presence and memory were no doubt critical ... written media were nevertheless an essential part of North Indian ... debate.[42]

Bayly invites us to recognize that the literate and the non-literate, the notables and officials, on the one hand, and the bazaar merchants and artisans on the other, were distinct but connected social formations whose opinions were represented as a matter of importance, It is a connection which carries over into the print media, when, in the 19th century, some of the 'vernacular press' comes to represent the views of the non-literate in the towns and the countryside. Shahid Amin gives a detailed account and careful analysis of how the vernacular press covered Chauri Chaura, the Mofussil town in Gorakhpur district in Eastern Uttar Predesh where violence in 1922 led Gandhi to call-off a massive non-cooperation campaign that was still gathering momentum. Amin shows how well into the 20th century Gandhi's words and deeds were 'translated' into the idioms and practices of a mainly non-literate town and village population.[43]

The Ashram as Public Sphere?

When Gandhi began to invent a people's politics in South Africa, one of his early moves was to establish a proto-type for the ashram, the Phoenix Settlement, located on a 100-acre farm 14 miles from Durban. In 1910 he established a second ashram, Tolstoy Farm, on 1100 acres in the Transvaal, 21 miles from Johannesburg. He created seven ashrams in all, two in South Africa, five in India.[44] With members drawn from many castes, classes, religions, occupations, regions, and languages,[45] ashrams provided retreats to those who wished to join a community dedicated to a new form of life, a life of simple living, service, and political activism. Some learned to be the disciplined, non-violent vanguard for the successful practice of satyagraha.

Is the 'communicative action' that Habermas says a public sphere and civil society require possible if many of those meant to participate in communicative action cannot read or write? By inventing satyagraha and reinventing the ashram, by creating social service organizations, by his mastery of signs and symbols, by making 'clothing matter',[46] and by his command of political theatre, Gandhi was able to reach beyond the literate, often English-speaking middle-class elites of urban India to the non-literate millions living in India's villages and towns.

Gandhi's version of a public sphere was not conditioned on literacy. Like the gurus of the bhakti [devotional] tradition who proceeded him, he was aware that public deliberations and cultural performance reach high levels of complexity under conditions of low literacy. Drama (travelling theatre),[47] domestic oral compositions (grandmother's tales),[48] and public oratory (the deliberations of caste and village panchayats) regularly engage ordinary non-literate people in complex and sophisticated communication.[49] To create a 'public' focused on matters of public concern under conditions of non-literacy requires forms of organization different from the coffee house, the literary society and the political journal, forms in which exemplification and performance play a visible role.

Gandhi's ashrams[50] and satyagrahas expanded the concept of public sphere beyond discursive exchanges of educated men. They featured exemplary performances whose enactment was designed to address the 'heart' as the well as the 'mind'. Ashrams prefigured how those from diverse social backgrounds could choose to live a new form of life. Satyagrahas were a form of deliberative action that engaged the contending parties in pursuit of situational truth.

A crucial feature for insuring the disinterested rationality of Habermas' public sphere is the insulation of the public from the private. The private is seen as the realm of interests such as, in Habermas' words, 'normative opinions' and 'collective prejudices'. Gandhi's concern to reach wider constituencies and his commitment to the undifferentiated nature of the public and private embodied in his concept of swaraj led him to transgress what was, for Habermas, a foundational dichotomy. The fact that the transgression of the boundary between the public and the private made moral sense in India has to be read against the complex meanings of public/ private found in Indian society. European conventional understandings can do little to help penetrate Indian assumptions and practices with respect to these concepts.

In India the meaning of privacy starts with the circumstances of the multi-generational 'joint' and extended family. Its collective norms and its living arrangements make privacy extremely difficult. It is easy and ordinary to observe quotidian acts and even intimate relationships. Surveillance is common. Rephrasing James Scott's telling metaphor, in India one can speak of 'seeing like a family'.[51] Privacy becomes problematic when the family constitutes an all-seeing community. Outside the family too, in villages, hamlets and *mohalla*s [neighbourhoods], most quotidian activity is carried out in the open—on verandas, in courtyards—in 'public' sight. Under such circumstances it becomes apparent that privacy is an invention of the bourgeois nuclear family whose members live in homes and rooms with doors that shut and curtains that close.[52]

Many nominally private practices in India have public meaning: the drawing of the *dupatta* [woman's head scarf] over the face to protect her modesty; the tying of a *dhoti* and the winding of a turban to signal place, caste or community; interdining with some and not others to mark purity and pollution boundaries or their transgression; wearing of a sacred thread to signal upper-caste twice-born status; riding or not riding a horse in a wedding procession to mark status. The most fundamental social transformations that Indian reformers sought to accomplish over the last hundred years have targeted what in the West would be designated private life.

In the colonial era, leading social reformers sought legislation in the public sphere that would change what they regarded as unjust or retrograde 'private' social practices. To enact their principles they defied convention by marrying a widow, by crossing the ocean, by staging inter-caste meals. As the feminists are wont to say, 'the personal is the political', a view that resulted in the Age of Consent Act, the Widow Remarriage Act, the Gains of Learning Act.

The claim that the 'personal is political' did not go uncontested. Those opposed to social reform held that family[53] matters were private and therefore beyond the reach of the colonial state. B.G. Ranade [1842-1901], a leading advocate of social reform in the early years of the Indian National Congress was forced to retreat when it became apparent that pressing ahead with his social reform agenda would split the organization and thereby jeopardize its principal goal, political freedom. A generation later, Gandhi restored Ranade's social reform agenda; 'private' matters were put back on the public agenda. The sharp distinction between the private and the public that Habermas invoked as an essential condition for the existence of a public sphere proved untenable under Indian conditions.

Gandhi's first ashrams[54] in South Africa—Phoenix Settlement, begun in 1904, and Tolstoy Farm, established in 1910—created public spheres by asking those who volunteered to adapt their private life to the ashram's material and moral purposes. Phoenix Settlement and Tolstoy Farm[55] were meant to be exemplary voluntary communities. Gandhi saw them as models for a diverse, pluralist India, an India willing and able to recognize, respect, and learn from difference. The negotiations entailed in adjusting private ways of life to norms and rules shared by the ashram community were discussed publicly. Starting with his first publication in South Africa, *Indian Opinion*,[56] and later in India, with *Navajivan* and *Young India*, Gandhi devoted considerable space in his publications to rendering the private public.[57]

The accounts in *Satyagraha in South Africa* and in *Indian Opinion* are replete with the quotidian details of negotiating the adjustment of private differences, bringing them into public view and shared practice. How to arrange the preparation of food, dining and cleaning up? By allowing every family to operate its own kitchen as religious and caste rules required? Most ashram volunteers came from caste backgrounds that forbade inter-dining on grounds of purity and pollution. And what about differences between those who were vegetarians and those who were meat-eaters? And who was to wash the spoiled dishes, regarded as polluted and polluting, and the dirty pots and pans? The conundrum of meat-eating versus vegetarianism appears to have been settled by Gandhi's usual negotiated consensus, a consensus not surprisingly in favour of vegetarianism.[58] Here is Gandhi's cheerful account of creating a public sphere for Tolstoy Farm:

> There was to be one single kitchen, and all were to dine in a single row. Everyone was to see to the cleaning of his own dish and other things. The common pots were to be cleaned by different parties in turn.[59]

The ashram and the satyagraha as vehicles for displaying a democratized public sphere became a new kind of political theatre. Gandhi moved their performances around India, recreating at various sites the drama of transgressing private commitments and challenging unjust laws to create democratized public spheres—in Champaran in 1917, in Ahmedabad in 1918, countrywide in 1919, during the Salt March in 1930.

Gandhi's political theatre was creating a new and distinctive form of the public sphere. It was marked by the visible practice of simple living; the performance of physical labour and polluting tasks; making and wearing khadi, doing for yourself; living with and learning from comrades of diverse backgrounds. The performances were to demonstrate the asceticism and discipline required for swaraj, sarvodaya, and the pursuit of situational truth.

Many of the bourgeois professionals who came to the nationalist cause because of Gandhi did so with Habermasian assumptions about the divisions between the public and private spheres. They were ready to collaborate with Gandhi but expected to do so in something like a bourgeois public sphere. Doing so would have shielded the private arenas of class, caste, and religion they brought with them behind a claim of privacy. But working with Gandhi entailed dismantling such boundaries. First the Harrow- and Cambridge-educated Jawaharlal Nehru, then this wealthy, Anglicized father, Motilal, shed their Savile Row suits and lifestyles to don the khadi of village India.

The exemplary performance of simplicity at Champaran, a centre of indigo-growing plantations in Bihar whose workers had called on Gandhi to save them from destitution, offers a well-known example of how Gandhi breached the private realm to create a democratized public sphere. The volunteers whom Gandhi had recruited to help him were advocates from prosperous upper-class and upper-caste backgrounds. They helped him to investigate the circumstances of indigo labourers and to bring court cases to challenge the laws that facilitated their exploitation. They assumed that they could serve the movement and keep their class and caste lifestyle in the realm of the private. Gandhi shamed them, teasing them into adopting the simple and egalitarian commonalities of ashram living. Here is how Gandhi tells the story:

The curious ways of living of my companions in the early days were a constant theme of raillery at their expense. Each of the vakils (advocates/lawyers) had a servant and a cook, and therefore a separate kitchen, and they often had their dinner as late as midnight. Though they paid their own expenses, the irregularity worried me, but as we had become close friends ... they received my ridicule in good part. Ultimately it was agreed that the servants should be dispensed with, that all the kitchens should be amalgamated, and regular hours should be observed ... it was also felt necessary to insist on simple meals.[60]

Rajendra Prasad, who was to become India's first President, was one of the advocates who came to help and live with Gandhi in Champaran. He wryly recalls his experiments with simplicity. The locals, he reports, were immensely amused as they watched him struggle to use a rope to lower a clay pot into the village well.[61]

The young city lawyers who signed up with Gandhi hadn't counted on cleaning their own chamber pots. The ashram as public sphere made greater demands than the coffee house. It challenged the Habermasian notion that the viability of the public sphere, its capacity to be the locus of communicative action and a source of the public good, required that private life and private interests be excluded from the public sphere. For Gandhi, the private sphere was the location of India's deepest inequalities and severest oppressions. Its arrangements and requirements blocked fellow feeling and common discourse. Transgressing the requirements of the private realm by instituting shared living arrangements at Tolstoy Farm and other ashrams made the political theatre of the ashram an exemplar for a democratized public sphere in India.

Satyagraha: Deliberation as Situational Truth

Gandhi's greatest invention may be satyagraha. His most historic satyagraha, a non-violent act of civil disobedience, shook the foundations of the British empire in India. From 12 March to 5 April 1930, Gandhi and the satyagrahis marched from Ahmedabad to the sea coast at Dandi where they broke the salt tax law by gathering contraband salt on the beach. On 3 May non-violent satyagrahis attempted to enter the government salt works at Dharsana. Webb Miller, a United Press correspondent. witnessed the event. His account was flashed around the world:

The column silently ignored the [police] warning and slowly walked forward ... Suddenly .... Scores of native police rushed upon the advancing marchers .... From where I stood I heard the sickening whacks of the clubs on unprotected skulls .... Those struck fell sprawling, unconscious or writhing in pain .... In two or three minutes the ground was quilted with bodies. Great patches of blood widened on their white clothes .... Then another column formed .... They marched slowly toward the police. Although every one knew that within a few minutes they would be beaten down, perhaps killed, I could detect no signs of wavering or fear.[62]

What did the satyagraha achieve? The salt works wasn't taken and the Salt Act in its entirety wasn't lifted. But by showing the moral power of non-violence in the face of coercive violence, the salt satyagraha had successfully opened a discussion about the legitimacy of British rule in India. In America those opposed to imperialism in general and those opposed to British imperialism in particular were impressed by Gandhi's methods and results.[63] In India, by February 1931 Lord Irwin, the Viceroy, had negotiated the Gandhi-Irwin pact that led to Round Table conferences in London to consider *inter alia* dominion status for India. In Britain, Winston Churchill, found it 'alarming and nauseating to see Mr Gandhi, a seditious middle temple lawyer, now posing as a fakir of a type well known in the east, striding half-naked, up the steps of the viceregal place, while still organizing and conducting a defiant campaign of civil disobedience, to parley on equal terms with the representative of the king-emperor'.[64]

Twenty-five years later, Martin Luther King could famously say of satyagraha that 'Gandhi was probably the first person in history to lift the love ethic of Jesus above mere interaction between individuals to a powerful and effective social force on a large scale .... I [had] discovered the method for social reform that I had been seeking ....'[65]

But what does Gandhi' satyagraha have to do with Jurgen Habermas' public sphere? Habermas' public sphere featured the literate disinterested few ('the bourgeois public') who could engage in what he called rational deliberation. Satyagraha brings about a deliberative process in which the non-literate interested may persuade each other by reasoning together. Satyagraha shifts the action to include participants beyond the bourgeois.

Satyagraha is not only a form of non-violent resistance and civil disobedience. It establishes relationships and opens a conversation. Satyagraha results in a deliberation process that forms or reforms individual wills.[66] It obliges adversaries to imagine themselves in each others' shoes and opens the possibility of reaching common ground via a situational truth.

Gandhi asks more of the deliberative process than the rationality that Habermas found sufficient. Gandhi is clear that mind without heart, reason without emotion, cannot be persuasive. In this Gandhi's position accords with the recent revival of Spinoza's view of the mind—body relationship, a revival which calls into questions Descartes' radical separation of mind from body. The neurologist-philosopher Antonio Damasio has argued in his recent book, *Looking for Spinoza: Joy, Sorrow and the Feeling Brain*, that Descartes was wrong to think that feeling is the enemy of reason, and that Spinoza was right to believe that feeling was thought's 'indispensable accomplice'.[67] Gandhi, in effect, critiques Habermas' [and Manin's] conception of deliberation by insisting that rationality without feeling cannot yield knowledge, truth, or the public good.

The heart must work together with the mind if deliberative processes are to produce shared truth. According to Gandhi:

Experience has shown that mere appeal to the reason produces no effect upon those who have settled convictions .... The *Satyagrahi* strives to reach the reason through the heart. The method of reaching the heart is to awaken public opinion. Public opinion ... is a mightier force than that of gunpowder.[68] [In another version of this position, Gandhi writes:] The conviction has been growing on me that things of fundamental importance to the people are not secured by reason alone, but have to be purchased with their suffering .... Suffering is infinitely more powerful than the law of the jungle for converting the opponent and opening up his ears, which are otherwise shut, to the voice of reason. Probably nobody had drawn up more petitions or espoused more forlorn causes than I, and I have come to this fundamental conclusion, that if you want something really important to be done, you must not merely satisfy the reason, you must move the heart also. The appeal of reason is more to the head, but the penetration of the heart comes from suffering. It opens up the inner understanding in man.[69]

Gandhi also rules out deliberation based on 'conversion by violence or compulsion'. 'Reason has to be strengthened by suffering ...', not by force. 'Therefore, there must be no trace of compulsion in our acts.' 'We should carry on the struggle', he says, 'on the lines of strict non-violence, i.e. by suffering in our own person. This is the meaning of *Satyagraha* ....'[70]

Gandhi is deeply concerned with ensuring that satyagraha, understood as a form of deliberation, be 'public' in the sense of disinterested and transparent. 'I want you to feel', he tells future satyagrahis, 'like loving your opponents, and the way to do it is to give them the same credit for honesty of purpose which you would claim for yourself'. 'I know that is a difficult task', he says. Once '... we begin to think of things as our opponents think of them, we shall be able to do them full justice. I know that this requires a detached state of mind, and it is very difficult to reach. Nevertheless, for a *Satyagrahi* it is absolutely essential'. We must, he says '... step into the shoes of our adversaries and understand their stand-point'.[71]

Gandhi, like Habermas, is in pursuit of truth, but Gandhi's truth is of a different kind. Habermas speaks of truth in the context of his thoughts about 'communicative action'. Communicative action involves *inter alia* various forms and levels of speech acts that yield 'truth, truthfulness, and rightness' in the context of Habermas' expectation that knowledge can be 'universally valid'.[72]

Gandhi's truth in the context of satyagraha is situational, not universal. Truth is what the satyagrahis and their adversaries find to be the common ground of their mutual understanding. It is the truth of a particular context.[73] Situational truth is arrived at, we have seen, after carefully researching the circumstances and the facts, listening to the adversary and 'putting yourself in his shoes', being self-critical, feeling with and for the adversary to establish a sense of fellow feeling, trusting and respecting the adversary, and opening his heart via self-suffering. If Gandhi's satyagraha as a deliberative process works, and, clearly, it sometimes did not work, the satyagrahi and the adversary come to share a common understanding of a situational truth.

How and why did Gandhi invent satyagraha? The ashram at Tolstoy Farm began as a voluntary, not compulsory, association. Discipline was helped by the fact that its volunteers were self-selected and shared its ethos of self-sacrifice and commitment to common goals.

Ashrams provided training for resisters and workshops for fashioning strategies and tactics of resistance. Volunteers observed routines and practiced discipline. They maintained the common enterprise by performing at assigned times common and individual labour on the farm or in the workshops. They were schooled to participate in risky political actions. They expected to be called upon to go on marches, attend meetings, and engage in civil disobedience by breaking unjust laws. Such acts would result in jail sentences which they anticipated and for which they were prepared.

Gandhi sometimes compared them to soldiers and they sometimes thought of him as a commander. But the military metaphor had its limits. It was much diluted by extended internal discussions about the anticipated risks and hardships that could result from resistant acts. Pressure to take risks was modified by more or less credible assertions that not doing so was acceptable. The habituation and discipline were critical. Satyagrahas were dangerous. Volunteers were arrested and jailed; sometimes they died. Jail could be and sometimes was difficult to endure. The capacity to be non-violent, particularly the 'new courage' to accept violence without retaliation had to be learned and cultivated.

Gandhi's first satyagraha was launched in 1913. It involved eleven women from Tolstoy Farm and sixteen volunteers from Phoenix Settlement, twelve men and four women, with Kasturba, Gandhi's wife, among them. They were protesting against the 'Black Acts' designed to stop migration from India, limit the movement of the Indian population to their home provinces [Natal and Transvaal], and to protest and oppose the discriminatory and oppressive three pound tax on 'free' [no longer indentured] Indians. All these causes were longstanding. The triggering event was a judgement by the Cape Supreme Court upholding Christian marriage among Indians but retrospectively invalidating Hindu, Muslim, and Parsi marriages. The decision rendered the 'wives' of such marriages kept women and the children of such marriages illegitimate.[74]

As a result of the court judgement the vanguard of the first satyagraha were women. The Phoenix and Tolstoy Farm women were incensed at the judgement. Gandhi spent long hours counselling them about the life-threatening risks involved in the march. But they insisted on going. 'The beauty of non-violent war', Gandhi once said, is 'that women can play the same part in it as men'.[75]

The sixteen-person Phoenix party, arrested for illegally crossing from Natal into the Transvaal, were sentenced to three months of hard labour. The women from Tolstoy Farm, mostly wives of former indentured labourers who had migrated from Madras [now Tamil Nadu], played lead roles in a political drama that inducted a non-literate constituency into the fight against racism and for social and political rights.

A fruit of ashram training and discipline was that a satyagraha could not easily be beheaded. Gandhi may have been the ashram's guiding spirit but he had succeeded in inculcating the spirit of swaraj. When the authorities arrested him during the first satyagraha campaign, his coordinating role was immediately filled by others. Ashram training was also apparent in the administrative and political skills evident in providing for thousands of marchers over many days, and above all in the discipline that kept the march non-violent.[76]

Here is Gandhi's retrospective self-evaluation [written in 1929] of Tolstoy Farm as the ashram that created a public sphere and launched the world's first satyagraha campaign:

Tolstoy Farm was never placed in the limelight, yet an institution which deserved it attracted public sympathy to itself. The Indians saw that the Tolstoy Farmers *were doing what they themselves were not prepared to do* [emphasis added] and what they looked upon in the light of hardship. The public confidence was a great asset to the movement when it was organized afresh on a large scale in 1913.[77]

The Coffee House and the Ashram: Looking Back, Looking Forward

We have used the coffee house as a metaphor for Habermas' 18th-century bourgeois public sphere. It was a public sphere whose publicness was made possible by the capacity for disinterestedness of literate and often literary persons whose education and class standing gave them the inclination and the means to concern themselves with the public good. Outside the coffee house, literary society, and political club where conversation was king, the printed word became an essential medium for communication and rational deliberation. We have used the ashram [and satyagraha] as a metaphor for Gandhi's democratized public sphere. It was a public sphere populated for the most part by the non-literate and the uneducated. In South Africa and India in Gandhi's time they were the hewers of wood and drawers of water. They were marked less by a shared class standing than by caste, religious, regional, and linguistic difference. Gandhi used the idealistic voluntarism of the ashram to induct persons who were strangers to each other into a new life dedicated to simple living, self-help, and service. The ashram's publicness was realized by shedding the private commitments that made them strangers to each other for shared commitments that made them an exemplary community. Gandhi created a public sphere among largely non-literate populations by amplifying the ashram as an exemplary community and by challenging racism, economic exploitation, and untouchability through satyagraha campaigns.

Yet we ought not to draw too sharp a distinction between the public spheres associated with the coffee house and ashram. Both are about civic virtue and realizing the public good. Gandhi would align with Habermas' concern about the public sphere falling victim to proliferating and increasingly powerful private interests and to the self-absorption of consumerism. But Habermas' commitment to the universal truths of Enlightenment rationalism as the foundation of the bourgeois public sphere stands in marked contrast with Gandhi's commitment to changing hearts as well as minds and to satyagraha's situational truth as the foundations for a democratized public sphere.

Voluntarism—free entry and exit—is a feature that the world of the coffee house and the world of the ashram share. Ashrams, writes Richard Taylor, 'may be the only traditional kind of Indian association [perhaps along with some *bhakti* groups] that are outside the ... conditions of ascriptive membership—at least in theory if not always in practice'.[78] Volunteers 'applied' to Gandhi's ashrams, alerted perhaps by the fame of Gandhi's life and projects. Some arrived in the spirit of novices entering a religious order, some in the spirit of Peace Corps volunteers. Neither caste nor religion nor nationality qualified or disqualified. Those for whom it was too much or too little left. Entry by merit, exit by choice.

The ashram's projects were based on a more holistic vision of how to improve the human condition than that of the coffee house. In the world of the coffee house, the political is separable from other spheres such as religion, caste, and other 'primal' solidarities. For Habermas the public sphere is concerned with politics, law, and institutional change. In the world of the ashram social change comes about more through swaraj, the moral transformation of the self, than through institutional change.

Gandhi formed his first ashram as the result of 'The Magic Spell of a Book?' This book was John Ruskin's *Unto This Last*, the four political economy essays that constituted his slashing attack on unregulated capitalism and modern society.[79] Gandhi made himself a promise that reaches well beyond political agendas: 'I determined to change my life in accordance with the ideals of the Book?'[80] The ashram was established in part to enable volunteers to practise a community of virtue: it was to be dedicated to Ruskin's notions that 'the good of the individual is contained in the good of all'; to the belief that all work is equally worthy; and to the conviction that the life of labour as exemplified by the tiller of the soil and the handcraftsman is the life worth living. Those who joined the ashram found that such commitments made the private public and the personal political. Caste differences based on purity and pollution gave way to inter-dining, washing one's own dishes, cleaning others' pots and pans, and disposing of one's own wastes. In the world of the ashram, private concerns and commitments helped define the public sphere.

Unlike in the world of the coffee house, in the world of the ashram the state was too frail to be the arena for realizing the public good. States could be more or less legitimate but none could survive without coercion and the threat of violence. In the world of the ashram, the individual in civil society becomes the decisive arena for change. States are constrained and directed by ideas and goals generated within and by civil society. Injustice such as belief in and the practice of untouchability can at best be marginally affected by the weak hand of legislation. Rational deliberation in the Habermasian public sphere can help to bring about legislation that threatens those who practise untouchability but it cannot change their hearts and minds. The public sphere associated with the ashram and with satyagraha provided a forum for deliberation that could and, on occasion, did change hearts and minds. It seems unlikely that the conditions that gave historic credibility to Habermas' conception of a bourgeois public sphere are likely to return. In this sense, it may have become an anachronism. Gandhi's concept of a democratized public sphere, because it is more in keeping with the Habermas 'normative ideal'[81] of a public sphere, seems to have a future.

Notes

[1] R.K. Prabhu and U.R. Rao, compilers, *The Mind of Mahatma Gandhi*, Ahmedabad: Navajivan Publishing House, 1976, p. 354; Anand T. Hingorani (ed.), *Service Before Self*, Bombay: Bhavan's Book University/*Gandhi for 21ˢᵗ Century*, vol. 22, 1998; Anand T. Hingorani (ed.), *The Village Reconstruction*, Bombay: Bhavan's Book University/*Gandhi for 21ˢᵗ Century*, vol. 14, 1998.

[2] See Chapter 8 of this book, 'This Worldly Asceticism and Political Modernization.'

[3] See Part IV, Ch. 18. 'The Magic Spell of a Book', in M.K. Gandhi, *An Autobiography or The Story of My Experiments With Truth*, London: Penguin, 1982, pp. 273–5.

[4] Martin Green, *Gandhi: Voice of a New Age Revolutionary*, New York: Continuum, 1993, p. 158.

Although familiar to Gandhians, the story of Phoenix's founding should be mentioned here. Gandhi had met Henry Polak, a young 'new age' Jewish immigrant from England to South Africa, in a vegetarian restaurant. Polak 'seemed to hold similar views on the essential things of life' and to promptly translate into practice 'anything that appealed to his intellect'. Polak gave Gandhi Ruskin's *Unto This Last* to read on the train journey from Johannesburg to Durban. 'The book', Gandhi tells us in his autobiography, 'was impossible to lay aside, once I had begun reading it. It gripped me. Johannesburg to Durban was a twenty-four-hour journey. The train reached there in the evening. I could not get any sleep that night. I determined to change my life in accordance with the ideals of the book'. M.K. Gandhi, *An Autobiography or The Story of My Experiments With Truth*, London: Penguin Books 1982, pp. 273–4.

'I now endeavoured', Gandhi writes, 'to draw to Phoenix those relations and friends who had come from India to try their fortune .... They had come in search of wealth, and it was therefore difficult to persuade them; but some agreed ... and there in spite of numerous odds *Indian Opinion* [which Gandhi had moved to Phoenix] continues [in 1927] to be published.' Gandhi, *Autobiography*, [Penguin edition], p. 276.

⁵ Martin Green tells us that 40,000 persons of Jewish origin entered South Africa, mostly from England, Germany, and the Russian empire, during Gandhi's years there. Most were attracted by the gold and diamond mines but a few were intellectuals, autodidacts rather than holders of academic degrees, interested in new ideas and ways of living. During the first decade of the 20th century, Gandhi's social and intellectual world was composed largely of such people, more than it was of the English Non-Conformist Protestants, who, James Hunt tells us, had influenced him in the 1890s, or the Indians with whom he was associated throughout his South African years. 'Gandhi's closest friends', Green says, 'were not Zionists, at least not during these years, but they were liberal in their Judaism, and saw the history of the Jews as constituting a call to them to recognize and alleviate the sufferings of similar groups—such as the Indians in the British empire .... The very broad historical and religious perspective ... [was] very congenial to Gandhi, and gave him an apprenticeship to idealistic politics quite different from the training of other Indian politicians of his generation.' Green, *Gandhi*, p. 152. James D. Hunt, *Gandhi and the Nonconformists: Encounters in South Africa*, New Delhi: Promilla & Co., 1986.

⁶ See Chapter IV. 'What is Swaraj?' in M.K. Gandhi, *Hind Swaraj and Other Writings*. Edited by Anthony J. Parel, Cambridge, UK: Cambridge University Press, 1997, pp. 27–8.

⁷ *Hind Swaraj*, p. 39.

⁸ Hannah Arendt, *On Violence*, New York, Harcourt Brace and World, 1969–70, p. 44.

⁹ Gene Sharp, *The Politics of Non-Violent Action, Part I: Power and Struggle*, Boston: Peter Sargent, 1973, p. 8.

[10] Most theorists of the modern, from Weber to Nehru, associated centralization with rationalization and bureaucratization. Their congruence, Weber wrote, goes, 'hand in hand with the concentration of the material means of management in the hands of the master. This concentration occurs, for instance, in the well-known and typical fashion, in the development of big capitalist enterprises .... A corresponding process occurs in public organizations.' Weber in H.H. Gerth and C. Wright Mills, editors and translators, *From Max Weber*, New York: Oxford University Press, 1946, p. 221.

[11] From *Harijan*, 28 July 1946, and *Harijan*, 26 July 1942, in Hingorani (ed.), *The Village Reconstruction*, pp. 115–17.

[12] John Keane, *Civil Society; Old Images, New Visions*, Stanford: Stanford University Press, p. 55.

[13] Among the works on civil society and the public sphere we have found helpful are: Neera Chandhoke, *State and Civil Society: Explorations in Political Theory*, New Delhi: Sage Publications, 1995; Neera Chandhoke, '*A Critique of the Notion of Civil Society as the "Third Sphere"*' in Rajesh Tandon and Ranjita Mohanty (eds), *Does Civil Society Matter?*, New Delhi: Sage Publications, 2003; Sunil Khilnani, 'The development of civil society', and Sudipta Kaviraj, 'In search of civil society', in Sudipta Kaviraj and Sunil Khilnani (eds), *Civil Society: History and Possibilities*, Cambridge, UK: Cambridge University Press, 2002; Carolyn M. Elliott, (ed.), *Civil Society and Democracy; A Reader*, New Delhi: Oxford University Press, 2003; Keith Michael Baker, 'Defining the Public Sphere in Eighteenth-Century France: Variations on a Theme by Habermas' in Craig Calhoun (ed.), *Habermas and the Public Sphere*, Cambridge, MA: MIT Press, 1992.

[14] Charles Taylor, 'Modes of Civil Society', *Public Culture*, III, 1, 1990, pp. 59–118.

[15] Antje Linkenbach, 'Ecological Movements and the Critique of Development: Agents and Interpreters' in *Thesis Eleven*, no. 39, 1994, pp. 63–85.

[16] *The Compact Edition of the Oxford English Dictionary*, Oxford: Oxford University Press, 1982.

[17] Robert Putnam, *Making Democracy Work; Civic Traditions in Modern Italy*, Princeton: Princeton University Press, 1993; James Coleman, *Foundations of Social Theory*, Cambridge, MA: Harvard University Press, 1990.

[18] For analysis in greater depth of the politics of categories see Susanne Hoeber Rudolph, 'The Imperialism of Categories: Situated Knowledge in a Globalizing World', presidential address, American Political Science Association, *Perspective on Politics*, vol. 3, no. 1 [March 2005]. See also Susanne Rudolph's defence of treating transnational religious movements as an aspect of transnational civil society, in *Transnational Religion and Fading States*, Boulder: Westview, 1997.

[19] The 'original' German version of Habermas' work on civil society and the public sphere was published in 1962 under the title *Strukturwandel der Öffentlichkeit*.

It deploys a more restrictive vision of civil society, focuses on narrowly political associations and features strongly rationalist and speech-act oriented dimensions. The 1962 book was published in English as *The Structural Transformation of the Public Sphere*, translated by Thomas Burger and Frederick Lawrence, Cambridge: MIT Press, 1989.

'The Habermas who appeared at a panel on his work in 1989 has expanded his horizons to include associations with mainly social ends.'

The institutional core of 'civil society' is constituted by voluntary unions outside the realm of the state and the economy and ranging ... from churches, cultural associations, and academies to independent media, sport and leisure clubs, debating societies, groups of concerned citizens, and grass roots petitioning drives all the way to occupational associations, political parties, labour unions, and 'alternative' institutions.

Craig Calhoun (ed.), *Habermas and the Public Sphere*, Cambridge, MA: MIT Press, 1996.

For Habermas most recent thinking about the public sphere and civil society see Chapter 8. 'Civil Society and the Public Sphere', particularly sections 8.3.1 and 8.3.2 [pp. 360–73] in his *Between Facts and Norms: Contributions to a Discourse Theory of Law and Democracy*, Cambridge, MA., MIT Press, 1998.

[20] Lloyd Rudolph found something similar, i. e. 'the politics of opinion' in 18th-century English and colonial American political life. His analysis went beyond the bourgeois public sphere of the coffee house to include 'radical' political associations and 'opinion out doors' in England and 'committees of correspondence' and 'sons of liberty' in the American colonies, He found that such manifestations of the public sphere were deliberative but not dis-interestedly rational in the Habermasian Enlightenment sense. See Lloyd I. Rudolph, 'The Origin of Party: From the Politics of Status to the Politics of Opinion in Eighteenth Century England and America', Ph.D. Dissertation, Department of Government, Harvard University, 1956.

See Markman Ellis, *The Coffee House; A Cultural History*, London: Weidenfeld and Nicolson, 2004, especially 1. First Encounters: George Sandys and the Coffee Houses of Constantinople and 3. The First English Coffee House.

[21] Habermas, 'Further Reflections on the Public Sphere' in Calhoun (ed.), *Habermas and the Public Sphere*, p. 422.

[22] Anil Seal, *The Emergence of Indian Nationalism: Competition and Collaboration in the Later Nineteenth Century*, Cambridge, UK: Cambridge University Press, 1968.

[23] Steven Seidman, *Jurgen Habermas on Society and Politics: A Reader*, Boston, MA: Beacon Press, 1989, p. 232.

[24] Geoff Eley 'Nations, Publics and Political Cultures; Placing Habermas in the Nineteenth Century', in Calhoun, *Habermas and the Public Sphere*, p. 293.

[25] *Jurgen Habermas ... A Reader*, p. 232.

[26] Deploring the 'refeudalization' on the public sphere, Habermas notes that 'today [publicness] has ... been enlisted in the aid of the secret policies of interest groups', *Jurgen Habermas ... A Reader*, p. 236. Much of this is reminiscent of the impatience with political bargaining that lies behind Max Weber's distaste for democratic politics.

[27] Eley, 'Nations', pp. 304–5.

[28] Eley, 'Nations', p. 302.

[29] Ben Lee, 'Textuality, Mediation, and Public Discourse,' in Craig Calhoun, (ed.), *Habermas and the Public Sphere*, Cambridge, MA: MIT Press, 1996, p. 417.

[30] Habermas had some doubts about such a single public interest surviving the downward trajectory of society, a trajectory that, in his view, entailed the assertion of non-public interests: 'The unresolved plurality of competing interests ... makes it doubtful whether there can ever emerge a general interest of the kind to which a public opinion could refer as a criterion.' Jurgen Habermas, 'Further Reflections on the Public Sphere' in Calhoun, *Habermas and the Public Sphere*, p. 441.

Fred R. Dallmayr in his 1984 essay [republished with 'slight revisions' in 1987, 'Life-World and Communicative Action' in Bhikhu Parekh and Thomas Pantham (eds), *Political Discourse; Explorations in India and Western Political Thought*, New Delhi: Sage Publications, 1987], anticipates this difficulty when he observes, in *Theory of Communicative Action*, 'the incoherence of the mixed perspective [of the objective truth available through rationality and the indeterminacy of 'life worlds'].

Habermas, according to Dallmayr, states that communicative agents cannot objectify or face frontally 'the horizon of their own life-world .... As interpreters they are with their speech acts part of the life-world, but they cannot refer to "something in the life world" in the same manner in which we refer to facts, norms or experiences .... Differently put: participants cannot distantiate language and culture in a way akin to their treatment of the totality of facts, norms or experiences about which communication is possible', pp. 169–70.

[31] Seidman, *Jurgen Habermas*, p. 236.

[32] Lee, 'Textuality', p. 416.

[33] John Keane, *Civil Society; Old Images, New Visions*, Stanford, AC: Standford University Press, 1998, p. 169.

[34] Habermas' aversion to divisive and debilitating private interests puts him on the side of Hobbes and Rousseau, who, from different premises, come to similar conclusions about private interests. As Hobbes would have it, they are like worms in the entrails of the body politic.

[35] Uday Singh Mehta, *Liberalism and Empire: A Study in Nineteenth-Century British Liberal Thought*, Chicago, IL: University of Chicago Press, 1999, p. 24.

[36] 'Beyond the Nation? Or With?' *Economic and Political Weekly*, 4–11 January 1997, pp. 30–4. Chatterjee's article recognizes the distinction between the traditional

definition of civil society and public sphere and the Gandhian variant of this definition which we are about to elaborate. But he would prefer, apparently in the interest of heuristic sharpness, to 'retain the term civil society [for] those characteristic institutions of modern associational life originating in western societies that are based on equality, autonomy, freedom of entry and exit, contract, deliberative procedures of decision-making, recognized rights and duties of members ... even though non-western countries provide 'numerous examples of the emergence of what could well be called civil-social institutions which nevertheless do not always conform to these principles'. It is a position that denies (on historical grounds? On normative grounds?) the fluidity and adaptability of 'traditional' institutions.

Chatterjee here adopts a different theoretical road than the one which we adopted in an earlier work where we argued that 'caste associations' represent a hybrid form of civil society [we referred to them as para-communities] by transgressing the dichotomy between ascribed and voluntary groups. See *The Modernity of Tradition: Political Development in India*, Chicago, IL: University of Chicago Press, 1967, 1983. The post-independence generation of Indian intellectuals to which Chatterjee 'belongs' is sufficiently close to the colonial experience to view the hybrid nature of many civil society institutions in India in a negative light. It seems that they regard the colonial dimension of India's historical experience and its contribution to hybridity as inimical to an authentic Indianness. By contrast, the IT generation is producing many observers for whom hybridity appears as 'natural' as it is desirable.

For the associational life and civil society of 'nationalist modernity' see Anil Seal, *The Emergence of Indian Nationalism.*

[37] C.A. Bayly, 'The Indian Ecumene; an Indigenous Public Sphere' in *Empire and Information; Intelligence Gathering and Social Communication in India, 1780–1870*, Cambridge, UK: Cambridge University Press, 1999, pp. 180–211.

[38] Karl Marx, 'The Eighteenth Brumaire of Louis Napoleon', *Selected Works*, New York, n.d., II, p. 415.

[39] Susan Wadley, *Struggling With Destiny in Karimpur; 1925–1984*, Berkeley, CA: University of California Press, 1994, p. 190.

Ralph Retzlaff's monograph in the 1960, *Village Government in India*, Bombay, Asia Publishing House, 1962, was based on the observation of such bodies. See pp. 24–5.

A more recent account of village panchayats is Bishnu Mohapatra, 'Social Connectedness, Civility and Democracy: A View from an Orissa Village', unpublished manuscript, Democracy and Social Capital in Segmented Societies: The Third International Conference', Vasasalen, Uppsala University, Sweden, 17–19 June 1999.

M.N. Srinivas in 'The Social System of a Mysore Village' and Kathleen Gough in 'The Social Structure of a Tanjore Villages' documented the dominance of higher castes in the consensus. In McKim Marriott (ed.), *Village India*, Chicago, IL:

University of Chicago Press, 1955. Wadley reports the decay of the ties of dependency ['the *jajmani* system'] that characterized the older village practice.

For a more sustained account of the consensus norm and of consensus procedures at the village level in India see Rudolph and Rudolph, *Modernity of Tradition*, pp. 187–201; 258–9.

[40] Bayly, 'Ecumene', p. 182.

[41] Ibid., p. 180.

[42] Ibid., p. 200.

[43] Shahid Amin, *Event, Metaphor, Memory: Chauri Chaura, 1922–1992*, New Delhi: Oxford University Press, 1996.

[44] Soon after Gandhi returned to India from South Africa in 1915 he founded Satyagraha Ashram at Ahmedabad. *Experiments*, pp. 395–436] 'I wanted to acquaint India with the method I had tried in South Africa' and the name, 'truth-force' explained 'our goal and our method of service'. [*Experiments*, p. 396; C.B. Dalal, *Gandhi: 1915–1948; A Detailed Chronology*, New Delhi: Bharatiya Vidya Bhavan, 1971, p. 15.] Plague drove the *satyagrahis* out of Kochrab village in 1917, and they subsequently settled at near-by Sabarmati. *Experiments*, p. 429. When Gandhi turned in 1933 to the condition of the untouchables, Sabarmati was dissolved and renamed Harijan Ashram—using Gandhi's name for untouchables. [*Chronology*, pp. 102, 104.] After three years at Wardha, from 1933–6, where the industrialist Jamnalal Bajaj made available a site, Gandhi's moveable community established a new ashram, Sevagram [or Segaon], near Wardha. Segaon was an untouchables' village whose circumstances symbolized the anti-untouchability campaign. [Martin Green (ed.), *Gandhi in India; in His Own Words*, Hanover, NH: University Press of New England, 1987, p. 116.]

More serious in its consequences for the viability of Gandhian ashrams in India was the addition of an untouchable family. The gesture has an artificial feel when read in the light of contemporary sensibilities. Post-Ambedkar and more recently, ex-untouchables are likely to reject upper-caste sponsorship. Gandhi's gesture proved costly; the life of the ashram hung by a thread. Gandhi recognized but took the risk when he solicited funds from among the Gujarati merchants and businessmen of Ahmedabad, where his first ashram in India was established.

'I made it clear to them that I should take the first opportunity of admitting an untouchable candidate to the ashram if he was otherwise worthy. "Where is the untouchable who will satisfy your condition?" said a *vaishnava* friend self-complacently.'

When Gandhi found such a 'humble and honest untouchable family' and inducted it into the ashram the funding came to an abrupt end. The vaishnava friend who had asked the question stopped his contributions, and there was talk of social boycott. Within the ashram, 'my wife and other women did not seem quite to relish the admission into the ashram of the untouchable friends'. Gandhi and the ashram were saved by Seth Ambalal Sarabhai, a wealthy merchant from Ahmedabad. Out of the blue, Sarabhai offered financial help and Gandhi was pleased to accept it. The public performance of diversity had been extremely risky, and it was indeed public: The Sarabhai intervention enabled him to proclaim '... to the world that the Ashram would not countenance untouchability'. In time, the orthodox had second thoughts and resumed their interest and support.

[45] Here is Gandhi's account of the volunteers at Tolstoy Farm. 'The settlers hailed from Gujarat, Tamilnad, Andhra-desh and North India, and there were Hindus, Musalmans, Parsis and Christians among them. About forty of them were young men, two or three old men, five women and twenty to thirty children of whom four or five were girls.' M.K. Gandhi, *Satyagraha in South Africa*, Ahmedabad: Navajivan Publishing House, 1928, p. 215.

For a continuation of this ethnic, religious, and social ecumenism, see Martin Green (ed.), *Gandhi in India; in His Own Words*, Hanover: University Press of New England, 1987, pp. 177–8.

[46] Emma Tarlo, *Clothing Matters; Dress and Identity in India*, Chicago, IL: University of Chicago Press, 1996, particularly Chapter 3, 'Gandhi and the Recreation of Indian Dress', pp. 62–93, and Chapter 4, 'Is Khadi the Solution?', pp. 94–128.

[47] See Susan Seizer, *Stigmas of the Tamil Stage: an ethnography of Special Drama artists in South India*, Durham, NC: Duke University Press, 2005 and Sameera Iyengar, Performing Presence: feminism and theatre in India, Ph.D., dissertation, Department of Anthropology, University of Chicago, 2001.

[48] See A.K. Ramanujan (ed.), 'Introduction', *Folktales from India: A Selection of Oral Tales from Twenty-two Languages*, New York: Pantheon, 1991.

[49] For a remarkable archive of judicial village rhetoric, see the documentary 'Courts and Councils', made by the University of Wisconsin and available from the Center of South Asian Studies.

[50] Gandhi founded seven ashrams in all, two in South Africa and five in India. For more on Gandhi's founding of ashrams see footnote 44.

[51] The reference is to James Scott, *Seeing Like A State*, New Haven, CT: Yale University Press, 1999.

[52] For ways of contextualizing private practices, see Philippe Aries and Georges Duby, general editors, *The History of Private Life*, Cambridge: Harvard-Belknap Press, 1990, 5 volumes, See particularly vol. IV. *From the fires of revolution to the Great War*, Midhelle Perrot (ed.), Arthur Goldhammer (trans.).

[53] Althusius is one of the few dissenters from the tradition that follows Aristotle, in which the family is *oikos* and pre-political, the polis is public and political. See Johannes Althusius, *Politica*, edited and translated by Frederick S. Carney, Indianapolis, Liberty Fund 1995. Althusius's pluralist view of the polity is constituted by a graduated set of socio-political units that start with the family as the basic unit. 'By politics alone arises the wisdom for governing and administering the family', p. 32.

[54] Gandhi's ashrams combined features of European 19th-centruy utopian settlements and colonies, which Gandhi learned about and visited during the years he spent in England [1888–91] studying to become a barrister, with the 'remembered' ashram of Kalidasa's 15th-century ascetic forest rishis, 20th-century activist NGOs; and the advance bivouac of a guerilla army.

In the 19th and 20th centuries ashrams took on a new life. They mixed classical models with more recent institutional forms and spiritual needs. The ashram travelled across denominational lines to Christians and New Agers. For an introduction to the forms ashrams took and a review of their historical manifestations see Richard Taylor, 'Modern Indian Ashrams', *Religion and Society*, XXXIII, 3, September 1986.

[55] Tolstoy Farm was named in response to Tolstoy's letter recognizing in Gandhi a spiritual heir. B. Srinivasan Murthy (ed.), *Mahatma Gandhi and Leo Tolstoy Letters*, Long Beach, CA: Long Beach Publications, 1987, p. 37. Phoenix Settlement and Tolstoy Farm announced not only the transnational links of Gandhi's social imagination but also the specific type of anti-modernist critics he meant to ally with.

The more ambitious normative goals—to transform the world by transforming the micro-context of everyday life—were linked to more quotidian political ones. Gandhi needed to house and economically sustain the press that produced *Indian Opinion*, the journal of news and opinion of his South African movement. Also Tolstoy Farm, established when it became clear that the freedom struggle in South Africa would be an effort of years, not days, gave a secure retreat to the dedicated satyagrahis and their families who were continually in and out of jail. 'On the one hand there were the Boer generals determined to yield not even an inch of ground, and on the other there were a handful of satyagrahis pledged to fight unto death or victory.' Locating the satyagrahis on the self-sustaining Tolstoy farm solved the practical problems of food and shelter even while providing a Benedictine sort of discipline. Gandhi, *Satyagraha*, p. 213; Green (ed.), *Gandhi in India*, p. 176.

[56] Gandhi's first journal was *Public Opinion*. Its name signals its place among the key agencies of civil society. Gandhi recognized that an unseen political performance has no effect. Hence the ashram's withdrawal from the world was conducted very publicly: 'We could not perhaps have educated the local Indian community, not kept Indians all over the world in touch with the course of events in South Africa in any other way, with the same ease and success as through *Indian Opinion*, which therefore was certainly a most useful and potent weapon in our struggle.'

Indian Opinion, as the quote above reminds us, functioned as a vehicle not merely of national but of transnational civil society, building a constituency in the homeland for the Indian diaspora in South Africa. His later journals for the Indian campaigns, *Navajivan* and *Young India*, reached a joint circulation of 40,000.

[57] Gandhi, *Satyagraha*, p. 134.

[58] It is not our purpose in the essay to systematically analyse Gandhi's rhetoric, much less his epistemology. It is worth noting, however, that Gandhi's accounts of the creation of ashram public spheres, what we refer to as negotiated voluntarism, report no agents. 'It was agreed', 'it was decided upon'. The decision to create a common kitchen at Champaran, for example, appears to have happened without the visible, active intervention of any advocate or persuader. Ashram decisions appear to be the fortuitous but appropriate result of spontaneous consensual deliberative action.

[59] Gandhi, *Satyagraha*, p. 216.

[60] M.K. Gandhi, *Autobiography: The Story of My Experiments With Truth*, Boston MA: Beacon Press, 1957, p. 417. See also observation in note 58 for how Gandhi arrived at such arrangements.

[61] Rajendra Prasad, 'Gandhi in Bihar', in Homer Jack (ed.), *The Gandhi Reader*, Bloomington, IN: Indiana University Press, 1956, pp. 149–59.

[62] The text of the Webb Miller dispatch from which these excerpts are taken appears on the internet site of Mike's World History—July 2003.

[63] For those in the US who took notice of Gandhi at this time see Chapter 3. 'Gandhi in the Mind of America'.

[64] Quote from 'Mahatma Gandhi Album; Churchill and Gandhi', at www.kamat.com/mmgandhi/churchill/htm.

William Manchester writes that Churchill in late 1930 and into 1931 'continuously assailed' Gandhi. Gandhi's cause and dedication were 'incomprehensible' to him. In his view the Mahatma was 'a malignant and subversive fanatic', a cynical manipulator of 'Brahmins who mouth and patter principles of Western Liberalism and pose as philosophic and democratic politicians.' Manchester, *Visions of Glory*, p. 849.

[65] Quoted in Bhiku Parekh, *Gandhi*, New York: Oxford University Press, 1997, p. 61.

[66] Jurgen Habermas, 'Further Reflections on the Public Sphere', translated by Thomas Burger, in Calhoun (ed.), *Habermas and the Public Sphere*, p. 446.

[67] Antonio Damasio, *Looking for Spinoza: Joy, Sorrow and the Feeling Brain*, New York: Harcourt, 2003. See Emily Eakin's excellent article, 'I Feel Therefore I Am; A Thinker Reunites Mind and Body,' *The New York Times/Arts and Idea*, 19 April 2003, page A 15, for an insightful account of Damasio's contribution to the Descartes/Spinoza, mind/body controversy.

[68] Anand T. Hingorani (ed.), *The Science of Satyagraha*, Bombay: Bhavan's Book University/Gandhi for 21st Century, vol. 4, 1998, pp. 90.

[69] Hingorani, *Satyagraha*, p. 90.

[70] Ibid., p. 92.

[71] Ibid.

⁷² Benjamin Lee glosses a Habermas view of truth this way: 'Habermas argues that developing an adequate theory of communicative action will involve balancing formal and empirical approaches in what he calls "formal pragmatics". This approach begins with three types of idealized speech oriented toward mutual understanding [constative, expressive, and regulative], their concomitant speaker attitudes [objectivating, expressive, and normconformative], and their corresponding validity claims [truth, truthfulness, and rightness]. Formal pragmatics is a reconstruction of "the universal pre-suppositions of communicative action"' as it is found in Jurgen Habermas. *The Theory of Communicative Action*, vol. 1, *Reason and the Rationalization of Society*, Boston: Beacon Press, 1984, p. 328.

'Larger structures of communicative action', Lee continues, 'such as science, law, and art, are each organized around a particular validity claim [truth, rightness, and truthfulness respectively ....']

In endnote 40 of his Introduction, Calhoun provides a short intellectual biography of Habermas. It includes this sentence: 'Habermas remained committed to the ideal of cumulative perfectible, and especially universally valid knowledge ...,' this in spite of his theory of 'life worlds' where what 'is' and what can be known about it is highly indeterminant. Calhoun, (ed.), *Habermas and the Public Sphere*, p. 407 and p. 46.

⁷³ For a gloss on Gandhi's construction of satyagraha and the kind of truth it yields that is supportive of the view taken here see Bhiku Parekh's chapter, '*Satyagraha*', in his *Gandhi*, New York: Oxford University Press, 1997, pp. 51–62. In our view his 1997 essay does a better job of explaining *satyagraha* than a 1989 essay on the subject, Chapter 6, 'Satyagraha and a Non-Rationalist Theory of Rationality', in his book, *Gandhi's Political Philosophy: A Critical Examination*, Notre Dame: University of Notre Dame Press, 1989. In the 1997 essay he is less committed to rationalism and to the 'critical' hypothetical arguments designed to show Gandhi as impractical and extreme that characterize his 1989 essay. Still, in the 1989 essay he can say, in commenting on the rationality of Gandhi's satyagraha, that Gandhi is unlike 'Most rationalists [who] ignore the moral and social context in which reason functions, and treat it as if it were a transcendental faculty operating in a psychological and social vacuum and in no way influenced by values, interests and prejudices', p. 164.

A few years earlier Thomas Pantham argued along lines followed here with respect to the Habermas—Gandhi relationship: 'Habermas assumes that the "polytheism of beliefs" can be overcome through "communicative rationality" .... We must ... according to Gandhi, act in the practico-political sphere on the basis of the assumption that our knowledge of truth is relative .... Through the direct actions of active non-violence [e.g. satyagraha] ... we can and must complement the rational-discursive methods of pursuing truth and rightness.' Thomas Pantham, 'Habermas' Practical Discourse and Gandhi's Satyagraha', in Bhiku Parekh and Thomas Pantham (ed.), *Political Discourse: Explorations in Indian and Western Political Thought*, New Delhi/Newbury Park/Beverly Hills/London: Sage Publications, 1987, p. 310.

[74] Gandhi, *Satyagraha*, p. 251 ff.

[75] Cited in Geoffrey Ashe, *Gandhi, a Biography*, New York: Cooper Square Press, 2000, p. 122.

[76] For the serial performance of the coordinating roles, see Gandhi, *Satyagraha*, pp. 274–86.

[77] Gandhi, *Satyagraha*, p. 236.

[78] Taylor, 'Modern Indian Ashrams', p. 20.

[79] See 'Go to Nature', Clive Wilmer's review of six books on Ruskin that herald the 'return' of this alternately celebrated and shunned Victorian figure, *Times Literary Supplement*, 7 April 2000, pp. 3–4.

[80] Gandhi, *Experiments*, p. 298.

[81] For the contrast between Habermas' historically situated public sphere and his 'normative ideal' public sphere, see Keith Michael Baker, 'Defining the Public Sphere in Eighteenth-Century France: Variations on a Theme by Habermas', in Calhoun (ed.), *Habermas*, pp. 182–4.

Part Two

5

The Fear of Cowardice

Like many thinkers and actors in the Indian tradition, Gandhi cared more for man's inner environment than his outer and was highly self-conscious about his effect on how Indians felt about themselves. The young Nehru, who often questioned the Mahatma's political strategy and tactics, concedes again and again his effect on the nationalist generation:

Much that he said we only partially accepted or sometimes did not accept at all. But all this was secondary. The essence of his teaching was fearlessness and truth and action allied to these .... So, suddenly as it were, that black pall of fear was lifted from the people's shoulders, not wholly, of course, but to an amazing degree .... It was a psychological change, almost as if an expert in psychoanalytic method had probed deep into the patient's past, found out the origins of his complexes, exposed them to his view, and thus rid him of that burden.[1]

The portrait of Gandhi probing the nation's historical subconscious is a telling one. Gandhi had a unique sensibility both for the nightmare terrors of the Indian psyche and for its commonplace daytime self-doubts. He understood both the fundamental fear of Indians that those Britons who judged them as lacking in basic components of moral worth—like courage—might be right and the more superficial doubts about their technical ability to do anything about removing the raj. The nightmare fears he understood in part by analogy with his own personal terrors, terrors involving especially the issue of courage. The shape that he gave to the national movement, above all the technique of satyagraha, had much more than strategic significance; it provided a path for action that 'solved' some problems of Indian self-esteem arising from acceptance of the negative judgements of Englishmen.

One result of British rule had been to strengthen the appearance and reality of non-violent cultural norms. By the middle of the nineteenth century the last vestiges of organized Indian military power had sunk from view. Kshatriya rule and culture, particularly after 1858, lost their violent capabilities and concerns. Under the sheltering umbrella of British guarantees, ceremony and conspicuous consumption atrophied the will and diverted the resources of India's fighting classes. Even while British rule was making clear that Indians lacked power, it strengthened the non-violent dimensions of Indian culture by providing educational and related service opportunities that required the skills and temperament of the office rather than the sceptre and sword. Adherence to non-violence, while conspicuous among the qualifications for reaching the eschatological goals of Sanskritic Hinduism, is only one of the social ideologies found in traditional thought. Violence, too, has occupied an important place in thought and history and has its share of legitimizing religious and secular norms. But as the psychological and moral effects of Britain's conquest and subjection of India spread and deepened, and Indians adapted to the roles the empire required, both Britons and Indians began to believe that non-violence and the corollaries the British attributed to it—passivity, weakness, and cowardice— were the norms of Indian culture and character. The belief led many Britons to think that the superiority of British power and culture was an inherent rather than a historical phenomenon. India's military heritage, the heroes and social ideology that legitimized the use of violence and the character and rule of those who practiced it were, if not forgotten, at least moved into the background. Within the literary heritage of Indian civilization the texts sanctifying the norms of the non-martial twice-born received the lion's share of scholarly and official attention. This image of India survived the sufficiently violent if disorganized and politically unproductive events of the 1857 Rebellion and the partition agitation of 1905. It was out of such circumstances and materials that the British constructed the unsystematic theory of imperialism that legitimized and explained British domination and Indian subjection.

The things that Britons had to say about India varied so widely that any attempt to distil their judgements seems presumptuous. And yet, in the second half of the nineteenth century and at the turning of the twentieth, even as the nationalist movement was gathering strength and even as new policy decisions by Britons carried India farther toward self-government, distinctive themes in British judgements of India emerged. These judgements distinguished between certain categories of Indians, especially between 'masculine' and 'feminine' races, between the 'natural' Indian leaders and the unrepresentative *babus* ('clerks') 'posing' as leaders, and between the 'real' Indians and the assimilated ones. In each case, the categories carried within themselves implications as to who was and was not with the angels. These themes are to be found more in the pronouncements of men like Lytton, Fitzjames Stephen, John Strachey, and Curzon, who were hostile to Indian self-rule, than Ripon or Allen Octavian Hume, who were sanguine on the same topic.

The distinction between masculine and feminine races is an especially pervasive theme in this unsystematic imperialist theory and appeared most frequently in connection with the Bengalis, whom most Englishmen knew best and who had most swiftly responded to English culture. The late Joseph Schumpeter remarked in his account of imperialism that many imperialists were feudal atavisms, men whose hunger for the chivalric life could not be accommodated by the middle-class civilization of nineteenth-century Europe and who turned to the new frontiers of the colonies for the challenge they could not find at home.[2] The picture one has of the precompetition wallahs, the early nineteenth-century English in India, clodhopping Collectors, trusty rifles slung over their shoulders, boar spears in their left hands, confirms this view.[3] Such men felt impatient with the allegedly unathletic Bengalis, and admiration for the muscular and venturesome tribal people of the Northwest. Although many came for reasons less romantic than feudal nostalgia, because of family traditions or interest in a remunerative and respectable career, and although many pursued timid Victorian and bureaucratic lifestyles rather than feudal virtues, practitioners of the swashbuckling style shaped the dominant image of Englishmen in India and, by contrast, the mirror image of Indians.

When Kipling, sedentary ideologue of the swashbuckling style, rhymed his verse and found that 'East is East and West is West, and never the twain shall meet', he added that there was, however, *one* equalizer of national difference: courage. The frontier Pathan and the English soldier of his ballad could understand one another as warriors: 'But there is neither East nor West, Border, nor Breed, nor Birth/When two strong men stand face to face, though they come from the ends of the earth.'[4] Englishmen fancied, though, that this levelling element was available only among a limited number of Indians.

By the second half of the century, venturesome Englishmen went to Africa as often as to India; and if men of Strachey's and Curzon's era speak with contempt of Bengali 'feminism', it is as much with the ambivalent masculinity produced by *fin de siècle* British public school training as with the knowledge gained from experience with Bengali character. There is an empirical basis for their perception. Much of Indian society, particularly that part made up of the non-martial twice-born castes, does seem to tolerate a larger component of feminine qualities in its men than most Western societies do, even while homosexuality appears to be a less significant issue in India than in more 'masculine' countries.[5] The differences in cultural patterning were sharpened by the compulsions of roles. Occupying inferior bureaucratic positions in the context of their conquest, Indians were obliged to nurse compliance, with its female implications, as a condition of success. In any case, a substantial number of the English felt ill at ease, or thought they ought to, among Indians who demonstrated a notable lack of interest in proving their manhood by overt signs of martial, leather-faced masculinity. They much preferred the 'races'—such as the Sikhs and Mohammedans and Rajputs and Pathans—that exhibited a more familiar aggressive spirit.

For a passage that exhibits this particular theme, one may turn to John Strachey's book *India*, a standard training assignment for Indian Civil Service probationers just before the turn of the century. Describing the diverse races of India, it begins with a quote from Macaulay characterizing the Bengalis:

The physical organization of the Bengali is feeble even to effeminacy. He lives in a constant vapor bath. His pursuits are sedentary, his limbs delicate, his movements languid. During many ages he has been trampled upon by men of bolder and more hardy breeds .... His mind bears a singular analogy to his body. It is weak even to helplessness for purposes of manly resistance; but its suppleness and tact move the children of sterner climates to admiration not unmingled with contempt ....[6]

Strachey himself proceeded to distinguish the more vigorous Mohammedans from the feeble (Hindu) Bengalis, only to be drawn back in a kind of horrified fascination to his previous subject:

The Mohammedan peasantry of the eastern portion of the province are men of far robuster character .... It has often been said, and it is probably true, that Bengal is the only country in the world where you can find a great population among whom personal cowardice is looked upon as in no way disgraceful. This is no invention of their enemies: the Bengalis have themselves no shame or scruple in declaring it to be a fact .... This for such reasons that Englishmen who know Bengal, and the extraordinary effeminacy of its people, find it difficult to treat seriously many of the political declamations in which English speaking Bengalis are often fond of indulging.[7]

The contrast to the supple, vapour-bathed creatures was to be found among the 'martial' races, the Sikhs, Pathans, Rajputs, and Muslims, peoples who either by caste ethic, religion, or geographic circumstance adhered to a more overtly aggressive world view.

The distinction between the martial and non-martial was no invention of the English. It had accumulated ethical and historical meaning in Hindu caste structure and culture, which inculcated a non-violent perspective in some castes and an aggressive one in others. But in English minds at the end of the century, the distinction was stressed as much for its instrumental utility in the imperialist theory as for its academic interest as a description of caste or regional character. The 'martial' races for the most part adhered to the British raj, not because they were martial—the unlikely collaboration of the Pathans with Gandhi must have come as a fearful shock to many Britons—but for political considerations, the Rajputs because they were the princes of states whose autonomy was threatened by a self-governed India, the Muslims because they feared a Hindu majority in an independent India.

Those described as the non-martial races produced nationalism. The allegedly non-violent Brahmans, Vaishyas, and Kayasths provided the shock troops of the pen, office and pocketbook to publicize, organize, and finance the message of national freedom and regeneration. They launched nationalist polemics in dailies and pamphlets and provided the speakers in official and unofficial public forums to attack government with the Mill and Mazzini inculcated in Anglicized university classes. The Indians whom Englishmen most frequently encountered, once they had established themselves on the subcontinent and the memory of armed resistance had faded, were those recruited to fill bureaucratic roles. By virtue of their tasks, they represented a deceptively one-sided picture of the traditions of the castes from which they were drawn. Beyond this, Englishmen seem to have excluded from their conscious and articulated perceptions evidence conducing to a different picture. Bengali Kayasths have been local notables with fighting traditions as predators and protectors as well as bureaucrats for Moghul and British rulers.[8] Other Bengali castes who served the British also possessed differentiated traditions. But because the imperial capital, Calcutta, was in Bengal it was not unnatural for many secretariat-centred Britons to form their impressions about Indians on the basis of their relations with some Bengalis, generalizing from their civil servants to castes as a whole, and from their regional impressions to India. Such obvious anomalies as, for example, applying non-martial epithets to nationalist Chitpavan Brahmans who spoke for a Maharashtra that had given Britain much pain on the field of battle were easily and often overlooked.

The masculine-feminine distinction overlapped those between 'natural' leader and 'unnatural' babu and between the 'real' Indian and the assimilated Indian. What could be more 'natural' in a leadership position than a sturdy Rajput whose fighting arm maintained his dominion over the land won by his forefathers and who stood in paternal and autocratic relationship to traditional followers? What less 'natural' than the socially mobile men seeking to add political power to traditional priestly, commercial, and literary power, the non-martial Brahmans, Vaishyas, and Kayasths whose new status was often a product of English-created opportunities and who claimed they could lead a parochial and traditional rural India in which they had no long inherited leadership ties? These *nouveau arrivé* politicians and thinkers were not even 'real' Indians. They had cut themselves off from India by successfully embracing Western, or more particularly English, ideas and manners. Britons greeted their success in doing so with the special brutality reserved by established classes for new men: if they failed to emulate, they showed their incapacity to appreciate and strive for higher ideals; if they emulate badly, they were easy targets for ridicule; and if they successfully modeled themselves on their masters, they lost their integrity by trying to be something they 'really' were not.

What is most significant about these distinctions, and what makes them relevant to the consideration of Gandhi, is that nationalist Indians half-accepted them. No ideology legitimizing superior-inferior relations is worth its salt unless it wins at least a grudging assent in the minds of the dominated. By this measure the unsystematic theory of imperialism was a notable success. Within twenty years of the deliberate exclusion of United Province Brahmans from the Bengal Army because of their leading role in the rebellion of 1857, the idea that Brahmans lacked fighting qualities had become prevailing opinion. Reading recent history back into an undifferentiated past, Indians came to believe that they lacked valor and moral worth. As the young Gandhi put it, 'It must be at the outset admitted that the Hindus as a rule are notoriously weak.'[9] Why inferiority in arms, technology, and organization, circumstances related to particular historical contexts that may be reversed, has led colonial peoples to more essentialist conclusions about themselves is not entirely clear. The fact that they frequently did come to such conclusions was one of the most degrading consequences of colonialism. This state of mind—a sense of impotence combined with the fear of moral unworthiness arising from impotence—was not unique to India. It provided a central theme in other nationalist movements and led to attempts—to use the Chinese nationalist phrase—at self-strengthening.

The Indian fear that their weakness was innate was fed by the scientism of late nineteenth-century post-Darwinian race theory. Ethnologists, particularly ethnologists of India, were fond of imputing a biological fixity to culturally transmitted traits. Further, men of the nationalist generation were by no means sure that they were 'natural' leaders or that they were still Indians. A good bit of the Hindu fundamentalism that suddenly gripped men like Sri Aurobindo, raised in an emphatic Western tradition, may be related to this quest to be 'really' Indian.

One of the first items on the agenda of nationalism once it stepped beyond the loyal, reasonable, but ineffectual parliamentarism of the early nationalists and began to grapple with the moral and emotional issues of Indian self-definition was the creation of an answer to the charge of national impotence. A variety of answers were formulated—among them the calisthenic muscle-building and aggressive Hindu spirit-building launched by the gymnastic societies of militant Brahmans at Poona, and Dayanand's Arya Samaj path. 'Our young men must be strong', Swami Vivekananda urged a generation. 'Religion will come afterwards .... You will be nearer to Heaven through football than through the study of the Gita.'[10] There was the ascetic soldiery of the novel *Ananda Math*, training in a forest Ashram, brave, celibate, sturdy, disciplined, which provided a model for future Hindu fundamentalist parties and the blood deeds of a terrorist generation in Bengal and the Punjab.

There seems to be some perverse historical dialectic in violent Bengali nationalism, as though the young men of Calcutta were saying no to Macaulay's and Strachey's assertions of their physical ineffectualness. But their refusal failed to convince. Britain could in good conscience manage young men who threw bombs, especially if they threw them at ladies on a Sunday afternoon. Violence did not in fact turn out to be an effective basis for rallying a mass Indian nationalism. These proofs of courage helped, but they did not help most people, and they did not suffice in the long run to build a sense of national self-esteem. Gandhi's formulation proved a better statement of the issue of courage, and spoke to the issues of potency and integrity as well, even if it did not speak to or for the entire country. Large sections of opinion in Bengal, Punjab, and Maharashtra continued to subscribe to violent methods. Some classes, like middleclass Muslims or non-Brahmans in Madras and elsewhere found his style or his followers too Hindu or Sanskritic; some intellectuals found his religious style and symbolism repugnant to their secular and rationalist values. Still others rejected civil disobedience in the name of establishmentarian or reformist loyalism. Yet Gandhi's approach succeeded in capturing control of nationalist ideology.

Two issues of self-esteem that afflicted Indian nationalism, strength and weakness and cultural integrity, 'afflicted' Gandhi in his own life. He confronted them over a period of some thirty-five years before they were fully mastered; his 'solution' helped the generations who knew him to deal with them as well. For him the issues of courage and integrity were connected, and he resolved them together. Much of his early life was spent deciding whether he could best master himself and his environment by embracing in greater or lesser measure a British life path or by committing himself to a certain kind of Indian way. The dilemmas of the young Gandhi did in many ways approximate those of the surrounding generations. They can be found in his autobiography, a document that makes clear that Gandhi meant to be simultaneously judged as a private and a public person.

The book he called *The Story of My Experiments with Truth* poses a puzzle for his Western readers. They think they are to read the autobiography of a political leader. Instead they found something so heavily concerned with the Mahatma's 'private' activities that it might better have been entitled 'Confessions'. Confessions are acceptable in saints, like Augustine, or in professional sensualists, like De Sade, or understandable in a tortured exhibitionist like Rousseau. But in a political man? The relative privacy and reserve of Nehru's autobiography seem more appropriate, not merely as a matter of taste, but as a matter of the life emphasis suitable for a public man. The Western reader is apt to conclude that *My Experiments with Truth* are evidence that the saintly man mattered more than the politician and that Gandhi cared more for his private virtue than his public efforts. But that conclusion rests on the belief, quite pervasive in Western estimates of Gandhi, that saintly striving and political effectiveness must conflict, cannot be merged, and that anyone who seeks to do both must be a fraud either in his pretensions to be a politician or in his pretensions to be a saintly man.

My Experiments with Truth may provide evidence to support different conclusions.[11] In the Indian context it is very much a *political* document, central to Gandhi's political concerns in a double sense, the function it served for him and that which it served for his public. It is from his 'experiments in the spiritual field' that he believed he had 'derived such power as I possess for working in the political field'.[12] And it was not only he who believed this. Many of his immediate and distant followers attributed his political effectiveness to his personal virtue. When thousands assembled to hear him in remote, rural areas, they did so because he was preceded by his reputation for saintliness. When he wrote the autobiography as weekly installments for his Gujarati journal *Navajivan*, with translations in his English journal *Young India*, he gave wider currency to his attempts at self-perfection.[13] The Gujarati original sold nearly fifty thousand copies by 1940, and the English twenty-six thousand by 1948, making it a best seller in the context of India's literacy and income levels.[14] The instalments provided reassurance that the conditions of his political strength had been long preparing and severely tested, even while they conveyed moral aphorisms to young men who would be virtuous. The autobiography, then, must be read with a particularly sensitive ear, one that hears what he has to say concerning his diet, or his relations to his wife, and considers what it might mean for his political style and for how that style was received. To relegate these remarks to the category of personal frills and curiosities that constitute the gossip rather than the serious significance of a great man is to miss what was central to his leadership.

The small princely state of Porbandar, in Kathiawad, where he was born in 1869, lies on the Arabian Sea, in the centre of an area that has always been open to the trade of Persia, Arabia, and Africa, on the one hand, and the interior of India, on the other. He was born a Vaishya, a member of the Modh Baniya caste, one of many trading castes that have flourished in that region because of the hospitable conditions for commerce. His grandfather, whose memory had taken on mythical grandeur for the family by the time Gandhi was a child, served, as members of Vaishya castes often did in western India and the Rajput states, as prime minister of a princely state.[15] Gandhi's father did the same, though with less distinction.

Gujarat resembled the 'burned-over' district of western New York in its religious eclecticism and susceptibility to intense religious experience and leadership; it is from its soil that both Swami Dayanand and Mahatma Gandhi sprang. Strains of Hindu, Jain, and Muslim belief found expression in a variety of sects that sought to transcend the clash of faiths through synthesis or syncretism.[16] The religious culture of Gandhi's family reflected many of these ideological forces and syncretic tendencies. Followers of Vaishnavism, a bhakti (devotional) path, they nevertheless adhered strictly to the social and ritual requirements of Brahmanic Hinduism. Jain ideas and practice powerfully influenced Gandhi, too, particularly through his mother: asceticism in religious and secular life; the importance of vows for religious merit and worldly discipline; and *syadvad*, the doctrine that all views of truth are partial, a doctrine that lies at the root of satyagraha. Putliba (Gandhi's mother) descended from the Pranami, or Satpranami, sect, whose eighteenth-century founder, Prannath, attempted to unify Islam and Hinduism in a Supreme God. Gandhi remembers, in his only visit to the sect's temple, the absence of images and the Koranic-like writing on the walls. Followers of Prannath were forbidden addictive drugs, tobacco, wine, meat, and extramarital relations.[17]

Of the many strands in Gujarat's eclectic and often competing religious cultures, the most powerful in shaping Gandhi's outlook and style was bhakti, the devotional path to religious experience and salvation. 'The culture of Kathiawar', Pyarelal writes, 'is saturated with the Krishna legend'.[18] Ota Bapa, Gandhi's grandfather, was a follower of the Vallabhacharya sect of Vaishnavism whose Krishna-Bhakti doctrine of love of and surrender to God, personified by Lord Krishna, makes Him accessible to all regardless of social standing of cultural background. Both he and Gandhi's father habitually read *Tulsi Ramayana*, a text that became Gandhi's favourite too.[19] It told of Rama's love for his devotees, his graciousness, his compassion for the humble, and his care for the poor. These qualities of bhakti have enabled it to appeal to democratic constituencies and to become the carrier of implicit social criticism of the hierarchy, social distance, and exclusivity of Brahmanic Hinduism.[20] Its contempt for classical Hindu social categories was expressed in the low caste social back-ground of many of those attracted to it, both leaders and followers, and in the substance of bhakti songs, its main means of communication. If bhakti, like chiliastic Christianity but unlike Gandhi's political strategy and methods, sublimated social discontent rather than channelling it in a rebellious or revolutionary direction, the mature Gandhi yet found in the bhakti tradition an orientation and a style that suited him and those to whom he spoke.

Gandhi's mother painstakingly observed the more rigorous demands of her faith. Her strong ascetic demands on herself—'self-suffering', as Gandhi was to call it when he made it part of his political method—seem to have been a central virtue in the Gandhi home. Mrs Gandhi fasted frequently and practiced other austerities. 'During the four months of *chaturmas* Putliba lived on one meal a day and fasted on every alternate day.'[21] The concern for non-violence also received impetus from her: Jain monks, with their emphasis on the sanctity of all life, frequented the house.[22]

'Self-suffering' was important in other ways to the family. If one member of the household was angry with another, he would punish him by imposing some penalty on himself. Thus young Gandhi, angry because his family failed to summon to dinner a friend whom Gandhi wished to invite—it may have been a Muslim friend, with whom the family could not dine without transgressing the caste ethic—ceased to eat mangoes for the season, though they were his favorite fruit. The family was duly distressed.[23] On another occasion, Gandhi, finding difficulty in confessing a minor theft to his father, wrote him a note. 'In this note not only did I confess my guilt, but I asked adequate punishment for it, and closed with a request to him not to punish himself for my offense.'[24] It was the father's self-suffering, not punishment, that he claims to have feared most, although it is possible that he may in fact have feared being beaten. Gandhi's father, in turn, had used the threat of self-punishment in his relations with the ruler he served by announcing he would go without food and drink until arrangements were made for his transport out of the state when his master was reluctant to accept his resignation.[25] And above all, self-suffering in the sense of self-sacrifice was a dominant theme in the life of a boy who, for some three years, daily spent most of his after school hours nursing a sick father—a theme to which we shall return.

Gandhi pictures himself as a shy, fearful, and pathetic child. 'I was a coward. I used to be haunted by the fear of thieves, ghosts and serpents. I did not dare stir out of doors at night. Darkness was a terror to me.'[26] He feared school and his schoolfellows: 'I used to be very shy and avoided all company. My books and my lessons were my sole companions. To be at school at the stroke of the hour and to run back home as soon as school closed—that was my daily habit. I literally ran back, because I could not bear to talk to anybody. I was even afraid lest anyone should poke fun at me.'[27] He shunned the actively virile and competitive sports, possibly, as we will presently see, because he was obliged to shun them. He participated in neither cricket nor gymnastics, which a headmaster made compulsory in line with English public school models. Gandhi's father, entertaining a rather different idea of what was good for the character of a young man, had him exempted from sports so the boy might come home and nurse him.[28] It was uncompetitive, unassertive walking that the young man learned to like, and gardening.[29]

His wife Kasturba, who he married at the age of thirteen, was no help in enhancing the self-esteem of a fearful child. She was willful and self-assertive, did not reciprocate his passion, and resolutely refused to be the deferential Hindu wife he had hoped for, adding to his sense that he could not command where others had traditionally done so.[30] His self-description pictures him as a boy of thirteen or fourteen who had failed to develop a sense of personal competence.

The Mahatma's description of the boy he was probably overstresses his timid nature. All accounts of his youth speak of his enormous energy, as well as his considerable independence.[31] He was the favoured child of both mother and father.[32] Capable of a self-confident naughtiness, he ran away from those sent to find him, scattered the utensils of the home shrine, including the image of the deity, scrawled on the floor, and committed other spirited pranks.[33]

Yet to judge from his subsequent actions one must conclude that he found inadequate support in his immediate environment for solving the issue of personal competence. He felt himself insufficiently strong and courageous and longed to be brave and masterful. The caste ethic of the Modh Baniyas as well as the family's faith closed many paths of assertive self-expression that might seem obvious to a boy beginning to become a man. Sexual expression, although formally sanctioned in marriage, was frowned upon. What one might call culinary masculinity, the eating of meat, was equally discouraged in a society that was vegetarian. The caste ethic, to say nothing of the local Jain influence stressing absolute non-violence, de-emphasized physical aggressiveness, which was in any case against young Mohandas' nature.[34] Not that Gandhi's environment provided no opportunities for self-assertion. The merchant castes of west India have found sufficient scope for assertiveness, even aggressiveness, within the bounds of commercial or bureaucratic caste roles. Members of Gandhi's family, despite the rhetoric of non-violence, allowed themselves aggressive behaviour, including his mother's willingness to see her boys defend themselves and Kaba Gandhi's willingness to beat an offender. But what the opportunities were is less important than how they appeared to Mohandas; he thought himself restricted.

Gandhi staged a massive revolt against his family, caste, and religious ethic in an effort to gain a more helpful perspective. Between the ages of thirteen and sixteen, he undertook a resolute programme of transgressing every article of the codes that mattered to those around him. The counsellor in revolt was Sheikh Mehtab, a Muslim, significantly enough, representing an ethic quite different from his own, the ethic of one of the 'martial races'.

The friendship was the most significant and enduring of Gandhi's youth, lasting well into his South African years. He sent Mehtab money from England[35] and brought him to South Africa. Mehtab came to live with him there until Gandhi, discovering his friend was bringing home prostitutes, threw him out.[36]

It is usual among Gandhi biographers to endorse the Mahatma's description of the relationship, that he took up Mehtab in order to reform him.[37] It is true in that Gandhi all his life tried to overcome men like Mehtab by 'reforming' them. But there was more to the relationship. On the evidence of Gandhi's own words, Mehtab was a model, and a model from whom he only gradually liberated himself. Mehtab was everything Gandhi was not— strong, athletic, self-confident, lusty, bold. As Gandhi writes, he was 'hardier, physically stronger, and more daring .... He could run long distances and extraordinarily fast. He was an adept in high and long jumping. He could put up with any amount of corporal punishment. He would often display his exploits to me and, as one is always dazzled when he sees in others the qualities he lacks himself, I was dazzled ....'[38]

Mehtab encouraged Gandhi to eat meat, saying that it would have a physiological effect in lending him new strength. 'You know how hardy I am, and how great a runner too. It is because I am a meat-eater.'[39] But there was a larger social context to the meat-eating issue. It had become attached to the problem of cultural virility for people other than Gandhi. Many people in Kathiawad, according to Gandhi, thought meat-eating was, so to speak, responsible for British imperialism, being the essence that made the Englishman strong. 'Behold the mighty Englishman; He rules the Indian small; Because being a meat eater; He is five cubits tall ...' went the ditty of Gandhi's school days. 'I wished to be strong and daring and wanted my countrymen also to be such, so that we might defeat the English and make India free.'[40] Actually, Gandhi did not have to look to British culture to discover that meat-eating 'produced' courage. The fighting castes of India, particularly the Kshatriyas, have always eaten meat, and it has always been thought to contribute to their strength. But meat-eating was not the only kind of demonstration of strength in which Mehtab supported Gandhi. There was also a brothel episode, presumably meant to lead Gandhi to a more zestful lustiness than the guilty pleasures of his legitimate bed. But Gandhi suffered a Holden Caulfieldesque experience of tentative approach and horrified retreat.[41]

This rebellion was a search for courage and competence, an attempt to overcome fearfulness and shyness through following an ethic other than the one to which Gandhi had been born, an ethic practiced by Englishmen and the 'martial races.' But it should be pointed out that the search for courage itself exacted a courage of another kind that the ultimately dependent Mehtab did not have. To revolt in secret against strongly held family prejudices over a period of three years required considerable inner strength, strength of the kind the mature Gandhi would have approved, though in the service of other objectives.[42] He demonstrated the same kind of courage, although he described himself as still a coward, when at the age of nineteen, after his father's death, he decided to go to England for an education. He was obliged to confront the opposition of the caste council at Bombay. In an open meeting where he appears to have been afflicted by little of the shyness he always attributed to himself, he faced the elders who forbade his English trip and who threatened all the sanctions of outcasting if he defied their verdict. 'I am helpless', he told them.[43]

In some respects, the English experience, during which Gandhi studied for the matriculation exam and was eventually admitted to the bar, represented an attempt to solve the issue of competence and self-esteem by acquiring a new cultural style and by escaping cultural ties that he still deemed in some way responsible for his incompetence and weakness. For three months after his arrival, he dedicated himself to a systematic effort to become an English gentleman, ordering clothing of the correct cut and a top hat in the Army and Navy stores and evening clothes in Bond Street, worrying about his unruly hair, which defied the civilizing brush, acquiring from his brother a gold double watch chain, spending time before the mirror in the morning tying his cravat, and taking dancing lessons so that he might be fit for elegant social intercourse and violin lessons to cultivate an ear for Western music so that he might hear the rhythm that escaped him when dancing. In the hope of overcoming his incapacity to communicate effectively, he took elocution lessons only to find that they helped him in neither public nor private speaking.[44]

Some of this systematic attempt to approximate urbane English manners stuck for a long time: the pictures of the young Gandhi, as a sixty-thousand-dollar-a-year lawyer in the South Africa of 1900[45]—one is apt to forget that he was capable of that kind of worldly success—which present a punctilious late-Edwardian appearance, bear witness to the experience. So did his English, which, after three years in South Africa, bore the marks of relatively cool English understatement. The writings of his early maturity strike quite a different note from the un-English moralizing of the autobiography, written after he had become the Mahatma and had returned to more Indian modes in all respects.[46] His family's clothing and the accoutrements of his house were Anglicized on his return to India. Less superficial aspects of English culture left a permanent mark. Throughout his life he remained a barrister, deeply influenced by ideas embedded within British law, administration, and political values, including respect for correct procedure, evidence, and rights, and for the distinctions and conflicts between private and public obligations.

But the attempts at Anglicization failed to satisfy Gandhi, partly because he could not make a go of it, partly because it didn't 'feel' right to him when he could. Besides, the England he met was not the England of public schools and playing fields, of clubs and sporting society, but an England closer to Kathiawad, an England of vegetarian Evangelicals and Theosophical reformers, an England suffering like Kathiawad from the effects of industrialization and protesting against them.[47] After three months he 'gave up' much of the Anglicization effort, although less than he suggests in the autobiography, and began a very gradual return to a personal style of life more in keeping with the ascetic, self-denying, and non-violent ethic that he had left behind when he began his rebellion at home almost seven years before.

He started to live very thriftily, partly through economic necessity, partly because the change 'harmonized my inward and outward life'.[48] Earlier, he had restricted himself to vegetarian restaurants because of a vow to his mother but had remained committed to meat-eating in the interest of reforming the Indian character.[49] Now he embraced vegetarianism by choice in a spirit that stressed a different kind of strength than that promised by meat. He began to rejoice in the effort of denying himself, in the strength of mastering his pleasures. He walked rather than rode to his studies[50] and took up moral and philosophic writings seriously for the first time, although more in the spirit of one seeking confirmation than of one seeking. He was moved by the biblical exhortation 'that ye resist not evil' and by passages urging self-suffering as a mode of conversion. Carlyle's hero impressed him as much by his austere living as by his bravery and greatness. He noted passages in the Gita condemning the senses and concluded 'that renunciation was the highest form or religion'.[51]

In this time lay the beginnings—it took another two decades to complete the process—of a rejection of any solutions to his personal dilemmas that were radically foreign to his early experiences in the Gujarat cultural setting of family, caste, and religion. Solutions drawn from England or from features of Indian culture closer to English culture began to recede. In this period lay the beginning, too, of his construction of an Indian definition for himself, a definition expressed in the Gandhi who in 1906 began political action in South Africa and in 1920 took charge of the Indian nationalist movement. In the long run, these new experiments lead to the development of a personal style consistent with a traditional Indian model rather than with the model of a London-touched barrister, which other Indian nationalists found congenial. The early experiments in vegetarian restaurants and the considered return to an un-English asceticism were not unrelated to those later appeals and techniques of agitation that touched traditional Indian sensibilities and perceptions.

By the end of the English experience, Gandhi had begun to learn that the English solution was not the one to resolve those personal dilemmas that had accompanied him to England. The man who returned to India, and spent several years in practice there, felt himself still a failure. 'But notwithstanding my study, there was no end to my helplessness and fear.'[52] Though he was a barrister-at-law, more highly qualified than a great many of the traditional *vakils* who had no such elevated training, he knew little Indian law and could not even master the fundamental skill of the courtroom lawyer—public speaking. In England, he had made several attempts to give public speeches, generally at vegetarian societies. Each time he failed.[53] On one occasion, to encourage himself, he decided to recite the anecdote of Addison, as diffident as Gandhi, who rose on the floor of Commons and tried to open his speech by saying, 'I conceive'. Three times the unfortunate man tried to open with the same phrase but could get no further. A wag rose and said: 'The gentleman conceived thrice but brought forth nothing.' Gandhi thought the story amusing; unfortunately, in his recitation of the anecdote he, too, got stuck and had to sit down abruptly.[54]

His first court case in India was a disaster; obliged to cross-examine plaintiff's witness in a petty case, he was unable to bring himself to open his mouth. 'My head was reeling and I felt as though the whole court was doing likewise. I could think of no question to ask. The judge must have laughed, and the *vakils* no doubt enjoyed the spectacle.'[55] His model in the law had something in common with the bold Sheikh Mehtab: Pherozeshah

Mehta, a strong and effective barrister, who dominated the Bombay bar with his vigorous courtroom style. Gandhi had heard that he roared like a lion in court. But the model seemed increasingly out of reach. He retreated from court work altogether to return, more or less defeated, to the backwaters of provincial Kathiawad, where he took up briefing cases for other lawyers, earning a respectable three hundred rupees per month but feeling that he was getting nowhere.[56] Yet a 23-year-old Indian in 1892 who considered himself a failure at three hundred rupees per month had high standards. At 24, a personal tiff with the political agent—an Englishman—at Porbandar convinced him that he had no future there.[57] He determined to retreat from the Indian situation. 'I wanted somehow to leave India.'[58] The flight seems to have come at the lowest moment of his life.

The low point was also the turning point. His first experiences in South Africa, where he went as a barrister for a Muslim firm, persuaded him that the humiliation and oppression of Indians in South Africa were worse than in India. He was discriminated against on trains and beaten by a white coachman who laughed at his legalistic insistence upon his rights.[59] Discussing his experience with other Indians, he discovered that the South African Indian community had suffered such humiliations for many years, pocketing insults as part of the conditions of trade. The discovery had a curious effect on his outlook. He recognized, rather suddenly it seems from the autobiography, that the skills that he had acquired in recent years, particularly a facile use of English, a familiarity with law codes and legal processes, and a belief that English justice must be enforced, were desperately needed and lacking among the Indian community. The South African Indians consisted of a merchant community and a much larger group of Tamil indentured labourers. Both lacked political consciousness and skills and were ineffectual at dealing with any part of the environment that transcended their economic tasks.[60] In this setting Gandhi, as the only Indian barrister, found himself to be the entire Indian professional middle classes.

Skills that in India had seemed ordinary here seemed extraordinary and enhanced Gandhi's self-estimate with an apocalyptic abruptness. Within three weeks of his arrival in South Africa, the shy boy of 24 suddenly called a public meeting of all Indians in Pretoria for the common discussion of their wrongs and oppressions in the Transvaal.[61] With a new-found authority, the man who had been unable to speak in public rose to sum up the problems of the community and propose an agenda for its amelioration. One has the sense that the overwhelming humiliations of the community around him suddenly carried him beyond the self-consciousness of his own failings, in a manner reminiscent of the 'cured' stutterer in Nikos Kazantzakis' *The Greek Passion* ('He Who Must Die'). While speaking in court was an exercise that would show whether he measured up to the standard set by famous barristers like Pherozeshah Mehta, a performance profoundly disturbing to a precarious ego, this speech had, ostensibly, nothing to do with his own standing. The new context, service, seems to have made it possible for the young man to do what he could not do when his own reputation was at stake. That service could lend him the effectiveness and potency he otherwise lacked must have had much to do with the life path he chose.[62] Away from home and the omnipresent memorials of early failure and performing a new task, he writes, 'I acquired some measure of my capacity.'

The South African experience helped him recognize that his salvation lay in devoting himself to the problems of those more helpless than he. As he did so, his capacity to act effectively and courageously grew. The techniques that expressed his new sense of competence rallied Indians to refute English charges of cowardice without, however, repairing to the English standard of courage. His style of leadership confounded the English charge that the new Indian middle classes had lost touch with their own people without, however, alienating those classes.

Notes

[1] Jawaharlal Nehru, *The Discovery of India*, New York: John Day Company, 1946, pp. 361–2.

[2] Joseph Schumpeter, 'The Sociology of Imperialism', in Heinz Norden and Paul Sweezy (trans.), *Social Classes and Imperialism*, New York: Augustus M. Kelley, 1951, pp. 65–98.

[3] Philip Woodruff's two volume work, *The Men Who Ruled India*, London: Jonathan Cape, 1953–4, admirably develops this picture.

[4] Rudyard Kipling, 'The Ballad of East and West', in *Rudyard Kipling's Verse*, New York: Anchor Books, 1940, p. 233.

[5] Percival Spear's *The Nabobs* (London, 1932), pp. 198–9, lists twenty-six quotations expressing European sentiments about Indians in the eighteenth century. Of these, ten include such allusion to weakness or feminine qualities as the following: 'Indians are a very sober people and effeminate ...' (Sieur Luillier, *A Voyage to the East Indies* (1702), p. 285), or the more perceptive, 'Tis a mistake to conclude that the natives of Hindustan want courage .... With respect to passive courage the inhabitants of these countries are perhaps possessed of a much larger share of it than

those of our own' (Major Rennell, Diary, Home Miscellaneous Series, No. 765, p. 182 (20 January 1768)). A.L. Basham has pointed out in *The Wonder That Was India*, London: Sidgwick and Jackson, 1954, p. 172, that homosexuality was rare in ancient India and certainly never became as widespread or legitimate as in Greece or Rome. What precisely the nature of contemporary behaviour is would have to be a matter of inquiry, but it is rarely mentioned in nineteenth- or twentieth-century accounts. Morris Carstairs suggests that it occurred in his village among children, was perhaps practiced on occasion among adults, and played a role in phantasy (*The Twice Born: A Study of a Community of High-Caste Hindus*, London: Hogarth Press, 1957, p. 167).

[6] John Strachey, *India, Its Administration and Progress*, London: Macmillan, 1888, pp. 411–12.

[7] Ibid., pp. 412–13.

[8] For the Traditions of the Bengali Kayasths, see Ronald Inden, 'The Kayasthas of Bengal: A Social History of Four Castes' (Ph.D. thesis, Department of History, University of Chicago, 1967).

[9] 'The Vegetarian', 28 February 1891, in *The Collected Works of Mahatma Gandhi*, Delhi, 1958—, I, p. 30.

[10] Swami Vivekananda, 'Lectures from Colombo to Almora', in *The Complete Works of Swami Vivekananda*, 3d ed.; Almora, 1922, III, 242.

[11] Erik H. Erikson has suggested the ways in which the autobiography acts not merely as a recollection of the past but as a cautionary meant to advise and guide young men, 'for the purpose of recreating oneself in the image of one's own method; and ... to make that image convincing' ('Gandhi's Autobiography: The Leader as a Child', *American Scholar*, XXXV, Autumn, 1966, p. 636).

[12] *Gandhi's Autobiography*, or, *The Story of My Experiments with Truth*, trans. from the Gujarati by Mahadev Desai, Washington, D.C., 1948, p. 4.

[13] Ibid., p. 3.

[14] This is in addition to the eight thousand copies the *Navajivan* and *Young India* serializations were selling when Gandhi wrote the autobiography (ibid., pp. ii, iii, and 581.)

[15] Prabhudas Gandhi, *My Childhood with Gandhi*, Ahmedabad: Navajivan Publishing House, 1957, Chapter 2.

[16] Pyarelal (Nair), *Mahatma Gandhi: The Early Phase*, Ahmedabad: Navajivan Publishing House, 1965, I, p. 173.

[17] Ibid., p. 214.

[18] Ibid., p. 117.

[19] Gandhi's grandfather Uttamchand was a follower of Khaki Bapa, of the order of Ramanand, a bhakta devoted to Rama; both Uttamchand and Gandhi's father, Kaba Gandhi, devoted their later years to reading the Ramayana (ibid., I, p. 179).

[20] The opposition between the bhakti cults and Brahmanic Hinduism is modified by the fact that orthodoxy, too, accepted bhakti as a path to God. See especially the Bhagavad Gita.

[21] D.G. Tendulkar, *Mahatma: Life of Mohandas Karamchand Gandhi*, Bombay: V.K. Jhaveri, 1951—, I, p. 28.

[22] Pyarelal, *Mahatma Gandhi: The Early Phase*, I, p. 214.

[23] Tendulkar, *Mahatma*, I, p. 31.

[24] *Gandhi's Autobiography*, p. 41. Gandhi's sister Raliatbehn, on the other hand, recalls that Gandhi was quite nervous about the prospect of a beating for this offence. (P. Gandhi, *My Childhood with Gandhi*, p. 22).

[25] P. Gandhi, *My Childhood with Gandhi*, p. 22.

[26] *Gandhi's Autobiography*, p. 33.

[27] Ibid., p. 15. Gandhi's relations with his age companions may have been affected by the fact that he would not fall in with the usual rough and tumble of youthful life. He could not be relied upon to tell white lies to cover up group pranks and would not strike back in any encounter. Whatever moral precocity was involved in these deviations received some positive recognition by his schoolmates, who used him regularly as a referee in games. These recollections spring from Gandhi's sister's memories (P. Gandhi, *My Childhood with Gandhi*, pp. 27–8). The memories are retrospective, recalled after Gandhi became 'Mahatma', and may deserve a little caution.

[28] *Gandhi's Autobiography*, p. 28.

[29] Pyarelal, *Mahatma Gandhi: The Early Phase*, I, p. 197.

[30] 'She could not go anywhere without my permission ... and Kasturbai was not the girl to brook any such thing. She made it a point to go out whenever and wherever she liked. More restraint on my part resulted in more liberty being taken by her ...' (ibid., p. 22).

[31] 'The first three children of Kaba Kaka and Putliba gave them little trouble, but young Mohan was a bit of a problem. Not that he was mischievous or one to annoy his elders. He was not a difficult child but he was exceedingly active and energetic. He was never at one place for long. As soon as he was able to walk about, it became difficult to keep track of him' (P. Gandhi, *My Childhood with Gandhi*, p. 25).

[32] 'I was my mother's pet child, first because I was the smallest of her children ...' (Gandhi as cited by Pyarelal, *Mahatma Gandhi: The Early Phase*, I, p. 193). Kaba Gandhi believed Mohandas would take his place: 'Manu will be the pride of our family; he will bring lustre to my name' (ibid., I, p. 202).

[33] Ibid., p. 195.

[34] Young Mohandas did not like to fight or hit back (ibid., p. 195).

[35] Ibid., p. 211.

[36] Louis Fischer, *The Life of Mahatma Gandhi*, London: Jonathan Cape, 1951, p. 75.

[37] *Gandhi's Autobiography*, p. 31.

[38] Ibid., pp. 32–3.

[39] Ibid., p. 32.

[40] Ibid., p. 34.

[41] Ibid., p. 37.

[42] 'The opposition to and abhorrence of meat-eating that existed in Gujarat among the Jains and Vaishnavas were to be seen nowhere else in India or outside in such strength' (ibid., p. 34.)

[43] Ibid., p. 58. The account that he gave to an interviewer from *The Vegetarian*, 20 June 1891, is slightly different. There he says he told the senior patel, who told him crossing the waters was against caste rules: '... If our brethren can go as far as Aden, why could not I go to England?' (*The Collected Works of Mahatma Gandhi*, I, p. 59).

[44] *Gandhi's Autobiography*, pp. 70–1. Gandhi in London 'was wearing a high silk top hat burnished bright, a Gladstonian collar, stiff and starched; a rather flashy tie displaying almost all the colors of the rainbow under which there was a fine striped silk shirt. He wore as his outer clothes a morning coat, a double breasted vest, and dark striped trousers to match. And not only patent leather boots but spats over them. He carried leather gloves and a silver mounted stick, but wore no spectacles. He was, to use the contemporary slang, a nut, a masher, a blood, a student more interested in fashion and frivolity than in his studies' (quoted in B.R. Nanda, *Mahatma Gandhi: A Biography*, London: Oxford University Press, 1958, p. 28).

[45] Fischer, in *The Life of Mahatma Gandhi*, says Gandhi earned five to six thousand pounds a year (p. 74).

[46] See, for example, 'The Grievances of the British Indians in South Africa—The Green Pamphlet,' written in 1896, in *The Collected Works of Mahatma Gandhi*, II, pp. 1–53.

[47] Chandra Devanesan, *The Making of the Mahatma*, Madras, 1969.

[48] *Gandhi's Autobiography*, p. 75.

[49] Ibid., p. 67.

[50] Ibid., p. 73.

[51] Ibid., p. 92.

[52] Ibid., p. 105.

[53] Ibid., p. 83.

[54] Ibid., p. 84.

[55] Ibid., p. 120.

[56] Ibid., p. 123.

[57] Ibid., p. 125.

[58] Ibid., p. 129.

[59] Ibid., pp. 140–1, 143–4.

[60] Gandhi's first South African client told him: 'What can we understand in these matters? We can only understand things that affect our trade .... We are after all lame men, being unlettered. We generally take in newspapers simply to ascertain the daily market rates, etc. What can we know of legislation? Our eyes and ears are the European attorneys here' (ibid., p. 173).

[61] Ibid., p. 157.

[62] A contributing factor in the success of the first speech may have been that Gandhi spoke in Gujarati. His audience consisted mainly of Memon Muslims, and 'very few amongst his audience knew English' (Tendulkar, *Mahatma*, I, p. 46; see also *Gandhi's Autobiography*, p. 158). It is interesting that when Gandhi returned to India in 1896, with three years of South African successes behind him, he failed once again to manage a public speech before a large Bombay audience (*Gandhi's Autobiography*, p. 216).

6

Gandhi and the New Courage

Indian nationalism had tried the paths of loyal constitutionalism and terrorist violence and found them wanting. Gandhi's answer was satyagraha ('truth force'), expressed through non-violent but non-constitutional direct action.[1] Satyagraha compels adherence to its cause not by mobilizing superior numbers or force but by mobilizing a general recognition of the justice of its cause. Civil disobedience under certain circumstances compels those who rule to confront the choice of enforcing what they themselves may suspect is injustice or altering policy and practice; for Gandhi, satyagraha was a means to awaken the best in an opponent. To resist, to retaliate or strike back if beaten, jailed, or killed, was at once to lack courage and to abandon the means to the common realization of justice. Satyagraha, Gandhi said, was 'the vindication of truth not by infliction of suffering on the opponent but on oneself.' Non-violent resistance to injustice is not unique to the East, much less to India, but it had an extraordinary appeal there during the three decades preceding Indian independence in 1947. Neither constitutional petition and protest nor violent acts of resistance and terrorism had been able to command popular support or unite nationalist leaders. Satyagraha did both, in part because Gandhi used it in relation to issues—urban labour grievances, rural tax relief, protests against untouchability—that mobilized new groups for nationalism, and in part because it expressed deeply embedded cultural values in an understandable and dramatic form. Central to these values were a definition of courage and a view of conflict resolution.

The prevailing Western definitions of courage, as well as definitions embraced by those Indians Englishmen called 'the martial races,' have generally stressed masterly aggressiveness, taking as their model the soldier willing and eager to charge with fixed bayonet the numerically superior enemy in a heroic act of self-assertion. The military analogy is merely the most extreme symbolic expression of a whole set of cultural attitudes—an aggressive, 'meat-eating', masterful personal style, overt self-expressiveness, self-confident lustiness—that go well beyond military action. The opposite cultural attitude, cultivated by sections of the explicitly and self-consciously non-martial castes and communities of Indian society, draws on self-control rather than self-expression, on self-suffering, and calls for restraint of the impulse to retaliate. It is misleading to see this willingness to suffer as a failure of will or surrender to fatalism, although it may have that meaning as well. Self-restraint may be and has been another way of mastering the environment, including the human environment. The Hindu who sat on *dharna* (a protest through fasting) at the house of an alleged oppressor, starving himself, was doing the very reverse of submitting. His courage was in some ways like that which Gandhi stressed. Not to retreat, to suffer pain without retaliation, to stay and suffer more in order to master a hostile or stubborn human reality—these expressions captured important elements of what Gandhi asked of India. Such courage relies for its effectiveness on the moral sensibilities, or at least capacity for guilt, of the more powerful perpetrator of injustice, using his conscience to reach and win him. Gandhi turned the moral tables on the English definition of courage by suggesting that aggression was the path to mastery of those without self-control, non-violent resistance the path of those with control.[2]

This kind of courage tends to go with other cultural practices and attitudes—vegetarianism, asceticism—found especially among the non-fighting twice-born castes, Brahmans, Vaishyas, and Kayasths, who provided the core of nationalist leadership.[3] The traditions of these castes were not, of course, uniform. The Brahmans of Maharashtra have often supported violent nationalism, as did the merchant castes of Punjab or the Kayasths and Vaidyas of Bengal. Tilak, Lala Lajpat Rai, and Subhas Bose mobilized different potentials in the same social groups, but with less effect. The Gandhian definition was more resonant with their style and capabilities. The more aggressive kind of courage is, of course, no monopoly of the West but has its counterpart in the ethic of certain Indian castes and communities, just as self-suffering courage has its Western equivalents. The Christian injunction to turn the other cheek, which so impressed Gandhi, is a compelling version of self-suffering—although it is perhaps more closely related to the tender ideals of meekness and love than the acerbic one of self-control.

Self-suffering courage is susceptible of two rather different moral emphases, one that is quite as aggressive in spirit, if not in form, as violence, and one without such overtones. As the traditional weapon of the Brahman, whose protest against oppressive rule was often fasting, self-injury, or even suicide, which would draw upon the oppressor the supernatural sanctions of having caused the death of a Brahman, it substituted spiritual violence for physical.[4] As used in many Indian homes, not merely Gandhi's, where family members sometimes expressed protest by abstaining from meals, it may substitute psychological violence for physical. For Gandhi, such satyagraha was nothing more than the passive resistance of the weak.[5] Satyagraha in his sense was to be purged of these connotations and infused with a positive moral task. Satyagrahis (those who practice satyagraha) were to act so as to elicit the better element in an opponent, rather than the worst, as violence would do. Ill will was the enemy of this effort and hence of satyagraha. To purge oneself of ill will was a task requiring strengths most men found hard to command. Gandhi demanded no less of himself and his followers, although he was under no illusion that either he or they always, or even usually, succeeded.

But beyond the distinction between English and Indian definitions of courage lie other cultural differences concerning the honorable and 'moral' way to manage conflict in general.[6] The belief that conflicts are best resolved through the frank confrontation of alternatives, the clear articulation of opposites, their clash and the victory of one alternative over the other, is embodied, at least in theory, in much of the adversary legal tradition of the West and in its political life. Traditional Indian ideas of conflict management in both politics and law, tend to stress arbitration, compromise, and the de-emphasis of overt clashes, of victories and defeats. The rhetoric, if not always the practice, of Indian foreign policy, the continued striving to 'restore' consensus processes in village affairs, and opposition to the 'evil' of partisanship are receding but still significant expressions of these traditional norms. Their desirability is related to the psychological attraction of self-control and harmlessness over aggressive self-assertion.

Resistance to the notion of conflict arises partly from the romance and reality that surround the image of the village in the minds of many Indians. When the council of five, the panchayat, spoke as one, it was said to be the voice of God; it gave expression to the consensus of the traditional moral order. If the consensus was often merely a rhetorical one that obscured real divisions, it was nonetheless valued. The apotheosized village republic, representative, deliberative, and harmonious, rested on the moral basis of *dharma*, of sanctified custom in which rank and distance, privilege and obligation, rights and duties, were acquired at birth and legitimized by religion.

Studies of village government document the resistance to adversary processes.[7] The consensual process, unlike the adversary, assumes that law will be found (not made) and decisions arrived at by some traditionally recruited body, such as the general panchayat dealing with village affairs or the caste panchayat dealing with the affairs of a single jati (subcaste). All who should be heard will be, and discussion will reveal what most, if not all, agree is the proper disposition of the problem. Discussion, according to one village study, continued until a satisfactory consensus could be arrived at or, in the event of a standoff between two powerful elements, until it was obvious that no agreement was possible.[8] In the meeting's ideal form there remains no opposition, for all have been convinced of the wisdom and necessity of the particular decision.[9] Support is determined not by a show of hands but by judging the participants' sense of moral fitness. Evidence, 'witness', and deliberation are important in establishing consensus, but without a common and intimate moral universe that legitimized the domination of some and the subjection of others, traditional consensus would be hard to realize.

Partisanship expressed through the adversary process in politics, government, and law proceeds on the quite different assumption that there are a variety of 'interested' answers and that the best one will emerge from the conflict of alternatives. The better each side mobilizes its arguments and resources and support, the better the victorious solution will be. The psychological quality of adversary relationships is self-interested and contentious; in a legislature, election, or court, one side wins and the other side loses. The relationship between opponents, at a certain level, is meant to be critical and combative, not conciliatory and accommodating; the arm's length relationship is an aspect of the adversary mode. Compromise, although it is often resorted to, is not the overt objective. There is a final accounting, a choosing between alternatives, and disagreement is exposed and emphasized by quantification through a vote.

To many Indians of Gandhi's time and since, establishing a consensus appeared to sustain and foster community solidarity and mutual accommo-dation, whereas adversary proceedings in politics and law appeared to sacrifice them by legitimizing partial statements of community purpose and interest. But this is too extreme a juxtaposition: to be viable, adversary proceedings must rest upon substantial, if sometimes, latent community agreement on values and procedure, and the process of consensual agreement often involves latent partiality and coercion. In the Indian village context especially, consensus was frequently acquiescence in the self-interested rule of a 'dominant caste'.[10] But the matter of appearance is important; many Indians view the 'traditional' consensual way as moral and the 'modern' adversary way as evil.

The suspicion of overt hostility seems to be as significant for the nation as the village and for the unconscious as the conscious. In his psychoanalytic study of the twice-born castes in a Rajasthan village, Morris Carstairs found two basic and interdependent patterns—one of mistrust and hostility, which destroyed mutual confidence and often erupted into violence, the other of self-restraint, which characteristically depended on a third person to intervene and bring the antagonists back to their senses. Here human conflict was evidently feared because of its propensity to release uncontrollable passions. 'When feelings of ill-will did find open expression ... the utter collapse of self-control [was] all the more remarkable for its contrast with the formality of normal exchanges.' The participants 'abandoned themselves to anger with a completeness which previously had been familiar to me only in the temper tantrums of young children. I was able to understand for the first time the epidemic of massacre and counter-massacre which had swept over this "non-violent" country only a few years ago.'[11] The severe emphasis on self-restraint, on formality and harmlessness, may well be allied to the omnipresent fear of loss of control. In Carstairs' account, it was the peacemaker who restored restraint by intervening 'between the disputants, reminding them how wrong it was to give way to anger, urging self-control and compromise'. He found the third-party role of mediator to be so regular of conflict in the village that it recurred in dreams. It was considered better to be the 'third party' to a dispute than the victor; 'in time, the verb *samjhana* (to impart instruction) became recognizable as an element in everyone's experience, providing a counterpoint to the prevailing distrust. The role of moral adviser, counseling moderation and control of one's passions, is one which compels an impulse to obey, and at the same time, a surrender, however temporary, of one's customary suspiciousness.'[12]

Gandhi began to embody these cultural themes concerning courage and conflict resolution in techniques of action relevant to his countrymen's problems in South Africa. Concluding his first big case, the one that had called him there, he believed be had found the path to his future work. Not only had the case been settled by arbitration out of court, but Gandhi had persuaded his client to take payment from the loser in installments so as not to ruin him. Both actions could have been justified on the mundane ground of ordinary legal or business prudence, but Gandhi did not choose to view the settlement in that light: 'My joy was boundless. I had learnt the true practice of law. I had learnt to find out the better side of human nature and to enter men's hearts. I realized that the true function of a lawyer was to unite parties driven asunder.'[13] The principle of adversary proceedings, that out of the conflict of two parties, each of whom tries to win by scoring off his opponent, justice will emerge, seemed to him a doubtful doctrine. 'The counsel on both sides were bound to rake up points of law in support of their own clients',[14] he complained. Solutions based on compromise seemed better because they rested on mutual confidence rather than institutionalized conflict.

A more mature Gandhi would formulate the approach in terms of *ahimsa*, the doctrine of harmlessness or non-violence translated into opposition to destructive conflict in general, not merely to physical violence. Had Gandhi developed a different, more aggressive personal style, had he been less diffident, bolder in court and public, he might have taken a different view of the issue of courage and the adversary mode and found himself with or at the head of Indians of quite a different sort. As it was, he turned what he once considered a failing in himself, an incapacity for aggressiveness, into a virtue and an effective political technique. His solutions were of a piece with the renewed concern for the harmlessness ethic of his youth and opposed to the path of aggressive self-assertion that he had tried and rejected.

What Gandhi concluded about the law, he applied thereafter to all other situations of conflict, including his struggles in South Africa and in India. The thread of compromise, of avoiding conflict to find areas of agreement that could produce settlement, remained central to his technique, sometimes to the despair of his followers, some of whom wanted to confront the issue and the enemy by taking a clear stand. To this technique, he added the 'witness' of self-suffering. A coercive technique and a means of psychic survival in his home, it was reminiscent of the traditional means that the non-martial classes used to cope with opposition and hostility. When Gandhi fasted or his followers suffered themselves to be beaten, he and they demonstrated the courage required for self-control rather than self-assertion. For those who described such behaviour as 'unmanly,' Gandhi reformulated the imputation. Such non-violence expressed not the impotence of man but the potency of woman: 'Has she not greater intuition, is she not more self-sacrificing, has she not greater powers of endurance, has she not greater courage?'[15] And the courage of non-violence was, moreover, apt. 'Self-suffering' touched the conscience of Englishmen as it might not that of some other imperial rulers.

Notes

[1] For a full-length and sympathetic treatment of Gandhi's philosophic and tactical contributions, see Joan V. Bondurant, *The Conquest of Violence; Gandhi's Philosophy of Conflict*, Princeton, N.J.: Princeton University Press, 1958.

[2] When with an old man's despair Gandhi watched the violence of partition, he questioned whether Indians had ever understood *his* non-violence. 'Gandhi then proceeded to say that it was indeed true that many English friends had warned him that the so-called non-violence of India was no more than the passivity of the weak, it was not the non-violence of the stout in heart who disdained to surrender their sense of human unity even in the midst of a conflict of interests but continued their effort to convert the opponent instead of coercing him into submission' (N.K. Bose, *My Days with Gandhi*, Calcutta: Nishana, 1953, p. 271).

[3] In Bihar, Kayasths, who constituted 1.18 per cent of the population of the state, constituted 54 per cent of the Bihar Pradesh Congress Executive Committee in 1934. Their disproportionate role in Indian nationalism, like that of other non-martial twice-born castes, was in the first instance due to the fact that they were the first to have Western education (see Rameshray Roy, 'Congress in Bihar' (Ph.D. thesis, Department of Political Science, University of California, 1965)).

For the nature of Gandhi's appeal to these men, see Rajendra Prasad, *Satyagraha in Champaran* (Ahmedabad: Navajivan Publishing House, 1949), and *At the Feet of Mahatma Gandhi* (Westport, CT: Greenwood, 1971). The Madras Congress until the 1940's was mainly Brahman. For the dominance of Congress politics by Brahmans, and especially the effect this had in limiting its appeal, see Eugene Irschick, *Politics and Social Conflict in South India: A Study of Tamil Separation and the non-Brahman Movement* (Berkeley: University of California Press, 1969). The Praja Mandals, Lok Parishads, and Harijan Sevak Sanghs (Congress-connected political and social service organizations in Rajasthan) were, through the nineteen-forties, dominated by Brahmans, Vaishyas, and Kayasths (see Rudolph and Rudolph, 'Rajputana under British Paramountcy: The Failure of Indirect Rule,' *Journal of Modern History*, XXXVIII (June, 1966).

[4] For a discussion of the moral and psychological subtleties of non-violence, see Joan Bondurant, 'Satyagraha versus Duragraha: The Limits of Symbolic Violence,' in Ramachandran and T.K. Mahadevan (eds), *Gandhi: His Relevance for Our Times*, Bombay: Bharatiya Vidya Bhavan, 1964, pp. 67–81.

[5] N.K. Bose, *My Days with Gandhi*, Calcutta: Nishana, 1953, p. 270.

[6] For an extended discussion, on which these pages draw, of Indian approaches to conflict management, see Susanne Hoeber Rudolph, 'Conflict and Consensus in Indian Politics', *World Politics*, XIII (April, 1961). Hugh Tinker suggests other threads of the conciliation ethic in his article 'Magnificent Failure? The Gandhian Ideal in India after Sixteen Years', *International Affairs*, XL (April, 1964), pp. 262–76. Vallabhbhai Patel had yet another interpretation of Gandhi's consensualism: 'You can work in harmony with everybody. It does not cost any effort. Vaniks (merchants) do not mind humbling themselves' (cited in *The Diary of Mahadev Desai*, trans. from the Gujarati and ed. V.G. Desai, Ahmedabad: Navajivan Publishing House, 1953, I, p. 53).

[7] See also Part III of Lloyd I. Rudolph and Susanne Hoeber Rudolph, *The Modernity of Tradition: Political Development in India*, Chicago: University of Chicago Press, 1967, pp. 251–92, for a discussion of a preference for consensus in the law. Ideas about political consensualism as opposed to adversary modes and partisanship have been most strikingly developed in the postindependence period by Jayaprakash Narayan, who argues for a neo-Rousseauist politics in the context of a radical decentralization of life lived in small-scale communities. See especially his 'Reconstruction of Indian Polity', in Bimla Prasad (ed.), *Socialism, Sarvodaya and Democracy*, New York: Asia Publishing House, 1964. A vigorous critique and defence of the essay may be found in W.H. Morris-Jones, 'The Unhappy Utopia: J.P. in Wonderland', *Economic Weekly*, June 25, 1960; and William Carpenter, 'Reconstruction of Indian Polity: Defense of J.P.', *Economic Weekly*, 4 February 1961.

[8] Ralph Retzlaff, *Village Government in India*, New York: Asia Publishing House, 1962, p. 24.

[9] Ibid., p. 25.

[10] The dominance of higher landowning castes and their special role in determining the nature of the 'consensus' are well documented. See, for example, M.N. Srinivas' discussion of the numerically and economically superior Okkaligas in 'The Social System of a Mysore Village,' and Kathleen Gough's discussion of the Tanjore Brahmans in 'The Social Structure of a Tanjore Village,' both in McKim Marriott (ed.), *Village India*, Chicago, 1955. These two studies make a useful contrast in that Srinivas indicates that economic power and numerical strength are as important as ritual superiority in determining dominant caste status with respect to village affairs.

[11] Morris Carstairs, *The Twice Born: A Study of a Community of High-Caste Hindus*, London: Hogarth Press, 1957, p. 46.

[12] Ibid., p. 47.

[13] *Gandhi's Autobiography*, trans. from the Gujarati by Mahadev Desai, Washington, D.C., 1948, p. 168.

[14] Ibid., p. 63.

[15] M.K. Gandhi, *Woman's Role in Society*, comp. R.K. Prabhu, Ahmedabad: Navajivan Publishing House, 1959, p. 8.

7

Self-Control and Political Potency

The distinction between 'real' and assimilated Indians, like that between the masculine and feminine races, left a psychic wound. Those Indians who became like Englishmen after being educated in Anglicized schools could no longer be respected nor respect themselves—so went the British imputation—because they no longer recognized their Indian birthright. The 'real' India of princes and peasants and martial races retained its integrity; the assimilated India of babus did not. How could the babus expect to lead, much less rule, India? The charge was telling one, especially in the decades before the turn of the century when nationalism and its leaders were strongly influenced by liberal England and its parliamentary life. However 'Indian' the private lives of Ranade, Gokhale, Srinivas Iyengar, and Surendranath Banerjee may have been, their public ideas, idiom, and often dress were those of cultivated English gentlemen. Their nationalism and political principles seemed not to speak to those who lacked their rather special intellectual and cultural experiences. It was convenient for Englishmen to characterize those experiences as somehow fraudulent. Their friends the 'real' Indians—peasants untouched by middle class intellectuality, traditional ruling classes—were generally indifferent to nationalist appeals and demands for responsible government, exhibiting instead a gratifying satisfaction with an administrative state managed by British civil servants.

The leadership of the political generation preceding Gandhi's, Tilak, Sri Aurobindo, Lala Lajpat Rai, and B.C. Pal, searched for a way to master the moral and strategic consequences of the distinction—and division—between 'real' and assimilated Indians. The issue was one of identity, of a national self-definition that could renew a sense of Indian distinctiveness while incorporating ideas suitable for a changing world. It was also one of political effectiveness, of reaching wider constituencies and broadening the base of nationalism. Both dimensions of the challenge pointed toward more traditional symbolism. Many of these leaders embraced traditional symbolism, often supporting, in consequence, conservative Hindu practices, exacerbating Hindu–Muslim relations, and countenancing violence.

Gandhi's response was shaped by such recent national experiences as the evocation of a hero (Shivaji) and religious symbolism by Tilak in Maharashtra, the appeal of sentiment in the politics and literature of the anti-partition movement in Bengal, and the reforming zeal with which the Arya Samaj was able to modify Hinduism in the Punjab and Uttar Pradesh. But unlike his predecessors Gandhi leavened traditional symbolism with reformist ideas, tried to find symbols and issues that would avoid Hindu-Muslim confrontations, and pursued a non-violent strategy. Even if he did not fully succeed, he did distinguish himself from his predecessors by infusing these inherited elements with the exceptionally remorseless moral vision of a 'religious'. Most striking symbolically was his resuscitation on a national plane of the style of a sanyasin, the ascetic seeking enlightenment and virtue. As in his reformulation of the issue of courage, he again responded dramatically to a telling British critique; he was a nationalist leader not cut off from his own people by assimilation.

There is no country whose people do not in some way worry about the private morality of their leaders. Gossip about the highly placed is never merely gossip; to some extent it reflects the assumption that there may be some continuity between a man's personal self-indulgence or self-constraint and his capacity to act disinterestedly in matters of state and the general welfare. But in modern times we have come to assume that the processes of differentiation that characterize our lives and that touch all our affairs have made private morals less relevant for public action. In the United States, it is assumed that if a senator or perhaps even a president pays attention to ladies other than his wife, doing so will not affect his capacity to manage affairs of state—provided he conducts himself with some circumspection and gives no cause for scandal. It is the differentiation of realms of conduct that suggests to us that conduct in one realm need not be affected by conduct in others.

Certain constitutional assumptions also lie behind the belief that private behaviour is to a point irrelevant to public, in a public man. The Western political tradition has been disposed to rely upon external rather than internal restraints, on institutional rather than ethical limits, to control those who wield power. The emphasis on institutional limitations—the balancing of branches of government or of class interests or of church and state—is already found in Greek and Roman thought and remains evident during the more ethically-oriented periods of medieval polity. Institutional limits have not, to be sure, been the exclusive means of restraining the arbitrary exercise of power. Political theorists in the West have emphasized the virtues kings must have and practice and have found in ethical restraints and their acceptance by kings the means to curb arbitrary action. But in the main, there has been a greater emphasis on institutional rather than on ethical means of ensuring that those who rule use their power for good rather than ill.

It is from 'experiments in the spiritual field', Gandhi wrote, 'that I derived such power as I possess for working in the political field'.[1] His belief that private morality had public consequences reflects the emphasis in traditional Hindu thought on ethical as against institutional restraints. Traditional Hindu political thought, the *dharmasastras* and the epics, stressed the importance of inner over external restraints on rulers, relying not upon countervailing institutions but upon ethical commands to guarantee the public spirit of traditional kings. In practice, of course, countervailing institutions did act as irregular restraints.[2]

Ethical commands had a private and a public variant. A king was commanded in private life to restrain his lust, control and master his passions, live simply, and rule his subjects justly. The *Manusmriti* declares 'that king [is] a just inflicter of punishment, who is truthful, who acts after due consideration, who is wise, and who knows the respective value of virtue, pleasure and wealth'.[3] 'For a king who is attached to the vices springing from love of pleasure, loses his wealth and his virtue, but he who is given to those arising from anger, loses even his life. Hunting, gambling, sleeping by day, censoriousness, excess with women, drunkenness, an inordinate love for dancing, singing, and music, and useless travel are the tenfold set of vices springing from love of pleasure.'[4] The king who overcomes attachment, who reigns with mind serene, who achieves that expunging of self-interest, can judge clearly and fairly the interest of others. (A problematic assumption, to be sure. There is no reason to believe that such virtue may not itself become a vested interest, seeking to propagate itself among subjects who would live more 'attached' lives or giving rise to that *hubris* of the disinterested, that their virtue gives them the right to prescribe for others. A prescription may not be loved any better for being imposed by one who has no 'interest' except in virtue.) The public variant of the ethic of restraint was the *rajadharma*, the commands that prescribed for kings what they must or must not do in their public function. There was an implicit assumption that a man who mastered himself could be relied upon to follow rajadharma.[5]

We are not concerned with whether these ethical hopes ever became operational restraints for most kings in distant or recent Indian history. The reputation of Indian princes in the last two hundred years would lead one to suppose that an ethic of self-restraint was honoured as much in the breach as in the realization. A reputation for a lively libidinal life may even have enhanced the status of princes and nobles by affording commoners a vicarious opportunity to consume and participate in those pleasures that did not usually come their way.

Yet ethical standards that are steadily breached need not lose their meaning. They remain an ideal, and if someone appears who can enact the ideal, he may fall heir to all the pent up hopes that have survived the experience of repeated disillusion; he may, indeed, command the more respect, inspire the more reverence, because the standard has remained unrealized. It is in this light that the public impact of Gandhi's asceticism must be understood. If Gandhi lived his private life in public, it was because both he and those who observed him believed that a man's claim to be just, to command others, to attain wisdom, was proportional to his capacity for self-rule.

Asceticism was thought to have a power-enhancing function, too. The practitioner of *tapasya* ('austerities') accumulated special powers. This belief rests on what might be called a theory of sexual and moral hydrostatics: The classic suggest, and many Hindus believe, that men are endowed with a certain amount of 'life force', which, if used up in passionate or lustful or self-seeking endeavours, will no longer be available for other and higher purposes. Freud, too, found the capacity for sublimation proportional to the diversion from more direct expression of libidinal energies. For him, the discontents arising from self-restraint were the prerequisite, the motor force, of civilization.[6] The *Manusmriti* states the same theory very graphically: 'But when one among all the organs slips away from control, thereby a man's wisdom slips away from him, even as the water flows through the one open foot of a water-carrier's skin.'[7]

The theory is no rarefied philosophic construct but enjoys popular acceptance. Morris Carstairs, in his study of the twice-born castes of a traditional Rajasthan village, and Joseph Elder, in his study of an Uttar Pradesh village, found much preoccupation with this life force. Carstairs' villagers conceptualized it in a prescientific medical theory as a thick viscous fluid stored in the head; a plentiful quantity of it was thought necessary for fitness and strength. It could be preserved by the practice of celibacy and the careful observance of ritual restraints and commandments and was diminished by ritual carelessness and sexual self-expression. It could also be enhanced by the consumption of certain foods. Unworldly devotees, by their austerity, accumulated such substantial quantities of this life force that they were believed to have special powers, believed to be capable, as ordinary men could not hope to be, of compelling the environment.[8]

Gandhi fully accepted the essentials of this theory: 'All power', he said, 'comes from the preservation and sublimation of the vitality that is responsible for the creation of life .... Perfectly controlled thought is itself power of the highest potency and becomes self-acting .... Such power is impossible in one who dissipates his energy in any way whatsoever'.[9] If he was able to compel the environment, it was because he practised *brahmacharya*, celibacy and more general self-restraint; if he was unable to do so, it was because of failures in control. 'It is my full conviction, that if only I had lived a life of unbroken *brahmacharya* all through, my energy and enthusiasm would have been a thousand fold greater and I should have been able to devote them all to the furtherance of my country's cause as my own.'[10]

In the late 1930s, when the nationalist movement was experiencing severe difficulties, Gandhi characteristically looked for the source of trouble not in society and history but in himself. 'A Congress leader said to me the other day, ... "how is it that in quality, the Congress is not what it used to be in 1920–5? It has deteriorated" ....' Special historical forces were part of the answer, but only a part: '... There must be power in the word of a *satyagraha* general—not the power that possession of limitless arms gives, but the power that purity of life, strict vigilance and ceaseless application produce. This is impossible without the observance of *brahmacharya* ...; *brahmacharya* here does not mean merely physical self-control. It means much more. It means complete control over all the senses. Thus an impure thought is a breach of *brahmacharya*, so is anger.' He had not achieved such complete control—a terrible self demand; had he succeeded, the movement, he thought, would not be encountering difficulties. 'I have not acquired that control over my thoughts that I need for my researches in non-violence. If my non-violence is to be contagious and infectious, I must acquire greater control over my thoughts. There is perhaps a flaw somewhere which accounts for the apparent failure of leadership adverted to in the opening sentence of this writing.'[11]

The ideal of self-restraint has not been confined to Indian public men; it seems to be broadly shared by Hindu Indians even though the intensity with which it is held varies by caste and locality. Its salience is greater among the higher than among the lower castes.[12] Among higher castes, those who share the more self-expressive Kshatriya (warrior-ruler) culture seem less responsive to the ideal of self-restraint than do the Brahmans, Vaishyas, and Kayasths, who formed so conspicuous a part of Gandhi's devoted lieutenants and followers.

Here, as in other areas of Indian life, the ideal asks more of men than most are able to manage. Not only are students, those who have withdrawn from society or those who live as recluses in distant places, asked to observe it, but so, too, to a lesser extent, are married householders. The result is that the ideal is not often fulfilled.[13] The felt disparity between the moral imperative and the capacity to realize it in daily life—a disparity that suggests that Indians are more prone than others to formulate ideals beyond the capacity of ordinary men, not that they are more erotic—also helps explain the impact of Gandhi's experiments: his achievement of a goal that many Indians recognize but do not realize became a form of vicarious fulfilment of an ego ideal.

The political effectiveness of Gandhian asceticism, then, lay partly in its expression of the traditional view of how rulers are restrained, partly in its coincidence with ideas about how a man's control over his environment might be enhanced, and partly in the fact that it vicariously achieved a personal moral ideal of many Indians. But there is yet another dimension. A great leader's capacity to compel his environment is related to his belief that he can do so. Such self-confidence creates the phenomenon social science calls 'charisma'. It involves, on the part of him who possesses it, a belief that he can perform, if not precisely superhuman, then at least extraordinary, deeds. Among those who perceive such self-confidence—the army calls it command presence—it produces a faith that he can indeed do what most men cannot.

In a curious way, the psychological chemistry of the relationship between the public man and his constituents is such that—if everything else is reasonably favourable—the belief produces its own justification. In response to such a leader, followers can sometimes mobilize resources within themselves that they do not ordinarily command, thus corroborating the faith that caused them to respond. The psychological logic of this is the reverse of that envisioned by Freud in his writings on leadership and mob psychology: that in a mass response to an apocalyptic call controls break down and libidinal energies are released in actions that express the lowest common moral denominator.[14] Rather, a great leader may mobilize in his followers unsuspected strengths and virtues, superego strivings not previously lived up to, which are made active by his moral challenge. The psychology of leadership has tended to neglect this dimension in its pursuit of the causes and consequences of the demagogue and his mass followers. The fear of mass response should not obscure the creative possibilities of charismatic leadership. Gandhi evoked in himself and those who 'heard' him responses that transcended the routine of ordinary life, producing extraordinary events and effects on character, which, metaphorically, can be described as 'magical'.

We are concerned not only with the abstract dimensions of the theory of asceticism but also with how Gandhi came to believe that through its practice he might compel the environment and how the cultural ideal of asceticism came to mean so much to the private man.

It seems fairly evident that Gandhi's extreme fearfulness and self-contempt as a child had much to do with his relations to an ailing father. Gandhi's marriage at the age of thirteen coincided with a stagecoach accident in which his father was seriously injured, never to recover fully.[15] The event itself was sufficiently symbolic and seemed so to the mature Gandhi, suggesting an inauspicious connection between the son's becoming a man and the beginning of the father's decline. Between the ages of thirteen and sixteen, Gandhi spent a substantial part of his free time nursing and ministering to his father's needs. 'Every night I massaged his legs and retired only when he asked me to do so or after he had fallen asleep .... I would only go out for an evening walk either when he permitted me or when he was feeling well.'[16] The father, at least in these years, appears to have discouraged the more venturesome and independent side of his son's activities and favoured those of service and nursing, which the young Gandhi shared with his mother. If Gandhi disliked active sports and ran home anxiously after school, the antipathy was probably partly inculcated. '... The reason of my dislike for gymnastics was my keen desire to serve as a nurse to my father. As soon as the school closed, I would hurry home and begin serving him. Compulsory exercise came directly in the way ....' And in case Gandhi's 'keen desire' should ever be overweighed by an interest in sports, 'my father wrote himself to the headmaster saying he wanted me at home after school ....'[17]

These restrictions on behalf of nursing, which among other things produced in Gandhi a lifelong love of nursing and medical ministrations— we learn to want to do what we have to do—may not have been easy to accept. What physical or temperamental endowments children bring with them seem in Gandhi's case to have been weighted to the energetic side. His older sister described him as a sprightly boy, active and adventuresome, a boy who liked to get away from home and climb trees and lead his own life. He was, says his sister, 'a bit of a problem ... exceedingly active and energetic. He was never at one place for long. As soon as he was able to walk about, it became difficult to keep track of him ....'[18] He was not, in short, the sort of boy to whom the home-bound tasks of regularly nursing a sick father are likely to have come easily and naturally.

The mature Gandhi looked back on this experience with a recollection that suggests he took bitter medicine: 'When I was younger than you are today,' he wrote to his son in 1901, 'I used to find real enjoyment in looking after my father. I have known no fun or pleasure since I was twelve'—a passage that seems to be saying two things at once.[19] The father was demanding and probably inspired fear and anger. 'I did not talk with him much. I was afraid to speak.'[20] Gandhi recalls that he found him short-tempered and remembers an occasion when the father responded with forgiveness rather than fury as one of the most striking and surprising of his youth.[21] A sense of unfreedom pervades the mature man's accounts of his youth: 'When they [the parents] are no more and I have found my freedom ...'; 'all happiness and pleasure should be sacrificed in devoted service to my parents.'[22]

That the story of Maharaja Harishchandra, a well-known classic tale acted by a passing traveling troupe, 'haunted' Gandhi as a boy may tell something about Gandhi's feeling for the relationship between father and son. He re-enacted it 'times without number'; his ideal was 'to go through all the ordeals Harishchandra went through.' The maharaja's endless misery and suffering, unlikely to speak to the mind and heart of a Western youth, apparently seemed to the young Gandhi a paradigm of existence and a moral guide. 'I literally believed in the story of Harishchandra.'[23] The story tells of the king's dreadful degradation as he seeks to satisfy the merciless and relentless demands of a saintly Brahman to whom he owes a debt. The Brahman's insistence on payment, that a promise must be honoured, is utterly untempered by common sense or charity. To those accustomed to an ethic of consequences related to human capacities, the Brahman's absolute ethic seems incomprehensible. Maharaja Harishchandra is driven from horror to horror in a descent for which Dante might have found words. His kingdom, wealth, wife, and child gone, he is to serve, as a final degradation, as an untouchable menial among fetid corpses in a cremation ground. Harishchandra's submission is total; he laments but accepts his fate. Self-suffering in the name of honouring duty and of pursuing truth, which Gandhi identified with each other, has its reward.[24] The gods themselves come to his side, rewarding his self-control, fortitude, and respect for truth with heaven itself.

The theme of a severe older man who imposes painful demands that must not be resisted recurs in the story of the boy Prahlad, whom Gandhi invoked repeatedly as a model of non-violence.[25] Prahlad, who loves God, is commanded by his father to deny him. When Prahlad refuses, the father has him trampled by elephants, and when he survives, he forces him to embrace a red-hot iron pillar. God springs from the pillar to save the boy and slay the father.

The parent who constrained may not have been easy to love or to respect with a full heart. Not only was he short tempered but also 'to a certain extent ... given to carnal pleasures. For he married for the fourth time when he was over forty'.[26] This passage from the autobiography seems mild enough until we recollect Gandhi's harsh view of the carnal life and note that Gandhi ignores an important consideration in his father's decision, the fact that he produced no male heir in his previous marriages and was without hope of having one unless he married again.[27] 'If you notice any purity in me', he said to a friend in 1932, 'I have inherited it from my mother, and not from my father.'[28]

Gandhi dealt with the constraint that he felt surrounded him by acceptance and rebellion, exploring both paths more or less simultaneously. He found a guide in his mother's qualities. She, too, sacrificed herself to an invalid requiring much care. It was her suffering and self-suffering and self-control, particularly the last, that he hoped to emulate.[29] But even while he was forcing himself to exhaust the depths of filial devotion, Gandhi set out on the previously discussed secret rebellion under the guidance of Sheikh Mehtab. He appeared for the nursing work and dutifully ministered each day. But he led a double life. In one, he experimented with everything that was forbidden in the other. Gandhi in his inner being and in his 'other' life was quite the reverse of the filial model pictured in the autobiography. His venturesomeness and independence survived the parental restraints—in secret and at a high cost to his conscience.

The demands made on Gandhi's filial devotion were not unique. The relationship between this particular Hindu son and his father gives expression to a more general pattern: service to an aging father who remains in charge of a joint family home after his sons have reached maturity and demands at least formal self-effacement of their masculinity and a commitment to devoted service. The pleasure of filial service is real. Like many cultural demands that initially require sacrifice and discipline, it becomes itself a satisfaction. Yet there may be limits to the kind or degree of self-effacement that can be expected. By the side of the satisfactions, and depending perhaps on the degree of devotion demanded, reside the more or less suppressed discontents of the effacement. The demands of the Hindu joint family, especially as they are expressed in the more ascetic sects and castes like Gandhi's, can require 'too much' of some sons. The circumstances of his father's illness, Gandhi's great sensitivity to the moral demands of the culture, and his innate vigor seem to have at once heightened the compulsions of filial devotion and the inner resistance to them. The conflict between duty and an insufficiently effaced self was exacerbated. That these events occurred during what a nineteenth-century novel would have called 'impressionable years' places them centrally in his development.

Gandhi speaks of the circumstances surrounding his father's death as a crisis that revealed to him his shameful moral insufficiency. The crisis represents a crucial turning point in his gradual commitment to asceticism. Its background included a father who commanded the personal ministrations of his son, superseding the claims of the young man's venturesomeness, and a son who had acquired the self-discipline to meet these demands with apparent equanimity and yet who, at great cost to his conscience, launched a secret massive rebellion. The circumstances themselves are quickly related. Gandhi, who had spent the afternoon as usual massaging his ailing and sinking father, left him to join his wife in their bedroom. She was pregnant and hence ritually impure and sexually forbidden. A short time later, he was summoned to his father's room by an uncle to find him dead. If 'animal passion had not blinded me, I should have been spared the torture of separation from my father during his last moments'. And, 'this shame of my carnal desire even at a critical hour of my father's death ... is a blot I have never been able to efface or forget, and I have always thought that although my devotion to my parents knew no bounds and I would have given up anything for it, yet it was weighed and found unpardonably wanting because my mind was at the same moment in the grip of lust'.[30] The child born after these events died.

The event confirmed Gandhi's readiness to believe that his venturesomeness, especially sexually, was in conflict with his duty to nurse and minister. He generalized this belief over time into the view that a life governed by desire conflicts with one governed by duty. Ministering to those who came to depend upon him as a public man was incompatible with anger and passion. His readiness to interpret his father's death in such terms had the weightiest cultural sanction: Those who acted in the grip of lust could not be guided by duty, whereas those who were capable of restraint could. The caste and sect from which Gandhi came perceived the expressive life in ways that could not balance this interpretation by providing a humane or sentimental view of sexuality. For Gandhi as for many others with similar backgrounds, sexuality was virtually an excretory function, not a vehicle for intimacy. If he slept with his wife, it was because he was weak and could not control his impurity, not because the experience provided a context to express their love. The fact that Gandhi's relationship with Kasturba and hers with him was based on duty and habit meant that the experiences of his own marriage could do little to dissuade him of this view. 'The husband', Gandhi later wrote, 'should avoid privacy with his wife. Little reflection is needed to show that the only possible motive for privacy between husband and wife is the desire for sexual enjoyment'.[31] Such a view of sexuality finds support in the culture and circumstances of the traditional arranged marriage and joint family households. Boys and girls were not taught nor did they have opportunities to learn the manners and mores appropriate for relations with those of similar age but opposite sex before their marriage was arranged to a stranger from within the caste fold. Respect for the older members of the joint family obliged the couple to avoid each other in the daytime and to deny if it should exist any overt expressions of the meaningfulness of their relationship. Before and after marriage there were often few opportunities for the creation of affection, understanding, and reciprocity, of the larger human context of sexuality, and thus it had no chance to stand for anything but itself.

His father's death not only spoke to Gandhi of the horrors of sensuality but also reached deeper into the recesses of his being. Its background, the imperfect realization of filial devotion through self-control and the 'descent' into self-expression, suggested to him that a culturally impermissible sentiment, lust, had been brought together with a psychologically and culturally impermissible sentiment, anger, and had produced an unthinkable result. 'Lust' had 'killed'; in some so far unconfronted recess of himself he had 'wanted' it to do so.

The circumstances surrounding his father's death moved Gandhi toward celibacy and the consensual mode. Their appeal and morality reach well beyond any particular life into Indian philosophic and historical thought and experience. To become a brahmacharya, to become not only a celibate but also one whose self-control extends to anger and aggression, was written large there. Such preoccupations 'incapacitated' him for a life of self-expression and aggressive self-assertion. That side of him that had experimented with the cultural style suggested by Sheikh Mehtab—meat-eating, sensualism, conflict and partisanship in law and politics, violent nationalism—fell into the shadow. They were the paradigms of the assertiveness from which he had been systematically and authoritatively deterred during the nursing years. Vegetarianism, brahmacharya, consensual modes in law and politics, non-violent nationalism, became the channels of venturesomeness and the means to affect and master the environment. They did not raise the spectre of forbidden conduct or the anger and fatal consequence that it 'produced.' It was among the Indians at Pretoria that Gandhi was able for the first time to speak in public. He could serve them, minister to their needs, ease their suffering, right their wrongs, modes of action that combined venturesomeness with duty.

When the mature Gandhi spoke of self-control, he had in mind not merely the control of the 'carnal self', although that was how he often put it. It was hatred and anger as much as sexual self-expression that he sought to pacify and control. Such emotions did not die easily in him. His capacity for fury at his wife and sons, in whom he could not bear to see the human frailties he would not tolerate in himself, remained long into his South African sojourn. It re-emerged to trouble him in his last years. Yet the energy that lay behind fury and his sexual desire was to be transformed into something constructive. A variety of observers commented over many years on the serenity to be found in Gandhi's presence.[32] But accounts of him by close disciples in his ashram suggest a man who gave them anything but peace; his serenity in great moments and in public life seems to have coexisted with great restlessness and testiness over the details of life. The serenity was, we must assume, most painfully constructed in part out of the necessity of mastering its opposite, internal war. Gandhi's techniques of public action in the nation sought to exclude anger. His private horror of private anger remained. Gandhi turned to the Gita, taking from it an ethic that could serve his private and public self: to become he 'who gives no trouble to the world, to whom the world causes no trouble, who is free from exultation, resentment, fear and vexation'.[33] To live it meant peace from the inner strife between filial duty and self-expression and enabled the public man to inspire the confidence and possess the authority that detachment brings.

There have been simpler explanations of Gandhi's serenity. Ritchie Calder, in *Medicine and Man*, writes: 'Whenever Mahatma Gandhi was under the stress of the modern world Rauwolfia would restore his philosophic detachment.'[34] This explanation seems to have gained a certain currency despite lack of supporting evidence. In view of Gandhi's profound suspicion of all stimulants or tranquilizers (from coffee through opium) because they distracted a moral man from his essential task of self-control[35] and in view of his belief that avoidance of temptation, by withdrawal from society as a wandering ascetic or as a forest recluse, was a less worthy means to gain self-control, such an explanation seems implausible. The same moral considerations that would have deflected him from becoming a eunuch to control his 'lust' would have deflected him from using a tranquilizer to produce serenity. At the level of ethics, serenity assumed for Gandhi the nature of a moral transcendence, not merely freedom from a case of nerves, and its moral significance would have been diminished by the employment of a chemical short cut. At the level of psychology, Gandhi valued self-control too highly, and feared its loss too much, to risk it for gains in what he would have regarded a specious serenity, specious because it involved a dulling of perception and the loss of control. The additional difficulty with the allegation is that none of the Gandhi literature provides evidence for it; one suspects that an era unfamiliar with the moral remorselessness of a 'religious' is too readily hospitable to a biochemical explanation.[36]

Gandhi ultimately took the vow of brahmacharya, of celibacy, at the age of thirty-seven.[37] His determination to do so was strengthened during the Zulu rebellion, when, as in the earlier Boer War, he undertook nursing service by forming an ambulance corps. '... The work', he wrote, 'set me furiously thinking in the direction of self-control', the self-control that so conspicuously failed him when he last nursed his father.[38] The brahmacharya vow culminated a gradual but growing commitment to asceticism. It began before Gandhi left for London as a young man of nineteen when he vowed to his mother that he would not touch meat, wine, or women.[39] It continued there with his principled return to vegetarianism and a growing awareness of and concern for ascetic living. His marriage, because it failed to provide a meaningful alternative to asceticism, strengthened rather than deflected him from the life course leading toward self-control. He gave institutional expression to the simple, unadorned life of limited wants in the Phoenix settlement, the utopian colony he established in South Africa and named after the bird who has no mate but renews life by a somewhat different procedure.[40] Those who lived there followed a Benedictine sort of discipline, each man serving according to his aptitude and calling and at the same time pursuing the Ruskinian virtues of dignity in labour and simplicity of wants.[41]

Phoenix and the brahmacharya vow were indispensable preconditions for his first great non-violent resistance campaign. 'Without Brahmacharya, the Satyagrahi will have no lustre, no inner strength to stand unarmed against the whole world ...; his strength will fail him at the right moment.'[42] He assumed that his capacity to compel the environment depended upon the degree of his self-perfection, the degree to which he had purged himself of lust, self-interest, and anger, and he prepared himself by self-imposed discipline. When things went wrong around him, when he felt helpless to shape events, he would conclude invariably that his impotence to do so was the consequence of a lapse into lustfulness or anger. In such moments, he would retreat to fast and observe other austerities, to renew that inner purity that could give him the strength to affect external events.

The relationship between Gandhi's asceticism and his belief that through it he might compel the environment is arrestingly illustrated by a series of events in his last years. He precipitated a scandal by asking at different times, several young women co-workers to share his bed.[43] The incidents tend to evoke either a kind of lascivious *Schadenfreude* or a protective silence.[44] More plausible is the view that they were almost desperate attempts by Gandhi to master tragic and overwhelming events by using an extreme version of an old remedy while relying on the reduced resources of an old man. The events coincide with the frightful period between 1946 and 1948, when, in the midst of the partition bloodshed, Gandhi at seventy-seven brought something like peace to Bengal by becoming what Lord Mountbatten called a One Man Boundary Force.[45]

He began in the Muslim majority area of Noakhali, where Hindus were being slaughtered, and continued in Bihar, where Hindus were doing the same to Muslims. The work was desperately taxing. His walks took him through riot devastated villages, over difficult countryside, and among people who had lost those nearest to them through ghastly brutalities practiced by neighbors on neighbours. Noakhali deeply shook his serenity: 'I find that I have not the patience and technique needed in these tragic circumstances; suffering and evil often overwhelm me and I stew in my own juice';[46] and again, 'the happenings in Noakhali succeeded in upsetting me; for there are moments when my heart gives way to anxiety and anger'.[47] Nirmal Bose, who worked with him in those days, speaks of him as preoccupied with a way to cope with these events—evidently as much the inner events, the wavering of serenity, the rise of anger, as the external events, the bloodshed all around. His capacity to affect the external, he was confident, rested on his capacity to control the internal. Desperate events required desperate remedies. He warned his friends that he was thinking of a bold and original experiment, 'whose heat will be great'.[48]

He asked Manu Gandhi, his nineteen-year-old grandniece, to share his bed. He appears to have regarded the matter at one and the same time as a test of his 'lust control', whether as a man he could withstand temptation, and of his success in creating in himself the feelings and perceptions of a mother, kin to woman, a test that suggests a certain ambiguity of self-definition. 'Manu Gandhi, my grandniece, shares the bed with me, strictly as my very blood ... as part of what might be my last *Yajna* [sacrifice]', he wrote to Acharya Kripalani.[49]

Gandhi had always held, in sharp contrast to some more orthodox views, that self-control was worthless if it was achieved by withdrawal from society and thus from temptation. Only self-control in the midst of temptation was worthy. Now he evidently increased temptation to test and thus strengthen himself. His activities were no secret, although many of his warmest adherents wished they were. He discussed the matter in two prayer meetings in February, 1947, telling his audience—Muslims among whom he was working for peace—that his granddaughter (-niece) shared his bed, that the prophet had discounted eunuchs who became such by an operation but welcomed those who became it by prayer.[50] The scandal seems to have made his task in Noakhali more difficult, and a number of his co-workers left him. These events, if anything, confirmed him in his belief that he had to persist. If he did not have the serenity to bear such disapproval, surely he was not yet master of himself. Bose heard him say to a visitor that 'the courage which made a man risk public disapproval when he felt he was right was undoubtedly of a superior order .... I get impatient and worried when I am confronted with silly arguments .... I sometimes flare up in anger. This should not be so. I am yet far from the state of *sthita prajna* (self-mastery).'[51]

These events are not characteristic of Gandhi at the height of his powers. Then, his experiments in self-mastery, while often unconventional, remorseless, and directed at the inner environment, were mingled with great common sense concerning their effect on the world around him. And he was often more sensitive to the proper use of human beings. But the logic of these events, even though executed with the declining moral and psychological capacities of an old man, illuminate the ascetic dimension of his character: to control his outer environment he must control the inner, testing it to the utmost limits.

Gandhi's meticulous concern for diet was related to his quest for sexual asceticism. He had a horror of drink because it threatened to undermine self-control. Moderate in his criticism of many things he found objectionable, he was wholly immoderate in his concern to realize temperance: 'Drugs and drink are the two arms of the devil with which he strikes his helpless slave into stupefaction and intoxication.'[52] This is not an unfamiliar point of view in men who place a high value on self-restraint. What is a little less obvious is the significance of his concern with food. The cultural context of the concern is the close connection classical Hinduism makes between ritual status and what goes on at either end of the alimentary canal. An extremely fastidious management of both input and output marks the practice of the higher castes. It is possible—although we have not been able independently to verify it—that Gandhi's mother carried this general cultural preoccupation with pollution to extraordinary extremes, deploring that she could not be like the honey bee, who converted all input into the purest output.[53] In her case, the preoccupation was associated with chronic constipation, as it was with Gandhi.

In the Indian cultural setting, the human processing of food has implications that go beyond ritual pollution and ritual rank. Food is also violent or non-violent, as Gandhi explicitly recognized in his early, tentative meat-eating experiments. Vegetarianism has a moral as well as a physiological and cultural dimension. Certain food doctrines concern the man of self-restraint.[54] It is generally believed that some foods, 'cool' foods, promote a cool disposition, one that is calm, undisturbed, unaggressive, resistant to lust,[55] whereas others produce a 'hot' disposition, aggressive, and lusty. The cool foods are thought to augment that part of life force conducive to saintly power, the hot that part of life force given to lust. 'Ghi (clarified butter) gave one a controlled strength, a power of mind and body that could enable one to perform acts bordering on the divine.'[56] Although opinion on which foods precisely are hot and cool is not fully consistent, the cool are mainly milk, clarified butter (ghi), curds, vegetables, and fruits.[57] Meat and strong spices figure prominently among the hot. The cool list was largely embodied in that developed by Gandhi and his followers in the twenties and also in the menu adopted at Phoenix settlement in South Africa at the beginning of the century.[58] The list of the twenties included sprouted wheat, sprouted gram, coconut, raisins, lemon, milk, fresh fruit, ghi, and honey. Gandhi even had doubts about milk, sharing the fear expressed in certain classical Hindu texts that milk is a stimulant.[59]

'Control of the palate', wrote Gandhi, 'is the first essential in the observance of the vow (of celibacy)', and '*brahmacharya* needed no effort on my part when I lived on fruits and nuts alone'.[60] This apparently unpolitical subject, too, then, had political relevance: what appeared to some as sheer food faddery was understood by many Indians who read or heard about it as an integral part of Gandhi's efforts at self-mastery and an index of his progress.

Gandhi's efforts to control his sexuality, to achieve, as it were, the serenity of neutrality, were reinforced by his very explicit feminine identification. He found his mother a more appealing figure than his father and tried to be like her rather than him.[61] 'But the manner in which my brahmacharya came to me irresistibly drew me to woman as the mother of man ...; every woman at once became sister or daughter to me.'[62] His love of nursing was the most prominent aspect of his maternal capacity: he welcomed all opportunities to practice this skill, acting as midwife at the birth of his fourth son, taking care of his wife and babies when they were ill. In his old age, he liked to think of himself as a mother to his grandniece, Manu, the girl who shared his bed as a daughter might her mother's and who had lost a mother. She has written a book entitled *Bapu—My Mother*.[63] He admired, first in his mother, then in women generally, their capacity for self-suffering. The admiration inspired confidence in women co-workers. When he converted self-suffering into a potent political weapon through non-violent resistance, its implication that it would be necessary to suffer violence without retaliation led him immediately to conclude that women would be most apt at it. 'Woman is the incarnation of *ahimsa* (non-violence). *Ahimsa* means infinite love, which again means infinite capacity for suffering.'[64] (Again, perhaps a curious definition of love.) His belief had enormous consequences for the politicization of Indian women, many of whom took part in public life for the first time during his non-violent resistance campaigns.

Gandhi built a life on rejecting the aggressive, 'masculine' aspect of the human potential, accepting instead the peaceful, communitarian, adaptive aspect associated—in the West—with the culture of women.[65] But if, in law, he adopted conciliation rather than the adversary mode or, in politics, he opposed partisanship and praised consensus, he did so to alter the environment, not in order to yield to it. If we stress Gandhi's feminine identification, it is not, as a friend of the rector of Justin remarks, to invite readers to jump over a Freudian moon. Indian culture appears to distribute somewhat differently among men and women those qualities that the West associates with male and female. Effective masculinity seems to be compatible with a broader range of human qualities than many Americans are inclined to accept. 'Male' and 'female' are not clear and self-evident, much less dichotomous, categories but open to great variations in cultural patterning. To insist that courage or assertiveness must be expressed in familiar patterns and idioms is to miss how others may express them. Gandhi's communitarian and peace-seeking ethic and method, 'in the manner of women,' evoked a broad and deep response in India.[66]

Notes

[1] See p. 197, n. 10.

[2] In Rajputana, the nobility acted as a restraint upon the activities of Maharajas, as did, in lesser ways, the Brahmans. But these restraints were irregular. See Lloyd I. Rudolph and Susanne Hoeber Rudolph, with Mohan Singh, 'A Bureaucratic Lineage in Princely India: Elite Formation and Conflict in a Patrimonial System,' *Journal of Asian Studies*, XXXIV, May 1975.

[3] Georg Bühler, *The Laws of Manu—Translated with Extracts from Seven Commentaries* vol. XXV of *The Sacred Books of the East*, Max Muller (ed.), Oxford, 1886, Chapter VII, vs. 26, p. 220.

[4] Ibid., vss. 46 and 47, p. 223.

[5] 'A king ... who is voluptuous, partial, and deceitful will be destroyed, even through the unjust punishment which he inflicts .... Punishment cannot be inflicted justly by one ... addicted to sensual pleasures' (ibid., vss. 27 and 30, p. 220).

[6] See Sigmund Freud, *Civilization and Its Discontents*. The idea of a sexual hydrostatics is developed in David Riesman, 'The Themes of Heroism and Weakness in the Structure of Freud's Thought,' in *Individualism Reconsidered*, Glencoe, Ill,

1954. The Freud comparison has a limit: for him, an excess of restraint produced pathology.

[7] Bühler, *The Laws of Manu*, Chapter II, vs. 99, p. 48.

[8] Morris Carstairs, *The Twice Born: A Study of a Community of High-Caste Hindus*, Bloomington: Indiana University Press (1957, reissued 1967), London, 1957, p. 86. Conversely, Joseph Elder found that in 'Rajpur' all castes shared the view that intercourse deprived a man of some of his soul stuff and thereby shortened his life ('Growing up in Rajpur', chapter of forthcoming book entitled 'Industrialism and Hindusim').

[9] Quoted in Pyarelal (Nair), *Mahatma Gandhi: The Last Phase*, Ahmedabad: Navajivan Publishing House, 1956, I, p. 573.

[10] M.K. Gandhi, *Self-Restraint v. Self-Indulgence*, Ahmedabad: Navajivan Publishing House, 1958, p. 56.

[11] *Harijan*, 23 July 1938, reprinted in ibid., pp. 150–1.

[12] 'My general impression was that conjugal intercourse occurred more frequently and was enjoyed more uninhibitedly among the lower castes than the higher castes' (Elder, 'Industrialism and Hinduism', p. 218).

[13] Carstairs suggests that the disparity between the ideal and its fulfillment produces 'the commonest expression of anxiety neurosis among the Hindu communities of Rajasthan, and perhaps elsewhere as well' (*The Twice Born*, p. 87).

[14] From Sigmund Freud, 'Group Psychology and the Analysis of the Ego.' The following quotations are from *General Selections from the Work of Sigmund Freud* (ed.), John Rickman (Anchor ed., 1957). 'What it [the group] demands of its heroes is strength, or even violence. It wants to be ruled and oppressed and to fear its masters .... All their individual inhibitions fall away and all the cruel, brutal, and destructive instincts are stirred.' The burden of Freud's argument lies in this direction, although he concedes that 'groups are also capable of high achievements in the shape of abnegation, unselfishness, and devotion to an ideal ...' (p. 173).

[15] *Gandhi's Autobiography*, trans. from the Gujarati by Mahadev Desai, Washington, DC, 1948, p. 20. He eventually died of a malignant growth, pp. 43–4.

[16] Ibid., p. 43; and D.G. Tendulkar, *Mahatma: Life of Mohandas Karamchand Gandhi*, Bombay, 1951—, I, pp. 27–8. Tendulkar says that Gandhi nursed his father for five years, which would carry the ailment back before the stagecoach accident.

[17] *Gandhi's Autobiography*, p. 28.

[18] Prabhudas Gandhi, *My Childhood with Gandhi*, Ahmedabad: Navajivan Publishing House, 1957, p. 25.

[19] Ibid., p. 31.

[20] Pyarelal (Nair), *Mahatma Gandhi: The Early Phase*, Ahmedabad: Navajivan Publishing House, 1965, I, p. 202.

[21] *Gandhi's Autobiography*, p. 12, and the incident of the stolen arm bracelet.

[22] Ibid., pp. 20, 36.

[23] Ibid., pp. 16–17. The story of Maharaja Harishchandra occurs in many versions. We have drawn on a translation of a Bengali version by Edward C. Dimock in *The Thief of Love*, Chicago: University of Chicago Press, 1963.

[24] '"Why should not all be truthful like Harishchandra?" was the question I asked myself day and night,' Gandhi writes in his autobiography. 'To follow truth and go through all the ordeals Harishchandra went through was the one ideal it [the play] inspired in me' (*Gandhi's Autobiography*, p. 17).

[25] Tendulkar, *Mahatma*, I, pp. 77, 169; II, pp. 4, 247, 378. The nearest equivalent in the Judaeo-Christian tradition to the virtues of Prahlad and Harishchandra is probably the virtue of Job—but he does not suffer at the hands of humans. We have stressed for the purpose of this account a particular set of relations in the two stories. But the tales speak for the psychology of the *bhakti* (devotional) cults more generally.

[26] *Gandhi's Autobiography*, p. 12.

[27] 'The first marriage,' Pyarelal writes, 'took place when he was fourteen; the second at the age of twenty-five, after the death of his first wife. From his first and second marriages he had two daughters; the third marriage proved issueless, and his wife was stricken with an incurable ailment which made her an invalid for life. Already then fortyish, without male issue or hope of having any, he yielded,' according to Pyarelal's version of these events, 'to the importunity of his elders and decided to remarry' (*Mahatma Gandhi: The Early Phase*, I, p. 186). P. Gandhi, a relative, tells us, however, that 'the elders in the family in Porbandar have no knowledge of the third marriage' (*My Childhood with Gandhi*, p. 18). Pyarelal, too, in the quotation above, does not make clear what happened to Gandhi's second wife. Gandhi's allegation of carnality rests not only on the fact of four marriages but also on his father's advanced age ('over forty') at the time of the fourth marriage. Here again Gandhi's feelings may have coloured his interpretation of the facts. Pyarelal describes Kaba Gandhi as 'fortyish' when he married Putliba, Gandhi's mother. Yet when Gandhi was born his father was forty-seven and had three previous children, two boys and a girl, by Putliba. The second of these children, Raliat, was 'Gandhiji's senior by seven years,' a fact that suggests that Gandhi's father may have been thirty-eight or nine at the time of the fourth marriage. See Pyarelal, *Mahatma Gandhi: The Early Phase*, I, 186–7, for the details of Kaba Gandhi's marriages and children.

[28] *The Diary of Mahadev Desai*, trans. from the Gujarati and ed. V.G. Desai, Ahmedabad, 1953, I, p. 52.

[29] *Gandhi's Autobiography*, pp. 12, 13.

[30] Ibid., pp. 45–6.

[31] Gandhi, *Self-Restraint v. Self-Indulgence*, p. 56.

[32] 'One cannot talk to Gandhi or listen to him or even see him from a distance without becoming aware both of the peace that is in him and of the energy he radiates' (Edmond Taylor, *Richer by Asia*, Boston: Houghton Muffin, 1947, p. 412).

[33] Mahadev Desai (trans. and ed.), *The Gita according to Gandhi*, Ahmedabad: Navajivan Publishing House, 1946), Chapter XII, vs. 15, p. 312.

[34] Calder, *Medicine and Man* (New York: Mentor, 1958), p. 50. Calder offers no source for the statement.

[35] See his *Drinks, Drugs and Gambling* by Bharatan Kumarappa (ed.), Ahmedabad: Navajivan Publishing House, 1952. He believed smoking stupefied and liked to cite the case of the hero in Tolstoy's *Kreuzer Sonata*, who kills once a cigarette has numbed his feelings (Pyarelal, *Mahatma Gandhi: The Early Phase*, I, p. 208).

[36] The one bit of evidence that could prove compatible with everything else we know about Gandhi is an account that he, among the many natural remedies he used in the course of his life, especially for constipation, may have incidentally taken Rauwolfia. Such evidence would carry this line of explanation no farther than the discovery of paragoric in a family's medicine chest would establish the existence of an opium habit.

[37] *Gandhi's Autobiography*, p. 254.

[38] Ibid.

[39] Ibid., p. 56.

[40] A fact that helped recommend the name to him (P. Gandhi, *My Childhood with Gandhi*, p. 37).

[41] Ibid., pp. 45–6.

[42] *Harijan*, 13 October 1940, p. 319; cited in Pyarelal (Nair), *Mahatma Gandhi: The Last Phase*, Ahmedabad, 1956, I, p. 570.

[43] 'He did for her everything that a mother usually does for her daughter. He supervised her education, her food, dress, rest, and sleep. For closer supervision and guidance he made her share the same bed with him' (Pyarelal, *Mahatma Gandhi: The Last Phase*, I, p. 576). 'Gandhiji said that it was indeed true that he permitted women workers to use his bed ...' (N.K. Bose, *My Days with Gandhi*, Calcutta: Nishana, 1953, p. 134).

[44] Arthur Koestler overstated the case when he wrote that 'the Gandhians ... were so thorough in effacing every trace of the scandal that [Nirmal Kumar] Bose's book is unobtainable in India' (*The Lotus and the Robot*, New York: Macmillan, 1961, p. 150n.). We obtained it by writing to a well-known Indian bookseller, and so did several colleagues. Pyarelal's book, a standard work that is everywhere available, discusses the matter in detail.

[45] Pyarelal (Nair), *Mahatma Gandhi: The Last Phase*, Ahmedabad, 1958, II, p. 382.

[46] Bose, *My Days with Gandhi*, p. 96.

[47] Ibid., p. 107.

[48] 'Referring to Manu, he said, that he had been telling her how he personally felt that he had reached the end of one chapter in his old life and a new one was about to begin. He was thinking of a bold and original experiment, whose "heat will be great." And only those who realize this and were prepared to remain at their posts, should be with him' (*My Days with Gandhi*, p. 116).

[49] Pyarelal, *Mahatma Gandhi: The Last Phase*, I, p. 581. Kripalani responded that he trusted Gandhi and that he was sure Gandhi had considered the danger that he might 'be employing human beings as means rather than as ends in themselves' (p. 582). One of his sceptical friends was reassured by the sight of Gandhi and Manu peacefully asleep. It is relevant for the meaning of these events that Gandhi's bedroom was not private and unaccessible but virtually a public room.

[50] Bose, *My Days with Gandhi*, p. 154. Bose, who acted as Gandhi's Bengali translator, chose not to translate these remarks, a procedure that greatly displeased Gandhi.

[51] Ibid., p. 159.

[52] Reprinted from *Harijan*, 10 May 1942, in *Gandhi, Drink, Drugs and Gambling*, p. 130.

[53] Ranjee (Gurdu Singh) Shahani, *Mr. Gandhi*, New York: Macmillan, 1961, p. 5. Shahani offers no citations.

[54] Many texts stress the connection between food and character, notably the Bhagavad Gita, which associates types of food with levels in the hierarchy of worshippers; see Gandhi's version, *The Gita according to Gandhi*, Chapter XVII, vss. 4–11, pp. 356–7. The categories of 'masculine' or 'lusty' foods are similar in other cultures: 'We Amhara are tough people. We love to eat hot pepper. We love to drink hard alcohol. We don't like smooth foods' (Donald N. Levine, 'The Concept of Masculinity in Ethiopian Culture' (paper delivered at the Fourteenth Annual Symposium of the Committee on Human Development)).

[55] Elder, 'Industrialism and Hinduism,' p. 217; Carstairs, *The Twice Born*, pp. 83, 84.

[56] Elder, 'Industrialism and Hinduism,' p. 186.

[57] Ibid., p. 217; Carstairs, *The Twice Born*, p. 84.

[58] P. Gandhi, *My Childhood with Gandhi*, pp. 36, 50.

[59] Reprinted from *Young India*, 18 July 1927, in *Diet and Diet Reform*, Ahmedabad, 1949, p. 13.

[60] Ibid.

[61] See *Gandhi's Autobiography*, Chapter 1, 'Birth and Parentage.'

[62] Bose, *My Days with Gandhi*, p. 109. Bose throughout offers a psychologically sophisticated account, in which he reveals himself as equally a social scientist and a sympathetic friend of Gandhi.

[63] Manubehn Gandhi, *Bapu—My Mother*, Ahmedabad: Navajivan Publishing House, 1955. She reports him as saying to her, 'Have I not become your mother? I have been father to many, but only to you I am a mother' (p. 3).

[64] *Harijan*, 24 February 1940.

[65] David Bakan, 'Agency and Communion in Human Sexuality', *The Duality of Human Existence*, Chicago: Rand McNally, 1966.

[66] Again it can be argued that these qualities are particularly appealing to the non-violent twice-born castes.

8

This-Worldly Asceticism and
Political Modernization

Many of those were Gandhi's followers in the nationalist movement accepted his political leadership even while rejecting or not hearing his message of religious commitment and social reform. With each passing generation his image and ideas have declined in public understanding and acceptance. One era's inspiration has become the next era's cliché. Post-Independence Indians have little regard for Gandhi's vision of India as a nation with a special 'spiritual' vocation and with the will and means to live simply in self-sufficient villages. One hears less and less in political discourse of the Vedas, Upanishads, and Gita or of the public relevance of the quest for union with the eternal. The conception of India as a spiritual nation formulated in the nineteenth and early twentieth century by Dayanand, Vivekananda, Tagore, Aurobindo, and Gandhi himself played a significant part in shaping India's national identity and helping her to make a name and place for herself in the world. With the coming of independence and democratic self-government, new age groups have emerged for whom the nationalist struggle, in which Gandhi played so central a part, has become a history book happening or the memory of old men's youth. Castes and classes have come to power whose cultural backgrounds, political experiences, and moral concerns are less rooted in the Sanskritic tradition and its ideological norms. They pursue goals that are increasingly instrumental. Self-sufficient villages stand in the way of their quest for a release from poverty and dependence. The other worldly concerns of Gandhian followers detract from the moral and material tasks of economic development and social mobility.

The men of power in India today also have little patience with Gandhi's post-industrial critique of industrial civilization and the alternatives he advocated. Living in an era when industrialized civilization was already well-established in the West, Gandhi was of a nation that was just beginning to industrialize. He could still hear and sympathize with the critics of early industrialism, Ruskin, Thoreau, and the European and American utopian socialists, who found that it brutalized men, alienating them from self and society and depriving them of the capacity to govern themselves. Like those who founded utopian colonies, he hoped to revitalize the village community economically and morally, transforming it into a viable and attractive alternative to urban and machine civilization. By freeing men from the dehumanizing tyranny of artificial wants and the production required to satisfy them, the Gandhian village would enable them to live simple, worthwhile lives in meaningful communities. These conceptions have influenced post-Independence policies, by providing some of the rationale and legitimation for political and economic decentralization.[1] But they are suspect as an unrealistic village romance that fails to appreciate how rapid industrial development can replace poverty with abundance and national weakness with national power. For many among India's intellectual and professional classes, the village is backward and conservative, a place where higher castes and classes dominate lower and new ideas and technology advance at a snail's pace, the place least rather than most likely to provide the inspiration and the means for tomorrow's utopia.

Both at home and abroad Gandhi's philosophy of non-violence has been more sympathetically and broadly received than has his apotheosis of village life. It helped to explain and legitimize, even if it was not the basis of, Nehru's non-aligned foreign policy, and it continues to influence the political tactics of organized political forces. Abroad, its most conspicuous influence has been on the ideas, strategy, and tactics of Martin Luther King in his struggle to win equal rights and opportunities for American blacks. Yet it, too, has been a casualty of events and forces. Gandhi was gunned down by a fundamentalist Hindu who thought he was too soft toward Muslims and Pakistan. Although just prior to his assassination Gandhi had been able to restore sanity and order in parts of Bengal and in Delhi, he had not been able to do so generally; the partition of India released the furies of communal hatred and vengeance, shattering the civilizing controls of respect for non-violence and for public force. In December 1961, Jawaharlal Nehru took the decision that he had been resisting for fourteen years, to use military force against the Portuguese colonial presence in Goa. In October 1962, the Chinese penetrated India's Himalayan frontiers, driving India's badly equipped and trained mountain forces to the plains of Assam. In September 1965, full-scale hostilities broke out between India and Pakistan. These encounters dramatically illustrated the limits of non-violence in international politics, weakened its hold on the Indian public mind, and undermined its place in official ideology. It still is invoked to help justify India's decision not to build nuclear weapons, but the threat of nuclear proliferation in the region and globally puts support for the policy at risk. The last ten years have witnessed the emergence of a vigorous new nationalism; it is more chauvinistic and parochial than that of Nehru, less tolerant, and more intemperate than that of Gandhi. It speaks especially to the urbanized young men who have benefited from expanding if deficient collegiate education. They and others more senior and influential would like India to have more muscle, larger armed forces and nuclear weapons to lick China, Pakistan, or whoever else might be looking for a fight.

On all these counts, spirituality, the self-sufficient village, and non-violence, Gandhi no longer speaks to the needs of the politically active classes of the sixties. For them Gandhi is a virtuous old gentleman, good in his time. His memory is being ritualized and devalued by proliferation of district town statues and stereotyped praise. But there is an aspect of Gandhi's character and work that is relevant to the political modernizer.

Gandhi's greatest contribution to political modernization was the one we have already discussed, helping India to acquire national coherence and identity, to become a nation, by showing Indians a way to courage, self-respect, and political potency. But because these contributions were rooted in the experience of imperial domination and coloured by Gandhi's transcendental morality and appeal to traditional ideas, they have become less meaningful to post-Independence generations. It is those aspects of Gandhi's leadership that relate to middle-level norms of conduct and to instrumental rather than ideological effectiveness that remain relevant. Obscured by the grand legacies of saintliness and independence, they require analysis and understanding not only because of their continuing significance but also because they were necessary conditions for Gandhi's greatness.

Gandhi's more mundane contributions to political modernization include introducing in the conduct of politics a work ethic and economizing behaviour with respect to time and resources, and making India's political structures more rational, democratic, and professional. A man with Gandhi's spiritual concerns might be supposed to show little interest in the more routine tasks of modern politics. Yet far from being incapacitated for mundane political entrepreneurship by his religious heritage, Gandhi drew from it a this-worldly asceticism. His efforts to build effective political organizations were associated with a psychological disposition toward work and efficiency that mobilized like propensities among those whose lives were affected by his example and teaching.

Gandhi approached his public work with the frame of mind of those modernizing men who confront all tasks with the calculation of the metronome and the balance sheet. While Weber and contemporary social psychologists associate industriousness and the economizing of time and resources with achievement drives rooted in 'Protestant' character, Gandhi came to them through familial and religious socialization in the Vaishnavite and Jain traditions of Gujarat. His life course does not support Weber's belief that 'it could not have occurred to a Hindu to prize the rational transformation of the world in accordance with matter-of-fact considerations and to undertake such transformation as an act of obedience to a divine will.'[2] The disposition to work, save, and rationally allocate time and resources in order to realize given goals is not necessarily modern. It appears, for example, among religious orders, both East and West, where self-control and asceticism in the service of spiritual ends find expression, as they did for Gandhi, in strict observance of schedules, hard work at physical, intellectual, or spiritual task, and the practice of thrift. Traditional merchant castes, too, such as Gandhi's, the Modh Baniyas, exhibit such psychological dispositions and habits. But it is also true that the elevation of these characteristics to universal virtues is particularly associated with the emergence of modern entrepreneurship and scientific technology and the expectations they raised that men could master their material and human environment. In the West, the preaching of these characteristics as virtues and attempts systematically to inculcate them into emerging generations through sermons, aphorisms, penny pamphlets, and public education began in the eighteenth century and peaked in the nineteenth.[3]

Much in the petty details of Gandhi's life corresponds to the practice of those eighteenth- and nineteenth-century figures in Britain and America whose lives and teaching popularized the Protestant ethic and applied technology. Preeminent among them in America was Benjamin Franklin. In *Poor Richard's Almanac* the inventor, people's philosopher, and statesman offered practical advice to the modernizing and mobile youth of a bustling, ambitious new nation. Some might boggle at the attempt to bracket Franklin and Gandhi, one a herald, the other a critic, of industrial civilization. At certain fundamental points, indeed, the two men undoubtedly were poles apart. Gandhi would not have enjoyed Parisian life, as did Franklin. And

Franklin's attitude was highly instrumental toward the practice of virtue. Gandhi would never have congratulated himself, as Franklin did, by saying: 'I cannot boast much success in acquiring the reality of [pridelessness] but I had a good deal with regard to the appearance of it.'[4] And Gandhi would have been scandalized by a similar Franklinism: 'Nothing [is] so likely to make a man's fortune as virtue.'[5] For Franklin, a practical man, moderation— in food, drink, and venery—was a virtue. For Gandhi, a religious who refused to separate means and ends, and found the passions a permanent threat, moderation in these areas of life was a shortfall from virtue. Food should be taken like medicine, privately and sparingly, not for pleasure but to sustain life.[6] Celibacy was too serious to be treated with 'moderation'. For Franklin, virtue was useful; for Gandhi, it was self-justifying.

These are important differences but they should not be allowed to obscure what the two men held in common; by exploring the points of congruence, Gandhi's contribution to Indian modernity can be better understood. Gandhi and Franklin subjected their environment to rigorous calculations that linked psychic and material expenditures to their returns. And, despite Franklin's contingent view of virtue, they shared a propensity to invest with moral, not merely utilitarian, implications the observance of certain 'Protestant' habits. Silence, order, resolution, frugality, industry, cleanliness, and chastity are seven of Franklin's virtues about which Gandhi would have been enthusiastic. However differently they viewed their ultimate fate, neither man proposed to let the control and mastery of his worldly environment escape him.

It is no accident that a large watch was among the few effects Gandhi valued in his lifetime and left behind at his death.[7] Gandhi was extremely meticulous about time, as it was measured by the clock, the more so as he found a good many of those about him indifferent to its compulsions. He employed his watch as a species of tyrant to regulate his own affairs and the lives of those associated with him. Arrivals and departures frequently were crises; Gandhi considered the normal practice of great public figures, to keep their audiences waiting, a transgression. Many were the arrangement committees and colleagues whom he upbraided for failures on this score. Introducing the venerable B.G. Tilak, who was late, to a conference in 1917, Gandhi remarked: 'I am not responsible for his being late. We demand *swaraj*. If one does not mind arriving late by three-quarters of an hour at a conference summoned for the purpose, one should not mind if *swaraj* too comes correspondingly late.'[8] Once, in his earlier work in 1917 among indigo workers in Bihar, when it became apparent that a decision to move himself and his co-workers would not be carried out by the end of the appointed day, he picked up his bedroll at ten o'clock at night and began to move his effects. His associates, for the most part from the upper castes and classes and accustomed to be waited on by servants and to adjust to their inefficiencies, were obliged willy-nilly to move themselves also.[9]

The timetable he blocked out for his first Indian ashram is faithful to his own schedule and recalls a similar affection for orderly schedules in Franklin. Their respective schedules read as follows:[10]

Gandhi			Franklin	
4	a.m.	Rising from bed	5	Rise, wash and address *Powerful Goodness!*
4:15 to 4:45	a.m.	Morning prayer	6	Contrive day's
5 to 6:10	a.m.	Bath, exercise, study		business, and take the
6:10 to 6:30	a.m.	Breakfast		resolution of the day;
6:30 to 7	a.m.	Women's prayer class		prosecute the present
7 to 10:30	a.m.	Body labour, education,		study, and breakfast
		and sanitation	7	
			8	Work
10:45 to 11:15	a.m.	Dinner	9	
12 to 4:30	p.m.	Body labour, including classes	10	
			11	
4:30 to 5:30	p.m.	Recreation	12	Read, or overlook my
5:30 to 6	p.m.	Supper	1	accounts, and dine.
6 to 7	p.m.	Recreation	2	Work
7 to 7:30	p.m.	Common worship	3	
7:30 to 9	p.m.	Recreation	4	
9	p.m.	Retiring bell	5	
			6	Put things in their places.
			7	Supper. Music or diversion,
			8	or conversation.
			9	Examination of the day.
			10	Sleep
			11	
			12	
			1	
			2	
			3	
			4	

Note: These hours are subject to change whenever necessary.

Franklin's timetable differs from Gandhi's mainly in its less picayune calibrations and in allowing more time for dining.

Gandhi took the timetable most seriously: 'All members', runs the first rule of the ashram, 'whether permanent or otherwise will turn every minute of their time to good account'.[11] A few days after Kasturbai died in jail in 1944, his morning meal was served at 11:45 rather than at 11:30; those responsible for the meal were lectured: 'You know she never sent me food late, even by one minute.'[12] Any item included in his schedule was ruthlessly attended to. In late 1946, when Hindu–Muslim disturbances had broken out in Bengal and Gandhi at 77 went to Noakhali district to try to restore peace, he began his day at 2:30 a.m. and took up Bengali lessons.[13] Manu Gandhi's diary records: 'After taking fruit juice, he began to pore over his Bengali primer. While doing so, he dozed off for about ten minutes .... At 7:25 we started on our day's march, reaching ... at 8:25 a.m. after a full one hour's walk. Immediately upon his arrival there, he again sat down to do his Bengali lesson.'[14] His secretary Pyarelal reports that, no matter how late the hour or how heavy the pressure of work, the Bengali lesson was never missed.[15] Manu Gandhi's diary entries, precise to the minute, stand witness to the microscopic relentlessness with which the Mahatma imposed on himself and those around him the discipline of calibrated time.

Gandhi's assiduous thrift expressed itself in the smallest and the largest matters. Like Franklin, he went over his accounts daily[16] and would have approved of the entire catalogue of savings aphorisms, from 'a penny saved is a penny earned' onward. The ashram rules not only linked cleanliness to thrift but also provided a practical Indian version of the saving-is-earning theme:

The split twigs used for toothbrushing should be washed well, and collected in a pot. When they dry up, they should be used for starting a fire, the idea being that nothing which can be used should be thrown away.[17]

Gandhi wrote hundreds of important communications on the reverse of old letters and memos. When he began the Natal Indian Congress, he self-consciously avoided the waste and ostentation that often accompanied new organizational beginnings in India. Instead of having receipt books and reports printed he ran them off on a cyclostyle machine in his office, 'knowing that in public work minor expenses at times absorbed large amounts ....' 'Such economy', he instructs the readers of his autobiography, 'is essential for every organization, and yet I know that it is not always exercised'.[18] In his correspondence with the industrialist G.D. Birla, from whom he extracted vast sums to support various nationalist and service enterprises, a good many letters concern themselves with the saving of bank charges on large transfers.[19]

He worried a good deal about accounting for the public funds with which he was entrusted, beginning in a small way in Natal: 'People never cared to have receipts for the amounts they paid, but we always insisted on the receipts being given. Every pie was thus clearly accounted for, and I dare say the account books for the year 1894 can be found intact even today.'[20] Returning to South Africa in 1896, he reported in detail to the Natal Indian Congress how he had spent the 75 pounds it had sanctioned toward his expenses, including 'Barber, 4 annas; Washerman, 8 annas; Pickwick pens, 6 annas; *Pankha* coolie, 2 annas; Theatre, Rs 4; Servant Lalu, Rs 10', and so forth.[21]

Gandhi, who tells us in the first sentence of his autobiography that he belongs to the baniya caste and is descended from shopkeepers, and who spent his formative professional years among Gujarati merchants in South Africa, showed a marked flare for acquiring as well as using money. An incident from the early days of the Natal Congress illustrates his persistence, use of strategy, and sense of timing:

On one occasion during this money raising tour the situation was rather difficult. We expected our host to contribute £6 [one-fourth Gandhi's initial monthly salary], but he refused to give anything more than £3. If we had accepted that amount from him, others would have followed suit, and our collections would have been spoiled. It was a late hour of the night, and we were all hungry. But how could we dine without having first obtained the amount we were bent on getting? All persuasion was useless. The host seemed to be adamant. Other merchants in the town reasoned with him, and we all sat up throughout the night, he as well as we determined not to budge one inch. Most of my co-workers were burning with rage, but they contained themselves. At last, when day was already breaking, the host yielded, paid down £6 and feasted us. This happened at Tongaat, but the repercussion of the incident was felt as far as Stanger on the North Coast and Charlestown in the interior. It also hastened our work of collection.[22]

Again, in 1919, at a critical point in Gandhi's Indian career, he demonstrated that he recognized the importance of mobilizing financial resources and had the will and the skill to do so. Pyarelal tells us that soon after the Jallianwala Bagh massacre a Congress decision to acquire the park for a memorial to those who had fallen required financial support from the businessmen of Amritsar. Swami Shraddhanand, 'the saffron-robed Savonarola of Northern India', told the assembled businessmen that 'India's glorious past and her lofty ancient cultural tradition' called upon them to rise to the occasion but his 'eloquence produced no ... results'. Pandit Madan Mohan Malaviya, founder and chancellor of the Banaras Hindu University and popularly known as 'the silver-tongued orator of the Congress', also cajoled the Amritsar business community, by telling its members that if they would only unloosen their purse strings dharma, artha, kama, and moksha, too, would be theirs, but to no avail. 'Finally, Gandhi spoke .... In level tones he told them that the target had been fixed. It had to be reached. If they failed in their duty he would sell his Ashram and make up the amount. He would not let the sanctity of the national resolve, to which he had been a party—so had they been too—be lightly treated .... The required amount [five lakhs of rupees] was subscribed on the spot.'[23]

'I must regard my participation in Congress proceedings at Amritsar', Gandhi confesses, 'as my real entrance into the Congress politics'. His experience there 'had shown that there were one or two things for which I had some aptitude'. Not only did he succeed in raising the money to acquire Jallianwala Bagh but he was also appointed one of the trustees to raise and administer an additional five lakhs to construct a national memorial there. Pandit Malaviya had the reputation of being Congress' best fund-raiser 'but I knew that I was not far behind him in that respect'. It was, Gandhi adds, 'in South Africa that I discovered my capacity in this direction'. Malaviya had succeeded by turning to India's rajas and maharajas; 'but I knew', Gandhi observes, 'that there was no question of approaching' them for donation for the memorial. It was under these circumstances that 'the main responsibility ... fell, as I had expected, on my shoulders'. Gandhi turned to the business community of Bombay and was again strikingly successful. 'The generous citizens of Bombay subscribed most liberally, and the memorial trust has at present a handsome credit balance in the bank.'[24]

Gandhi's ascendancy in the Congress was associated not only with his organizational and idiomatic skills and popular touch but also with his financial capacities. More than any other Congress leader, he had access to the purses (as well as the hearts and minds) of India's business communities, an access he used to generate financial support for Congress even while recruiting merchants, traders, and industrialists into organizations and activities associated with nationalism and social reform. While there was no doubt a conservative political dimension to this support, it is difficult to see how, with public patronage and resources in British hands, the professionalization of Congress politics could have been achieved otherwise.

Evidence of Gandhi's industriousness and productivity can be found in his rigid adherence to schedules; the frequency and pace of his interviews: the volume of letters, reports, petitions, and articles that issued from his pen; the number and scope of his tours; and his leadership and management of literary, reform, and spiritual and political organizations and activities. Ordinarily Gandhi maintained his schedule while on tour, doing his daily writing on trains and in way stations. The collected works, which will run to some one hundred volumes, greatly understate the level of his productivity because speeches and statements that did not enter into the public record and letters that were not directed to officials who filed them or to adherents who saved them will not be recorded there. The enormous volume of replies to unknown or obscure inquirers—Nirmal Kumar Bose recalls that in Noakhali he 'refreshed' himself with a six-page letter to an unknown young man seeking his advice on marriage arrangements—and a significant volume of public mail are simply lost.[25] In the busy days of the nationalist movement, many who might have kept records found it hard to do so between jail terms; others were not disposed to keep files. But we do know that it took some half-dozen well-trained assistants to help him handle his daily mail and that he took keeping up with it very seriously.

He did a great deal, and he applied exacting standards of accuracy, clarity, and efficiency to all of it. 'His energy', Pyarelal tells us, 'was phenomenal .... One day I actually counted 56 letters which he had written in his own hand'. In the midst of din and disorder, his 'remarkable faculty of switching on and off his mind to and from anything at will and to remain unaffected by his surroundings' enabled him to carry on with his usual pace and efficiency. 'He had a passion for precision and thoroughness in the minutest details ... and enforced military discipline and clock-work regularity in his own case and expected the same from those around him .... He insisted on his desk being always clear and woe to anyone of his staff who referred to him a letter more than forty-eight hours old .... Any reply of more than five or ten lines was a rule consigned to the waste paper basket. The address was no less minutely scrutinized. Not to know ... the exact location of an out of the way place in India was regarded as a culpable failure. Vagueness about train timings or the exact time it took for the post to reach its destination by a particular route was another cardinal sin ....'[26] His public reports, petitions, and demands reflect the capacity for orderly clear argument and meticulous care for facts that he had developed as a successful lawyer.[27]

Gandhi's this-worldly asceticism took its meaning in the context of larger motives and meanings. Those who practice it cannot know direct rewards but they remain alert for signs of grace. Gandhi associated his reception by the Indian people with the potency of his charisma and saw it as a visible recognition that his worldly asceticism made him worthy. Public influence was the coin in which he measured his worldly success. 'The incomparable love that I have received has made it clear to me that they in whom truth and the spirit of service are manifested in their fullness will assuredly sway the hearts of men and so accomplish their chosen task.'[28]

But Gandhi was never certain that he was one of those in whom the spirit of truth and service was sufficiently manifest. Some of the energy that he invested in worldly asceticism must have arisen from this uncertainty. It is in his relationship to darshan (view of an auspicious object, such as a temple deity, king, or holy man from which the viewer gains merit or good fortune) that these uncertainties become clear. Soon after his return to India in 1915, Gandhi first confronted his darshan dilemma—whether his capacity to give and people's eagerness to receive darshan was a worldly sign of his spiritual achievements or whether it was an expression of his vanity and their irrationality. At the Kumbha Mela, a vast religious assemblage of pilgrims and sadhus held once every twelve years, darshan seekers did not allow him a minute to call his own. It was then, he tells us, 'that I realized what a deep impression my humble services in South Africa had made throughout the whole of India'. And, in almost the same breath: '... The *darshanvalas'* blind love has often made me angry, and ... sore at heart.'[29]

Four years later, as he was establishing his ascendancy in the nationalist movement, Gandhi found, on the one hand, that 'the affection that I am receiving from men and women here in Lahore [and throughout the Punjab] puts me to shame', and on the other, that 'the unique faith of India and the frankness and generosity of our people enchant me'. Not only did 'young and old ... come all day to have *darshan* of [Gandhi]', but also it was impossible for him to go out alone. 'I simply cannot check them', he complained. More disturbing was the thought that he knew of nothing in himself that made him 'worthy of giving *darshan*'; he found it 'intolerable' that they should want *darshan* from a 'mere servant'. Nor did the people 'profit in any way by having *darshan*'. 'If I keep on giving *darshan*', he commented ominously, 'my work will suffer'.[30] A month later, in Wazirabad, he had grown tired of *darshan*. '... In the end we had to keep the doors closed ...; it is not possible simultaneously to work and to give *darshan*.'[31]

'No man', he stated flatly, 'is great enough to give it'. He found that he was embarrassed by the experience and wanted to put a stop to it. But to do so would hurt people's feelings, and he had 'not yet found it possible to do this'. Perhaps his courage was 'inadequate' or his judgement 'clouded'; more likely 'my principle of non-violence does not allow me to hurt people's feelings. 'I do', he protested, '... make every effort to extricate myself from this dilemma.' But his solution, tentatively stated in 1919 but developed into a habit over the years, was not to choose between darshan and work but to try to do both: 'At present, even when people come for *darshan*, I continue to write and do other work.'[32]

However much Gandhi found himself unworthy of darshan and giving it a threat to his work and serenity, he could not escape the feeling that it expressed in worldly terms some measure of other worldly approbation, that it was a sign of grace. 'Man's instinctive urge to worship', he found 'admirable'.[33] The test for worship was the worthiness of its object, and Gandhi found it hard to accept that he and those who came to him for darshan were engaged in a mutual fraud upon each other. 'It is perfectly clear to me that this relationship is the miracle wrought by even a small measure of devotion to truth and service .... I am making a prodigious effort to live up to these two principles.'[34]

Toward the end of his life, as he was leaving for Noakhali to try to still the communal passions unleashed by partition, the old man in a train was still not certain whether his spiritual virtue and worldly asceticism made him worthy of such attention. But he persisted, mindful of the possibility that he might be and in the belief that effortfulness would make it so:

The journey proved to be as strenuous as many had feared. There were mammoth crowds at all big stations on the way. At places it was like a swarming ant-heap of humanity as far as the eye could reach. The crowd clambered on the roofs of the carriages, choked the windows, broke glass, smashed shutters and yelled and shouted till one's ears split. They pulled the alarm-chain again and again for *darshan*, making it necessary to disconnect the vacuum brakes .... Later in the evening, Gandhiji sat with his fingers thrust in his ears to keep out the shouting when it became unbearable. But when it was proposed to him that the lights be switched off to discourage *darshan* seekers, he turned down the suggestion by saying that the simple faith of the masses demanded that he should serve them with the last ounce of his energy ....[35]

Gandhi's version of this-worldly asceticism led him to rationalize and extend the organizational bases of Indian political life. Soon after Gandhi returned to India in 1915 he recognized that Congress could not achieve the goals of national mobilization, social reform, and political freedom as long as it depended exclusively on talking shops by, for, and among the English-educated elite. Legislative debates at the centre and in the provinces and the formulation of resolutions at Congress annual sessions could not, by themselves, realize these goals. Until opinion was organizationally related to the aspirations and objective needs of popular social and economic forces, it could be neither legitimate nor politically effective. One of Gandhi's most important contributions to political modernization was to help Congress become a mass political organization, manned by fulltime political workers and capable of mobilizing public opinion and bringing it to bear on governmental policy and administration. All that has been said and written about Gandhi's shifting the arena and method of Indian politics from persuasion of the government by elites to direct action among the people has obscured a parallel and equally important shift that he inaugurated, building a political organization.

Gandhi began building political organizations well before he entered Indian politics. Visiting India from South Africa in 1901, he was disappointed by what he witnessed at a session of the Indian National Congress. An association of political amateurs in an era that was ready for political professionals, the Congress provided an annual forum for liberal nationalists to address adherents and sympathizers but found it difficult to translate words into action because it lacked the continuity and specialization that permanent structures and full-time personnel make possible. 'The Congress', Gandhi observed, 'would meet three days every year and then go to sleep. What training could one have out of a three day's show once a year?'[36] He deplored Congress' slovenly procedures and its subordination of efficiency to ceremony. 'I also noticed the huge waste of time here .... There was little regard for economy of energy. More than one did the work of one, and many an important thing was no one's business at all.'[37] Too many people came and too few had the inclination or the means to take the business at hand seriously. 'The procedure was far from pleasing to me .... There was hardly any difference between visitors and delegates. Everyone raised his hand and all resolutions passed unanimously.'[38]

Gandhi had established his first political organization seven years earlier, in 1894.[39] The Natal National Congress was a cadre organization, meticulously organized, that demanded of its members a continuous and high level of commitment. At the end of its first year it had a membership of 228 drawn from the prosperous middle-class section of the South African Indian community.[40] Those who failed to pay their subscription or missed six consecutive meetings were struck off the rolls.[41] The subscription was substantial; at three pounds per year (paid in advance) it represented, for example, 1 per cent of the salary Gandhi received in 1894, a salary that enabled him to maintain the style of life characteristic of the white middle classes.[42] A number of middle-class merchants participated in door-to-door canvassing, a labour that Gandhi evidently considered good experience for testing their commitment.[43] The Congress met monthly to discuss policy and pass on expenditures.[44] Its objective were not unlike those of the caste associations emerging in India: it published and distributed pamphlets on problems confronting Indians as a subject community facing dominant white South Africans; provided legal assistance to indentured Indians; represented Indian interest in legislative and administrative contexts; and worked to upgrade the manners and life style of the community.[45]

Recognizing that political consciousness and organization without political skills inhibited personal confidence and public effectiveness, Gandhi worked to repair the political skills of Natal Congressmen. 'People had no experience of taking part in public discussions .... Everyone hesitated to stand up to speak. I explained to them the rules of procedure at meetings .... They realized that it was an education for them, and many who had never been accustomed to speaking before an audience soon acquired the habit of thinking and speaking publicly ....'[46]

The meetings were conducted in Gujarati; if expatriate Gujarati merchants without formal schooling were to participate, there was no other choice.[47] These early experiences contributed to Gandhi's recognition that the use of English inhibited the Indian National Congress and to his optimism concerning the effect the use of regional languages would have on political participation and national consciousness.

Gandhi extended the reach of the Congress by proliferating branches in ten centres outside the territorial jurisdiction of the parent Natal organization.[48] These new structures retained the vanguard qualities of the original organization by being composed of a few, well-placed, committed, and active members.

On his return to India in 1915 he applied the ideas and methods that he had developed in South Africa to the first political organization he joined, the Gujarat Sabha, converting it from an ad hoc society that met annually to pass resolutions into a permanent structure whose executive conducted a year-long programme of activities.[49] Gandhi was quite explicit about his intention to make politics more professional and to associate it with permanent specialized structures:

Conferences do not, as a rule, at the end of their deliberations leave behind them an executive body, and even when such a body is appointed, it is, to use the language of the late Mr Gokhale, composed of men who are amateurs. What we need is men who would make it their business to give effect to the resolutions of such conferences. If such men came forward in great numbers, then and then only will such conferences be a credit to the country and produce lasting results. At present there is much waste of energy.[50]

If the professional revolutionary and the professional politician represent two types of the modern political specialist, the Gandhian professional embodies qualities of both without fully resembling either. The professional revolutionary was first given historical expression in the seventeenth century by the 'saints' of the English civil war and subsequently elaborated upon by the Jacobin and Bolshevik of the French and Russian revolutions.[51] The professional politician developed out of the experience with competitive democratic politics in western Europe and America.[52] The Gandhian model of politics as a vocation emerged in the years immediately following his return to India in 1915. Although in its particulars this type was related to the Indian cultural context, it has more general application as an example of the professionalization of peaceable ideal politics. Its concern for spiritual meaning, its emphasis on service, its insistence on non-violent means, and its suspicion of power distinguish the Gandhian from the other two models.

Like professional revolutionaries, Gandhian professionals gave the highest priority in their personal lives and public actions to ideologically defined ends, but unlike revolutionaries, they gave equal priority to non-violent means. Modern political specialists, regardless of type, must attend to the requirements of mobilizing and representing particular classes, communities, and interests. For professional politicians, this task tends to become an end in itself since it is the prescribed means for acquiring power. For revolutionaries, mobilization and representation are options to be used under certain historical conditions. Gandhians used mobilization and representation as a means to help realize certain ideal goals, such as national freedom or social justice, by making their claims more legitimate and effective. Like revolutionaries but unlike politicians, Gandhians placed self-sacrifice above self-assertion and service to the cause and those whom it was to benefit above considerations of personal popularity or advantage.

Gandhian professionals can also be distinguished from both revolutionaries and politicians by their orientation toward power. Revolutionaries must seek and use power if they are to model a new society; it is good societies that produce good men, and power is a necessary instrument for the realization of good societies. Politicians, too, must seek and use power. In establishing their mandate to govern, to realize certain ideal and material goals, and to allocate resources, patronage, and honour, politicians find the pursuit and deployment of power an integral part of their work. For Gandhians, the desire for power, like any other passion (such as sex or anger) destroyed self-control; without self-control neither serenity nor mastery of the environment nor virtue was possible. By aspiring to power, a man demonstrated his unfitness to exercise it. To seek and use power instrumentally, to put it in the service of worthy ends, was possible, but the danger of attachment to power had to be constantly guarded against. The uses of power were, in any case, limited; the cure for the ills that afflicted state or society lay in changing men's inner environment, their hearts and minds, not their laws and institutions. Virtuous men made for a virtuous society, just as virtuous rulers were the ultimate guarantee of good government.

None of these three modern political specialists can admit that the possession and use of power is an end in itself; their legitimacies depend upon its use in achieving objectives that transcend power. Yet revolutionaries and politicians recognize power as an integral and necessary aspect of their role, whereas Gandhians do not. Gandhi managed the incompatibility between the corruption inherent in seeking power and his insistence that organizational power was a prerequisite for political effectiveness by a contingent and temporary relationship to political and other organizations. His example in building organizations, such as the Natal Congress or the Gujarat Sabha, ashrams, service societies, and the Congress itself, and then leaving them to the direction of others, or disbanding them when he thought their goals had been realized (as he attempted to do with the Congress in 1948 after Independence), set the standard for the relationship of Gandhian professionals to organizational and political power.

When Gandhi in 1920 was able to bring his organizational ideas to bear on the Indian National Congress, he proceeded to make its structure and procedure more rational, professional, and democratic.[53] The nationalist leaders of each province had been drawn from narrow strata of the English-educated whose connections with popular, 'vernacular' structures, opinion, and organized interests were tenuous and haphazard. No one was disturbed by the overrepresentation that followed when the host provinces of Congress annual sessions sent more delegates than those more distant. The Congress, Gandhi objected, placed 'no limit to the number of delegates that each province could return'.[54] Election to the Subjects Committee, then the Congress' highest executive organ, was not based on any explicit principles of representation or procedure; 'there was', Gandhi observed, 'hardly any difference between visitors and delegates'.[55] Most business was settled beforehand by informal gatherings of Congress notables.[56] Gandhi relates the fate in 1901 of his resolution before the Subjects Committee:

'So have we done?' said Sir Pherozshah Mehta.

'No, no, there is still the resolution on South Africa ...,' cried out Gokhale.

'Have you seen the resolution?' asked Sir Pherozshah.

'Of course.'

'Do you like it?'

'It is quite good.'

'Well, then, let us have it, Gandhi.'

I read it trembling.

Gokhale supported it.

'Unanimously passed', cried out everyone.[57]

Even the battles of 1905–6 between moderates and extremists, battles prophetic of those to come over the conflicting claims of alternate strategies, leaders, ideologies, and regions for dominance within the organization, did not elicit efforts to rationalize representation, procedure, and membership.

Gandhi's draft of a new constitution provided for manageable size, defined procedures, and 'scientific' representation. 'Without that', he wrote, 'the Congress will remain an unwieldy body and we would not be able to carry the weight we otherwise could .... I have attempted to give the Congress a representative character such as would make its demands irresistible'.[58] Although he was obliged to accept six thousand rather than one thousand as the limit on the number of delegates to attend annual sessions, he did succeed in introducing regular procedures for the selection of delegates and the president by creating an orderly, graduated structure of party organizations with fixed jurisdiction, rights, and responsibilities.[59] He also succeeded in establishing rules for the selection of the Subjects Committee and for voting at annual sessions and in converting the informal committee of notables into a new executive organ, the Working Committee.[60]

The structural core of Gandhi's democratization of the Congress lay in the proliferation of units capable of attracting and channelling a mass membership base. The Subjects committee, Annual Session, Provincial Congress Committees (PCC's), and District Congress Committees (DCC's) were already in existence, but they were geared to a limited membership.[61] Gandhi expected that 'the delegates will be elected only through the choice of millions .... Every person wishing to join a unit of the Congress is given the right to do so by paying the fee of four annas [about .08 cents in 1920] and signing the Congress creed.'[62] The pre-1920 PCC's could not accommodate a mass membership base because their boundaries, which coincided with the administrative boundaries of British India, cut across those of language, with the result that English literacy was virtually a prerequisite for participation. 'In so far as Congress is concerned', Gandhi held, 'we should re-divide India into provinces on a linguistic basis'.[63] His constitution did so, creating twenty-one Provincial Congress Committees each corresponding to a linguistic region. The new PCC's succeeded, although not as much as Gandhi expected they would, in transforming Congress from an elite to a popular organization.[64] Part of the difficulty, then as now, lay in creating structures below the District Congress Committees that could be assigned powers and responsibilities capable of attracting sufficient devotion to insure continuity and effectiveness.[65]

Gandhi also moved to remedy the lack of professional staff and continuous attention to business. 'The Congress', he observed, '... had practically no machinery functioning during the interval between session and session';[66] 'only one of the three general secretaries was a functioning secretary, and even he was not a whole timer'.[67] Gandhi urged that 'the secretaries of the Provincial Congress Committees and the District Congress Committees should, so far as possible, be whole-time workers, and may, if necessary, be paid out of the Provincial or District funds.'[68] He also provided for the national and state organs meeting throughout the year; the Working Committee and the All-India Congress Committee (the AICC, which assumed most of the responsibilities of the Subjects Committee) were to meet periodically and the PCC's at least once a month.[69]

Gandhi's reform of Congress in 1920 may not have made it into as popular and representative a political structure as was his intention,[70] but there is no question that he did succeed in changing it from an elite to a mass organization. In doing so he not only changed fundamentally the character of the nationalist struggle for independence but also modernized Indian politics by moving it in a professional and democratic direction and by providing the organizational base, procedures, and habits for national politics.

Notes

[1] Balwant Rai Mehta, chairman of the team established to consider the possibilities of decentralizing political decision-making, was an old Gandhian worker from Gujarat. The team proposed schemes which served as the pattern for subsequent legislation establishing panchayati raj (local political authorities) at the district, development block, and village levels (Government of India, Planning Commission, Committee on Plan Projects, *Report of the Team for the Study of Community Projects and National Extension Service*, New Delhi, 1957).

[2] Max Weber, *The Religion of India: The Sociology of Hinduism and Buddhism*, trans. and ed. H.H. Gerth and D. Martindale (Glencoe: Free Press, 1958), p. 326. In his classic but much disputed *The Protestant Ethic and the Spirit of Capitalism*, trans. Talcott Parsons, New York, 1958, he argued that the modernization that flowed from industrial capitalism in the West was rooted in Protestant 'this-worldly asceticism,' the sanctification of the asceticism and acquisitiveness that made for business success. Weber found in Hinduism the mirror image of Protestant Christianity. Despite his awareness and appreciation of elements of Indian culture and society that were conducive to sanctified asceticism and acquisitiveness, he concluded that 'it could not have occurred to a Hindu to see the economic success he had attained in his calling as a sign of his salvation' (*The Religion of India*, p. 326). Milton Singer observes that 'on prima facie grounds one could make a pretty plausible case for the thesis that Hindu metaphysics should produce just those kinds of "character" and "character traits" which Weber regarded as necessary for modern industrial society .... But I do not think that such a *prima facie* argument is any more conclusive than the opposite argument, which holds that Hindu metaphysics cannot produce a "capitalist spirit" in a good Hindu' ('Religion and Social Change in India: The Max Weber Thesis, Phase Three,' *Economic Development and Cultural Change*, July, 1966, p. 501). See also his important review article of Weber's *The Religion of India*, in *American Anthropologist*, LXIII, February, 1961, and Amar Kumar Singh's very able criticism of the Weber thesis in an Indian context, 'Hindu Culture and Economic Development in India,' *Conspectus*, III, no. 1, 1967.

David McClelland's *The Achieving Society*, Princeton, N.J., 1961 is probably the leading example of the use of the Weber thesis by social psychologists. He finds that 'Hinduism explictly teaches that concern with earthly achievements is a snare and a delusion. It is hard to see how they [Hindu parents] would set high standards of excellence for their son's performance, or show great pleasure over his achievements or displeasure at his failures' (p. 357). McClelland's exemption of Jains and Vaishnavas, who provide some of India's most successful businessmen, is difficult to appreciate since it is not at all clear that their metaphysics, practice, and socialization differ from those of Brahmans in respects critical for McClelland's theory of the need for achievement.

[3] See, for example, Reinhard Bendix, *Work and Authority in Industry*, New York: John Wiley and Sons, 1956, and Robert Kiefer Webb, *The British Working Class Reader, 1790–1848*, London: Augustus M. Kelley, 1955.

[4] Leonard Labaree (ed.), *The Autobiography of Benjamin Franklin* (New Haven, Conn.: Yale University Press, 1964), p. 159.

[5] Charles L. Sanford, *Benjamin Franklin and the American Character*, Boston: DC Heath and Company, 1955, p. 18.

[6] 'His diet', Pyarelal writes, 'consisted of goat's milk, raisins and fruit and was weighed out and measured with a druggist's exactness and care. The menu for each meal was adjusted carefully according to how the system had responded to the previous meal, the amount of sleep he had or expected to have, and the physical or mental strain already undergone or in prospect'; *Mahatma Gandhi: The Early Phase*, Ahmedabad: Navajivan Publishing House, 1965, I, p. 12.

[7] Nirmal Kumar Bose, Gandhi's able—and sceptical—secretary in Bengal in the mid-forties has developed the theme of Gandhi's preoccupation with time and with the watch (in a lecture, South Asia Seminar, University of Chicago, Spring, 1965).

[8] 'Speech at Gujarat Political Conference,' in *The Collected Works of Mahatma Gandhi*, Delhi, 1958—, XIV, p. 48.

[9] Rajendra Prasad, 'Gandhi in Bihar,' in Homer A. Jack (ed.), *The Gandhi Reader*, Bloomington, Ind.: Indiana University Press, 1956, pp. 149–50.

[10] M.K. Gandhi, *Ashram Observances in Action*, Ahmedabad, 1955, pp. 123–4, and Sanford, *Benjamin Franklin and the American Character*, p. 16. Gandhi did, however adjust his schedule when he was on tour or in action politically.

[11] Gandhi, *Ashram Observances in Action*, p. 147.

[12] Mukulbhai Kalarthi (comp.), *Ba and Bapu*, Ahmedabad: Navajivan Publishing House, 1962, p. 105.

[13] Pyarelal (Nair), *Mahatma Gandhi: The Last Phase*, 2nd edn, Ahmedabad: Navajivan Publishing House, 1966, I, p. 118.

[14] February 2, 1947, cited in ibid., p. 44.

[15] Ibid., p. 41.

[16] Ibid.

[17] Gandhi, *Ashram Observances in Action*, p. 151.

[18] *Gandhi's Autobiography, or, The Story of My Experiments with Truth*, trans. from the Gujarati by Mahadev Desai, Washington, DC, 1948, p. 188.

[19] G.D. Birla, *In the Shadow of the Mahatma*, Bombay: Orient Longman, 1953, pp. 1–16, 89, 93.

[20] *Gandhi's Autobiography*, p. 188.

[21] Pyarelal, *Mahatma Gandhi: The Early Phase*, I, p. 730.

[22] *Gandhi's Autobiography*, p. 187.

[23] Pyarelal, *Mahatma Gandhi: The Early Phase*, I, p. 6; *The Collected Works of Mahatma Gandhi*, XVI, p. 468.

[24] *The Collected Works of Mahatma Gandhi*, XVI, pp. 596–7.

[25] From a lecture by N.K. Bose, South Asia Seminar University of Chicago Spring, 1965.

[26] Pyarelal, *Mahatma Gandhi: The Early Phase*, I, p. 12.

[27] See, for various examples, 'Extracts from Minutes of Chamaparan Agrarian Enquiry Committee,' *The Collected Works of Mahatma Gandhi*, XIII, *passim*; 'Letter to the Secretary, Passenger Grievances Committee, Rangoon, July 25, 1917' (with reference to the bad lot of deck passengers of the British India Steam Navigation Service), ibid., pp. 476–8; and 'Report of the Commissioners Appointed by the Punjab Sub-Committee of the Indian National Congress' (1920), *ibid.*, XVII, pp. 114–292.

[28] 'Punjab Letter,' *Navajivan*, 11 November 1919, in *The Collected Works of Mahatma Gandhi*, XVI, p. 282.

[29] *Gandhi's Autobiography*, p. 187.

[30] 'Punjab Letter,' *Navajivan*, 11 November 1919, p. 282.

[31] 'Punjab Letter,' *Navajivan*, 7 December 1919, in *The Collected Works of Mahatma Gandhi*, XVI, p. 325.

[32] 'Punjab Letter', *Navajivan*, 11 November 1919, pp. 282–3.

[33] Ibid., p. 282.

[34] Ibid., p. 283.

[35] Pyarelal, *Mahatma Gandhi: The Last Phase*, I, p. 4.

[36] *Gandhi's Autobiography*, p. 274.

[37] Ibid., pp. 278–9.

[38] Ibid., p. 281.

[39] Pyarelal, *Mahatma Gandhi: The Early Phase*, I, p. 435.

[40] Ibid., p. 489.

[41] Ibid., p. 436.

[42] Ibid., p. 431.

[43] *Gandhi's Autobiography*, p. 186. The group included Messrs. Dawud Muhammed, Moosa, Haji Adam, Mohamed Casam Jeeva, Parsi Rustomji, and Gandhi (*Pyarelal, Mahatma Gandhi: The Early Phase*, I, p. 437). That Gandhi's

early political experiences should have placed him with men who were not intellectuals, who were conservative, merchants, and mainly Muslim, helps explain his later propensity to believe that these groups, in addition to the liberal, Anglicized, intellectual Hindus, could be won over to the nationalist movement.

[44] Pyarelal, *Mahatma Gandhi: The Early Phase*, I, p. 436.

[45] Ibid., pp. 436, 438.

[46] *Gandhi's Autobiography*, p. 187.

[47] Pyarelal, *Mahatma Gandhi: The Early Phase*, I, p. 439.

[48] Ibid., p. 442.

[49] N.D. Parikh, *Sardar Vallabhbhai Patel*, Ahmedabad: Navajivan Publishing House, 1955, p.43. It is this programme that drew Patel, subsequently one of the Congress' great organizational talents and a man impatient with bodies of a deliberative nature only.

[50] 'Speech at Gujarat Political Conference, (Godhra, November 3, 1917),' in *The Collected Works of Mahatma Gandhi*, XIV, pp. 49–50.

[51] See Michael Walzer, 'Puritanism as a Revolutionary Ideology,' in Judith Shklar (ed.), *Political Theory and Ideology*, New York: Macmillan, 1966, p. 64, where he argues that the saints were entrepreneurs, but in politics, not economics. His view of the saints as political specialists is elaborated in *The Revolution of the Saints: A Study in the Origins of Radical Politics*, Cambridge: Harvard University Press, 1965.

[52] See Max Weber, *Politics as a Vocation*, Philadephia: Fortress Press, 1965, in which he describes types of professional politicians, particularly the lawyer, journalist, and 'demagogue' of the postdemocratic era.

[53] At the Congress session in December 1919, Gandhi was asked to revise the constitution of the Congress (*The Collected Works of Mahatma Gandhi*, XVII, p. 487, n. 2).

[54] *Gandhi's Autobiography*, p. 598.

[55] Ibid., p. 282.

[56] Ibid., p. 596.

[57] Ibid., p. 281.

[58] Letter from Gandhi to N.C. Kelkar, July 2, 1920, in *The Collected Works of Mahatma Gandhi*, XVIII, p. 3.

[59] *Gandhi's Autobiography*, p. 613.

[60] The new All-India Congress Committee (AICC) became the Subjects Committee; its procedures were fixed; delegates alone were permitted to vote; and their qualifications had to be ascertained (see articles XXV, XXVI, XII, and XI, respectively, of the Congress Constitution adopted at Nagpur (*The Collected Works of Mahatma Gandhi*, XIX, pp. 190–8)). Article XXIV of the Nagpur Constitution provides for the Working Committee (ibid., p. 197).

[61] Constitution of 1908: Arts. 4, 6–8 (PCC's), 9–12 (DCC's), 24–5 (Subjects committee), in M.V. Ramana Rao, *Development of the Congress Constitution*, New Delhi, 1958, pp. 13–14.

[62] 'Nagpur Congress,' *Navajivan*, 1 January 1921, in *The Collected Works of Mahatma Gandhi*, XIX, p. 207.

[63] Letter from Gandhi to Chairman, AICC, September 25, 1920, in ibid., XVIII, p. 289.

[64] 'Nagpur Constitution,' Article V, in ibid., XIX, p. 191.

[65] For the party arrangements at the DCC and *taluka* or *tehsil* level (smaller administrative units within a province), see 'Draft Model Rules for Provincial Congress Committees,' in ibid., XIX, pp. 217–19. The elections to the PCC's and the AICC were to be indirect, DCC's electing PCC's and these electing the AICC (see Nagpur Constitution, Article XIX, in ibid., XIX, pp. 195).

[66] *Gandhi's Autobiography*, p. 597.

[67] Ibid.

[68] 'Draft Model Rules for Provincial Congress Committees,' pp. 218–19.

[69] Ibid., p. 219.

[70] Gopal Krishna points out that the Congress membership in the high recruitment year of 1921 was only 1,945,865 ('The Development of the Indian National Congress as a Mass Organization, 1918–23', *Journal of Asian Studies*, XXV, May, 1966, pp. 419–20).

Index